UNDERSTANDING
ANTIQUES

UNDERSTANDING
ANTIQUES

*An Introductory Guide
to Furniture, Ceramics, Glass,
Timepieces, and Silver*

LUCILLA WATSON

CHANCELLOR
PRESS

Edited and designed by the
Artists House Division of
Mitchell Beazley International Ltd

This 1993 edition published by Chancellor Press
part of Reed International Ltd
Michelin House
81 Fulham Road
London SW3 6RB

EXECUTIVE MANAGERS	Kelly Flynn
	Susan Egerton-Jones
ART EDITOR	Julie Williamson
EDITOR	Derek Derbyshire
PRODUCTION	Peter Phillips
PICTURE RESEARCH	Anne-Marie Erhlich
	Meg Price Whitlock
	Caroline Smith
ADDITIONAL RESEARCH	Stephen Bowden

ISBN 1 85152 387 1

Typeset by Hourds Typographica, Stafford
Reproduction by La Cromalito s.n.c., Milan
Produced by Mandarin Offset

CONTENTS

INTRODUCTION

*W*hen thinking of "going in for antiques" people are often afraid of making mistakes; they are very worried about what will be a good buy, what they should look out for and generally how they should go about the whole business. I think you should never buy anything unless you like and want to own it; buying something simply because it is a good investment is missing half the point of being an antique collector. Antiques are to be enjoyed; a collection should grow slowly, with each purchase being a memorable event and a pleasure.

To anyone who has a feeling for things of the past but little knowledge, I would say, don't rush into buying straight away. Go to antiques fairs as often as you can and visit antique shops. Don't be afraid to browse. Dealers are used to it, they don't expect every customer who walks in off the street to snap up the first Pembroke table or Chelsea bowl they see! If the dealer is not busy, he or she might well be happy to chat about the pieces in the shop; after all you may not be a customer this time but when you are ready to buy you'll be back if he or she has been helpful. On the other hand, it is unreasonable to expect a dealer to leave a "real" customer to give time to talk to you about every item which catches your eye if you aren't serious. They are in business to make a living!

You have already made a clever move by acquiring a copy of *Understanding Antiques*, covering as it does the whole spectrum from furniture to ceramics, silver and glass. A good general guide such as this will give you an overview of the whole subject. You will learn something of the history and development of all aspects of antiques, come to differentiate between the various periods and to recognize factory marks and hallmarks. As your knowledge increases so will your confidence in your own judgment, and consequently your pleasure in buying and collecting. You will be able to talk to dealers and to other collectors; and the more you talk to people in the know the more you will develop your own expertise and gradually find yourself drawn more to one area than another. Perhaps silver will become your speciality or a particular aspect of ceramics. You may care to base a collection round a hobby or interest – perhaps fishing or sewing. Obviously what you collect will be dictated by how much you can afford to spend and the available space to house your treasures as well as by your interest.

My own passion is pottery and porcelain, particularly English blue and white. My collection began in a very modest and purely instinctive way when I was a student. I knew I liked certain things and bought when I could afford them. As I had little money at the time, many of the pieces were imperfect and within my price range. Some of these pieces are, in fact, quite rare and are now considered valuable in spite of minor damage.

I have, over the years, made pottery and porcelain my speciality and although my knowledge has become quite extensive, there are always new discoveries being made and consequently more and more to learn. The more deeply I go into the subject the more satisfaction and sheer enjoyment I gain from it.

Furnishing your home with antiques can be especially rewarding – we all have to have furniture, so why not choose some antique pieces to blend with your interior? In this way you will create a really individual environment. Even if you have a very modern home, a single stunning item of antique furniture can make a dramatic focal point in a room.

Of course, as well as giving you great pleasure your antiques are also a good investment. They are becoming rarer all the time and if they are damaged or destroyed you cannot just pop to the nearest chain store to replace them. New pieces of furniture, porcelain and so on become secondhand as soon as you get them home; antiques simply become older and more desirable. So by starting a collection you are not only providing yourself with a fulfilling hobby, but are investing your money in a way which is much more fun than dealing in stocks and shares.

I hope that for you, as for me, searching out and collecting antiques will be a journey of discovery and that each item you buy will help you put together a picture of how our forebears lived, worked and played, and how they decorated and furnished their homes. Handling, understanding and loving objects from the past gives us a true sense of history and our own place in it . . .

Bon voyage!

Judith Miller

PREFACE

Antiques hold an almost universal yet often mysterious fascination. Their attraction may be obvious enough, but their historical or stylistic significance is often less well appreciated since descriptions and dates, periods and styles, taken in isolation, can all too easily appear meaningless. It is the aim of this book to describe the most frequently encountered categories of antiques and, by placing them in the context of their period and styles, make them easily understood.

The Pocket Guide to Antiques – Bevis Hillier's excellent instant reference for the uninitiated collector – was the major source and inspiration for this book, which in turn traces in pictures and text the evolution of the predominating styles in the popular categories of antiques: furniture and mirrors, ceramics, glass, clocks and watches, and silver. Taking in developments in North America and the Far East as well as in Europe, it presents an international view leading the reader through each category, country by country and century by century.

Of course, it should not be thought that styles changed overnight and that, once established, they were adopted everywhere. Nor should it be assumed that, for example, all cabinet-makers, all silversmiths or all porcelain factories adopted new styles simultaneously. Innovations tended to develop in the larger cities, with the provincial regions often lagging behind and

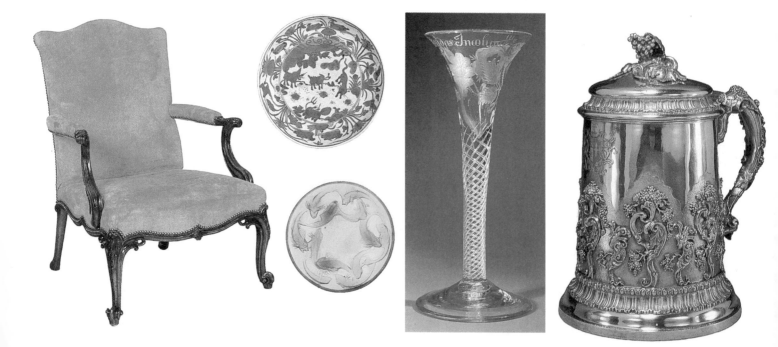

adopting and adapting at a slightly later date new styles that had become the rage in London, or Paris, or Philadelphia, for instance. Moreover, the most distinctive stylistic developments in the antiques of today – so very often the luxury items of previous centuries – catered primarily for the tastes of the aristocracy and the wealthy. Only they could afford such pieces and only they had the leisure to enjoy them. For this stratum of society, delight in the appearance of a fine piece of furniture or exquisite dinner service tended to eclipse its functional value. Further down the social scale, where furnishings and equipment served a mainly functional purpose, innovations and dynamic stylistic changes played but a minor role though craftsmanship was often of a high order.

This book does not attempt to cover the history of more humble, everyday furnishings and household objects. Rather, by presenting an overall view of the predominant "luxury" styles of previous centuries, it will ensure that we will have a better understanding of all antiques and will be able to recognise the major national and international influences over the centuries.

LUCILLA WATSON

FURNITURE
& MIRRORS

In this section the major furniture-making countries of the world
are organized alphabetically, the important periods of
furniture-making are explored and the finest examples of design,
decoration and craftsmanship are illustrated. The incorporation of
increasingly sophisticated mirrors and mirror frames into room
furnishing is also featured.

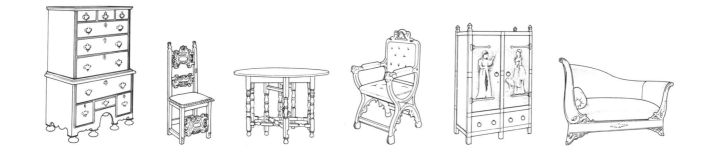

AMERICA

From 1620 until the Revolution of 1775, the majority of the settlers in America were British, and the chairs, tables, chests and cupboards with which they furnished their homes were of English design, adapted to American conditions. Furniture was too bulky to ship across the Atlantic in quantity, and imported furniture tended to shrink in the American climate and had no resistance to the insects encountered.

American furniture is generally less showy than the most sophisticated English furniture. And American country-made furniture is usually straightforward and functional and less subject to changing styles than pieces made in towns and cities.

The 17th century

This oak armchair, of the Brewster type, (below) was made in New England in the mid-17th century. Oak was the most popular wood with American furniture-makers at this time, although pine and maple were also used.

The earliest surviving American furniture dates from about 1650–70. Examples show prominent Jacobean features as much in design and construction as in panelling and carved decoration.

The woods used were primarily oak, pine and maple. Oak, which is lighter than the English variety, predominated. The finest pieces of early American furniture include: oak chests, often with one or two drawers below, and decorated with carving in low relief; Jacobean court cupboards, with a closed section below and open storage space above, generally decorated with mouldings, panelling, bosses and bulbous columns; press cupboards, similar to court cupboards; and chests of drawers, also decorated with mouldings and panelling. Early American tables fall into three categories; trestle dining tables, gate-leg tables and smaller, sturdy four-legged tables. Legs and stretchers were often spiral-twisted or turned on the lathe to produce mouldings.

The simplest seating furniture took the form of benches and stools, but there was also the wainscot chair, a three-legged armchair, and two other types of armchair, the Carver and the Brewster (both named after two Pilgrim fathers, who are reputed

This early 18th-century gate-leg table has the paint-brush feet often used at this time. Both legs and stretchers are decorated with elaborate turning.

to have brought them to America in the *Mayflower*). The Carver-type chair usually had a single row of vertical spindles in the back. The Brewster had two rows, with further spindles below the seat and under each arm. The luxurious chair, caned and high-backed, with turned and carved decoration, known as the "Boston Chair", came into vogue later in the 17th century.

By the end of the 17th century, styles were changing and new forms of decoration developing. This was the beginning of the William and Mary period in America, a phase in furniture history which was already finished in England.

Left: a 17th-century panelled oak and pine press made in two parts. The single drawer on the lower section has applied panels and half spindles.

*The central panel of the late 17th-century oak and pine chest (**right**) is decorated with a Tudor rose, The top is hinged and there is a long drawer underneath.*

The 18th century

The William and Mary style spread from England to America during the last decade of the 17th century, and remained popular in America until about 1720. It was a Dutch-influenced style, but Dutch styles were not new to America.

The William and Mary style is most easily recognizable by ball feet on furniture. It was also a style more refined than its Jacobean antecedent. Americans liked this style because it was less bulky and more suitable for smaller houses. Walnut, rather than oak, became the usual wood, carved or in veneers, but maple was also used.

Styles of chair design developed rapidly in the William and Mary period. Cane was used as a seating material and upholstered easy chairs appeared. Slat-backed or ladder-backed chairs, known in the Jacobean period, became more common; drop-leaf tables came into vogue, and the range of chests also developed. By the beginning of the 18th century there were three varieties of chest: the high chest (or tallboy, as it came to be known), the bureau dressing table (or lowboy), and the *Kas*. The high chest was a tall chest of drawers on a high four- or six-legged stand, often with burr walnut or maple veneers. The bureau dressing table was a truncated version of the high chest with only a single drawer

*The child's walnut desk (**above**) dates from the William and Mary period.*

Left: a painted – green – and carved maple bannister-back side chair with rush seat, made in New England 1740–60.

or shallow layers of drawers. The *Kas*, brought to America by Dutch settlers, was a large press, or wardrobe, of simple construction, sometimes painted with flowers or fruit.

Ball feet, characteristic of the American William and Mary period, were used for chairs, tables and some chests. The elegant paint-brush foot, carved in the shape of an outward-curving paint brush, is also sometimes seen in furniture of the period.

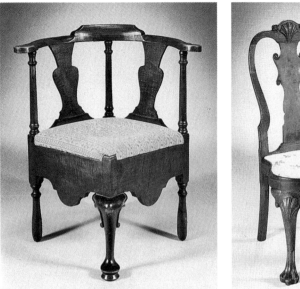

*The tiger maple corner chair (**above**), from Rhode Island, and the walnut side chair (**above right**), from Philadelphia, show two variations on the Queen Anne cabriole leg. The corner chair's single cabriole leg ends in a pad and disc foot, and the legs of the side chair have trifid feet. The carved splat and shell motif on legs and rail were fashionable touches of the period.*

Furniture produced between about 1720 and about 1760 is known in America as "Queen Anne", even though she died in 1714. American styles again lagged behind those in England.

Furniture for the richer American homes became more elegant, and the cabriole leg appeared in almost all forms of furniture. One exception was the American form of Windsor chair, with its angled legs and round spindled back. An ingenious variant on this type was the writing-arm Windsor chair, an American invention with its right arm fashioned as a desk top, fitted with a candle-stand and drawers below for sand and quills. Other chairs were generally smaller than those in England at this time, the most elegant ones being made in Philadelphia, and ladder-backs in dining chairs tended to be replaced by a single vertical carved splat.

On highboys and lowboys, six turned legs gave way to four cabriole legs, the missing legs surviving only as pendant drops below the drawers. Further ornamentation in the American Queen Anne period is seen in shell motifs added to cabriole legs, boat-shaped handles in place of Jacobean tear-drop pulls, and arched panels in writing desks and clothes cupboards. Gate-leg tables were replaced by drop-leaf tables.

The Queen Anne period, ending about 1760, was followed by American Chippendale, which continued until about 1790. (In America, collectors hardly ever use the term "Georgian", as in English furniture history.) The Chippendale manner, studied by American makers in Chippendale's *Gentleman and Cabinet-Maker's Director*, was most markedly practised in Philadelphia between 1760 and 1776. Fine cabinet-makers there included Thomas Affleck, John Folwell, Benjamin Randolph and William Savery. American Chippendale is more restrained than English: the rococo element of the style appeared too frivolous against America's puritan tradition. American Chippendale is seen to best effect in chairs with rails in the form of Cupid's bow, claw-and-ball feet, and Gothic or *chinoiserie* splats. The "Marlborough" leg, a straight tapering leg of square section, also appeared.

Softwood was generally used for the main construction of case furniture (in contrast to the use of hardwoods in England) and dowel-and-tenon construction continued to be used in America until the late 18th century. Mahogany was used for the finest furniture, while local woods, such as tulipwood, maple and cherry, were used for country furniture, which now also took on simplified Chippendale features. Another rustic design was

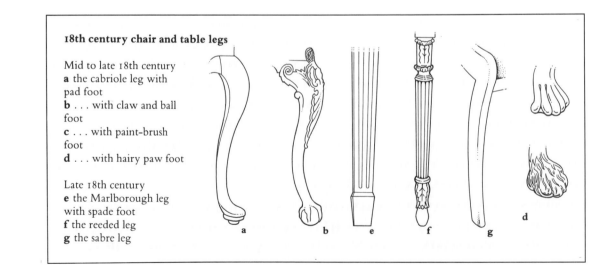

18th century chair and table legs

Mid to late 18th century
a the cabriole leg with pad foot
b . . . with claw and ball foot
c . . . with paint-brush foot
d . . . with hairy paw foot

Late 18th century
e the Marlborough leg with spade foot
f the reeded leg
g the sabre leg

the *Schrank*, introduced in the mid-18th century by settlers. It was a wardrobe, similar to the *Kas*, and was often painted with flowers.

Philadelphia and Newport, Rhode Island, were the main centres of furniture manufacture in the 18th century. Notable among their products were highboys, block-fronted secretaries, drop-fronted desks, and chests-on-chests. The best known Newport cabinet-makers were the Townsend-Goddard family of craftsmen. It was John Townsend who was responsible for the handsome block-fronted secretaries, chests and desks in which the centre of the front curves gently inwards while the right- and left-hand portions curve gently outwards.

In England in the last decades of the 18th century, the Chippendale style was followed by the neo-classicism of Robert Adam. But the designs of this influential architect and designer were not published in America, and the style was not widely adopted. The Revolution had in any case broken Anglo-American relations and, after the resumption of trade with England in 1784, fashion in England had moved on to the styles of Adam's successors, George Hepplewhite and Thomas Sheraton, styles which America now took up and used in combination.

Like the Adam style, the Hepplewhite and Sheraton styles are neo-classical in inspiration. American cabinet-makers now produced square-backed or shield-backed chairs, for example, with much reeding on rails and arms, and cabriole legs were replaced by the straight or slightly curving sabre leg. Serpentine chests made their first appearance. There was also a new type of desk, the tambour, with rolling doors made up of vertical strips of wood glued to canvas.

Below left: a fine cherry-wood secretaire, probably made in Connecticut in the mid to late 18th century. The general form of the desk follows the Chippendale style, but the sunburst let in to the lower drawer and the paint-brush feet are American in character.

Below: simplicity and elegance in a Chippendale-style mahogany Pembroke table probably made by John Townsend of Newport, Rhode Island, in the mid to late 18th century. Here is a good example of the straight, square Marlborough leg, in this case with simple fluting.

The Federal Period (1790–1830)

By the end of the 18th century, lowboys and highboys, which had become unfashionable, were replaced by smaller chests of drawers. Large numbers of small, occasional tables were also produced. Tulipwood, poplar and white pine were sometimes used instead of mahogany, and, after about 1790, carved mahogany was often replaced by painting, veneering and inlay.

It was towards the end of the 18th century, in New York, that Duncan Phyfe (1768–1854), one of the Federal Period's most important cabinet makers, began to make furniture. Phyfe worked

*The mahogany chair by Benjamin Randolph (**above**) shows the influence of Chippendale's designs.*

Below: this mahogany work table of the early 19th century, has Duncan Phyfe's label. The drawer on the front is a dummy; the top lifts to reveal a fitted interior with hinged work surface and a variety of compartments.

initially in the Hepplewhite and Sheraton style, still tending to use mahogany when other makers had abandoned it. Phyfe's importance as a maker continued into the 19th century, when new styles, the French Directoire and Empire, also came into vogue.

The 19th century

Furniture in the Hepplewhite and Sheraton styles, which had appeared towards the end of the 18th century, continued in vogue in the first decades of the 19th century, but, from about 1805 to about 1825, some American furniture came under the influence of the French Directoire style.

The American adoption of the Directoire style is most apparent in chairs and sofas, in which concave "sabre-shaped" curves predominate. In chairs, every line, except for the seat, was curved, and lyre-or vase-shape motifs were often used in the backs. Duncan Phyfe, who took up the Directoire

style when it came into vogue, often used the lyre motif in his pieces. Charles-Honoré Lannuier (*fl.* 1780–1819), a French immigrant who worked in New York, was another important exponent of the Directoire style in America.

Perhaps because of the Revolution, America was disinclined to copy the English fashions of the time. American cabinet-makers thus tended to reject English Regency and were attracted instead to the bulky and showy Napoleonic Empire style, from France. Inclined to be square or rectangular, with sumptuous veneers, American furniture in the later Federal period became increasingly gross; and Duncan Phyfe scathingly called it "butcher furniture". Charles-Honoré Lannuier, who had

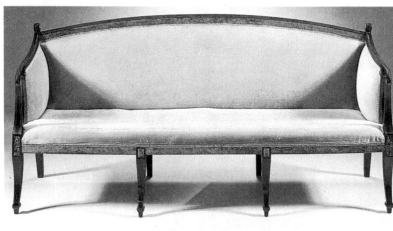

Above: inlaid mahogany and birch veneer settee. Sabre-shaped legs highlight the European influence in late 18th- and early 19th-century American furniture.

*This inlaid mahogany chest-of-drawers (**right**) was made in New Hampshire around 1810.*

*The simplicity of Shaker furniture (**above, right**) contrasts sharply with the Empire mahogany pier table with mirrored back (**below, right**).*

followed the earlier Directoire style, now made furniture in a mixture of Directoire and Empire styles.

But throughout the epoch of the great 19th-century fashions in American furniture – Hepplewhite and Sheraton, Directoire and Empire – other, different ideas about furniture and interior design had been taking shape. Indeed, while furniture made for the most developed tastes was seen as much as a work of art as a furnishing piece, furniture for more modest levels of society was plainer, reflected the many immigrant influences and remained functional.

In contrast to the showiness of the Empire style, for instance, the furniture made by the Shakers from the early 19th century was lean and functional, and usually of pine, maple, walnut or fruitwood. The aim of the Shakers, a religious, celibate sect, was to create furniture of the utmost simplicity, with no decoration except paints and stains in primary colours. Shaker chairs and tables are distinguished by their slender lines, sound construction and smooth finishes.

In the later part of the 19th century, some exuberant pieces of furniture were produced and designs often followed those of past styles not least among which was the Gothic.

John Henry Belter, who opened a shop in New York in 1844, was an important manufacturer who created an elaborately carved variant of the neo-rococo style using rosewood bent into curves and laminated. Belter is best known for his "parlour suites". At least two of his competitors, Charles A. Baudouine and Joseph Meeks and Sons, copied his technique and style, while Alexandre Roux, in New York, drew upon a vast range of historical themes. Cast-iron furniture, made from the 1840s to the early 20th century, took the form of beds, hatracks and garden chairs and benches.

The late 19th and early 20th centuries

Towards the end of the 19th century, the English Arts and Crafts movement, which promoted the superiority of the hand-made over the machine-made, was embraced by American craftsmen. Japanese motifs and designs were also beginning to be seen in furniture design, including that of Christian Herter, a leading New York manufacturer. other influential designers following the Arts and Crafts ideals were Gustav Stickley, Elbert Hubbard

and Harvey Ellis, all of whom made relatively simple, elegant, well-crafted pieces. Though the movement flourished, hand-made furniture remained expensive, and factory-made pieces were produced on a large scale.

Meanwhile, from the late 19th century, Art Nouveau, with its swirling, plant-like forms, was attracting the attention of designers all over America. The style was named after a shop, *L'Art Nouveau,* in Paris. By contrast to the products of the Arts and Crafts tradition, Art Nouveau furniture often appeared elaborate. Charles Rohlfs, for example, created some pieces of fantastic elaboration.

By the 1920s, Art Deco had arrived, with its bright colours and angular shapes. The term "Art Deco" came from the Paris exhibition which introduced the style to Europe – the "Exposition des Arts Décoratifs". America now led the way in architecture, with the skyscraper; Frank Lloyd Wright, primarily an architect, designed furniture with simple outlines, to go with his buildings. Donald Deskey's furniture for Radio City Music Hall, New York (1933) shows Art Deco in its most mature form. Architectural involvement in furniture was also seen in the design of Paul T. Frankl, who designed wooden bookcases in the form of skyscrapers.

*This elaborately carved neo-rococo side chair in rosewood from John Henry Belter (**above, left**) was made at the height of his success.*

Above right: *a later chair in oak by Charles Rohlfs is a good example of Art Nouveau style.*

CHINA AND JAPAN

*This Ming dynasty rosewood armchair (**left**) has a tall serpentine back and rattan seat. Chinese taste favoured simplicity of line.*

***Below:** an eight-fold black lacquer screen decorated in gold dating from about 1750. Many screens were exported to Europe – some being cut up and used in other items of furniture.*

*The fabulous carved red lacquer throne (**above**) – now in the Victoria and Albert Museum – was made for the 18th-century emperor Chen-Lung. Unlike most Chinese pieces, palace furniture – which tended to be massive – was not made to be taken apart and packed up There are pictorial panels on the back and sides of the throne. This (**above, left**) is the one on the back.*

China

The best surviving Chinese furniture dates from the 15th century to the 18th century. It is solid and well made, completely at odds with the erroneous European equation of the delicate and flimsy with the quintessentially Chinese.

Much of the best Chinese furniture was made of polished rosewood and a greyish-brown timber which the Chinese called "chicken-wing-wood". Although veneering is rare, the Chinese used coloured woods, often in combination. Bamboo furniture and lacquered furniture, which was insect-resistant, were popular in southern China.

The Chinese were expert joiners who constructed their furniture mainly by mortise-and-tenon joints, with occasional dovetailing and a little glue. The joints are usually hidden. Mortise-and-tenon joints are particularly appropriate to Chinese furniture for two reasons: firstly because this method of construction allowed the wood to expand and contract without damage in humid conditions and rapidly changing temperatures; secondly, because it allowed furniture to be taken apart easily and packed up, a necessary convenience in view of the Chinese habit of travelling from place to place. A further characteristic of Chinese

Left: a 17th century circular lacquer folding centre table. It has a folding base and is decorated with red and green flowers, bats and leaves on a black background.

Above: a Meiji period (1868–1912) panelled, silver-cased kodansu cabinet with drawers, from Japan. The sides are decorated with birds and branches on a gold ground.

Above: a very elaborate Japanese lacquer side cabinet made at the end of the 19th century. It is decorated with pictorial earthenware panels.

furniture is that it was made without the aid of the lathe (which only reached China, from Europe, late in the 19th century). The legs of Chinese trestle tables, for example, are never perfectly circular, and there is no turning in Chinese joinery. Because of the Chinese habit of venerating their ancestors, a lot of earlier Chinese furniture was also copied in later centuries.

Chinese furniture was often designed to be set against the walls. There was a wide variety of cupboards, for storing possessions, and chests, in which clothes were kept. There were three kinds of chair: a chair with a box-frame base and a straight back and arms; a box-frame chair with swinging curved back (called an "abbot's chair"); and a collapsible type with a round or straight back. Chinese tables were of the trestle type, with roughly cylindrical legs, or of frame and stretcher construction, often with square legs and carved decoration.

The Chinese taste was generally for plainness, and heavily ornate furniture was most often made for export. Nevertheless, some lavish lacquer furniture, such as low thrones and beds, was made for palaces in the 17th and 18th centuries. Unlike much other Chinese furniture, palace furniture, which tended to be massive, was not made to be dismantled. Lacquered screens, known to us as "Coromandel" screens, were particularly ornate and played an important part in interior design.

Japan

By comparison with Western styles, Japanese interiors were simply and sparsely furnished. Japanese furniture was movable, so that the look of a room could be changed with little effort, and even the Japanese fireplace – a charcoal burner – could be moved around the room. Walls were also movable and consisted of a paper-covered framework. As in China, screens were an important part of the decor. They were made of strong paper and were generally about 1.5 metres high. Some were decorated by painters such as Maruyama Okyo.

There were no chairs in the Japanese home. Seating was on mats spread on the floor and because of this most other Japanese furniture is low. There were low tables, less than 20 centimetres (8 inches) off the ground, and low writing desks and reading stands, often lacquered and inlaid. Storage furniture took the form of a small cabinet known as a *kodansu,* and a small chest on short legs, known as a *karabitsu,* both of light construction, with lacquered wood. Japanese lacquer made for home use rather than export is of unrivalled quality, but standards declined sharply after about 1870 when pieces were mass-produced for export to Europe.

ENGLAND

Right: two oak court cupboards, or buffets, dating from about 1620. Rarely, if ever, is the decoration on court cupboards identical. The two pairs of figure supports are an unusual feature in the nearer illustration; the upper pair represent Hope and Faith. However, the supports in the other example are of typically bulbous form. Arcading, on the lower shelf, and gadrooning, on the middle shelf are common features of the period.

This panelled armchair, c. 1640, is a magnificent example of the carver's art.

The Age of Oak

Oak was the staple material of English furniture from the Middle Ages until the second half of the 17th century. Oak trees have long been abundant in England, and the toughness and strength of their wood is reflected in the robust design of early English furniture. Construction was by mortise and tenon, secured by dowels and, until the late 17th century, furniture was made by joiners (or carpenters) rather than by specialist cabinet-makers.

Oak furniture of the 16th and 17th centuries consists mostly of chairs and stools, chests, cupboards, tables and beds. Shapes had changed little since medieval times but, from the 16th century, Renaissance decoration, in the form of carvings, was added. The medieval practice of gilding and painting furniture was also continued for a time.

Early chairs, known as back-stools (stools with backs), have no arms and many have a box-like construction, derived from chests. Another early type, developed in the late 16th century, was the wainscot chair, with arms and a planked seat. The

farthingale chair, with back support raised clear of the seat, appeared at the beginning of the 17th century; it had no arms, so that women with wide skirts could be seated without difficulty. Four-legged joint (or joined) stools, with stretchers, were also common during the 16th and 17th centuries. Benches, of similar construction, were also made.

Chests, the descendants of primitive dug-outs, were framed and planked from the 13th century, and panelled from the 15th century. Cupboards were originally "cup-boards" – sideboards for displaying silver or pewter – with no doors or enclosed spaces. In the late 16th century the three-tiered open court cupboard appeared, and was often elaborately carved. Aumbries and livery cupboards, both of them variations on the court cupboard, were used for storing food. Tall press cupboards, often with shelves, held clothes and valuables. A dole cupboard was hung on the wall for dispensing charity food. The term "dole cupboard" is often wrongly applied to another type of food cupboard which is correctly known as a food hutch.

Trestle tables, easy to clear and store, originated in the Middle Ages and continued to be used by

Left: *an elegant and richly carved bed such as this added grandeur to the 16th and 17th-century Englishman's bedroom, when beds tended to become increasingly elaborate. The carving and moulding on this one are relatively restrained. It is a tester bed, in which the headboard and end posts support a canopy or tester.*

Above: *rich upholstery gives this James I x-frame chair a luxuriant appearance. The handy x-frame, which could be folded for storage or carrying, was probably invented by the Ancient Egyptians and has been popular ever since.*

humbler members of English society until the 17th century. Frame tables, with four legs joined by stretchers, had been known since the 14th century but came into regular use during the 1600s.

The bed developed from the simple box to the "wainscot", with panelled bedsteads at both ends, and then to the "post", similar to the traditional four-poster bed. The "stump" bed was low-slung, and the "truckle" (or "trundle") had wooden wheels. Beds were prized items of furniture in the 16th- and 17th-century English house. The "post" bed, with its rich hangings and bedding, was of course, the grandest. Bed posts, head-boards and canopies were richly carved.

Decoration on most early oak furniture took the form of turning and carving. Inlay was sometimes also used, although it was generally inferior to French or Italian work.

The legs of joint stools and gate-leg tables, for example, were often turned on the lathe to produce contours. Carving, sometimes very elaborate, took the form of festoons, swags and imaginary figures drawn from pagan and Classical sources. Romayne work, roundels enclosing carved profile heads, was characteristic of Henry VIII's reign. Strapwork, a low-relief geometrical decoration,

Gateleg tables, like this one (above), first appeared in the 16th century and remained popular throughout the 17th and into the 18th century.

appeared from the Netherlands in Elizabethan times. Arcading, pilasters and panels appeared on chests and cupboards, while beds, tables and cupboards sported grotesquely bulbous legs.

By the early 17th century, the Jacobean period, decoration became more restrained, even reaching sobriety towards the middle of the century and before the Restoration.

The Age of Walnut

Although walnut had been used to a limited extent in the 16th century, its fashionable days date from about 1670. The compact nature and attractive colouring of walnut made it very desirable for cabinet-work and veneering. By contrast to most oak furniture, with its robust construction and bold ornamentation, walnut furniture has a refined aspect. By the second half of the 17th century there was a distinction between joiners, or ordinary craftsmen, and cabinet-makers, or furniture craftsmen. It was the cabinet-makers who were responsible for the finest furniture of the time.

Charles II became king in 1660. While in exile in France, Charles and his court had become acquainted with the splendours of the Louis XIV style. On his return, flamboyant tastes caught on in England.

English taste was to receive another injection of flamboyance with the arrival of the baroque style later in the 17th century. In 1685, the Revocation of the Edict of Nantes forced the Protestant Huguenots to leave France. Many of them settled in England and the craftsmen among them brought over the new baroque style, which soon became established in England. The baroque was a style of sweeping curves and heavy ornamentation, which is seen at its grandest in the work of Daniel Marot, one of many Huguenot refugee craftsmen.

The late 17th century was also the great age of lacquered and marquetry furniture. Strong marquetry colours and naturalistic, often floral motifs were used at first, but by 1700 colours were more subdued and naturalistic patterns were replaced by arabesques and "seaweed", or "endive" marquetry.

Gate-leg tables, often with "barley-sugar" twisted legs, were popular during Charles II's reign, and chairs were given elaborate carved and turned decoration. From about 1675, S-shaped scroll designs (known as "Flemish" scrolls) were applied to the front legs of chairs. Chairs made during the William and Mary period were simpler, with a backward tilt. Turned legs, and woven cane seats and backs remained popular for chairs, while chests had ball- or bun-shaped feet. Many chairs were expensively upholstered, as were the new day-beds (couches). From 1660, small tables, known as occasional tables, were made for tea-drinking, cards and dressing.

The greatest age of walnut furniture coincides with Anne's reign (1702–14). Fine walnut veneers reached their peak. Walnut was also used for chests, chests-on-stands, chairs, bureaux and cabi-

These late 17th-century tables contrast strongly with the sturdy appearance of much oak furniture of earlier times. Representing a new, more elegant development in furniture design, they demonstrate the effective use of marquetry and parquetry which flourished between the late 17th and early 18th centuries. The floral motifs in the marquetry (left) are picked out in walnut and stained ivory on an ebony ground. Oyster veneer, cross-cut from roots and small branches, is used to create an abstract, symmetrical pattern in the William and Mary table (right).

Right: *a fine example of a William and Mary high-backed dining chair. Wooden backs, ornately carved and pierced as here, are less common than canework backs. The curved x-stretchers and ball feet, also seen in the two tables (opposite left), are also notable features of the period.*

Bureaux, or desks, appeared in the mid to late 17th century. The walnut bureau, c. 1710, (below) is basically a writing box on a chest of drawers and evolved from the writing box on stand.

nets. A major feature of Queen Anne chairs and cabinets was the cabriole leg, sometimes embellished with carvings on the knee. Chairs often had solid splats and removable stuffed seats.

Writing bureaux became especially popular in the second half of the 17th century. The earliest writing bureaux, essentially an extension of a writing box on legs, had a fall front and rested on a stand. Queen Anne examples often stood on a chest of drawers and had elaborate interiors, sometimes with secret compartments. A bookcase top could be added to form a bureau–bookcase.

Above: *an early 18th-century walnut secretaire cabinet. The door, set with a mirror, opens to reveal compartments; the upper "drawer" pulls down on a hinge to provide the writing surface, and the lower drawers provide extra storage.*

Left: *an early 18th-century walnut dining chair. The cabriole legs with shell motif, the claw and ball feet and the highly figured veneers on the backrail are all characteristic of the period.*

Right: this massive mahogany pier table with marble top was made in about 1740, and presages the "Age of Mahogany". Such features as the extravagantly carved cabriole legs and the ornate, rather clumsy swags and mask were to be rejected by the great names in furniture design later in the century.

In total contrast to the pier table, this late 18th-century satinwood library desk (*above*) is light and graceful even when compared to more usual mahogany examples of the period. The beauty of the wood is further brought out by contrasting woods inlaid in the sides and top.

Right: the fashion for classical features and architectural outlines was a striking change from the curves and excessive ornament seen in furniture of the earlier 18th century. This mid-18th-century cabinet is a clear example of the neo-classical style.

The Age of Mahogany and Satinwood

From about 1725 both walnut and mahogany were used for fine furniture, but a blight affecting walnut trees in France made walnut difficult to obtain so that, by about 1750, mahogany had become the prized material, and was used for the best cabinet work. The many attractions of mahogany included a fine patina, a range of attractive colouration and natural durability. The size of the trees from which it was cut made it ideal for table tops and large wardrobes, and the fine figurations of the wood also made it desirable for veneers. Two main varieties were used: "Spanish", or "Jamaican", mahogany, from the West Indies, notably Santo Domingo, and Cuba.

From about 1765 to the end of the century, satinwood, a pale straw-coloured wood from Puerto Rico, rivalled mahogany in the manufacture of high-quality furniture. For veneers and bandings decorative woods like tulipwood, Brazilian rosewood, kingwood and purplewood were used, and ebony and fruitwoods were used for marquetry. Painted furniture was most often made of beech, while pine was usual for carved and gilded furniture.

The 18th century, perhaps more than any other, was a time of experiment and innovation in furniture design, and the years 1740 to 1800 represent a

William Kent was an apprentice coach painter before he ran away to study portraiture and painting in London and Rome. Returning to England he began by painting allegorical murals before turning to architecture and landscape gardening. He was not universally liked – Hogarth described him as a "contemptible dauber". But his charm and skill brought him fame, and he rose to be principal painter to the crown, as well as master-carpenter, architect, and keeper of the King's pictures.

The ponderous animal motifs, shells, leaves and scrolls of this giltwood console table, made in about 1730, reflect the exuberant style of William Kent. By Kent's standards, however, this would have been a relatively simple piece.

golden age of English furniture-making. The Industrial Revolution was imminent and England's prospering middle and professional classes were acquiring grand houses and demanding suitably elegant furniture. By about 1750, the desk, with drawers or cupboards either side of the kneehole, had become an important feature of the rich man's library. Chairs were made in a profusion of styles. Chests of drawers, now in mahogany, were another development. Up to about 1750, they were still mainly straight-fronted, but serpentine-shaped commodes based on French designs came in soon after the middle of the century.

Commodes in the neo-classical style often had fine inlay-work, with circles or ovals depicting mythological scenes. From the 1730s, case furniture was often topped by a broken pediment. Small tea tables became increasingly popular before the middle of the century, as did breakfast tables, and later in the century sideboards and Pembroke tables appeared.

For the first time, furniture was designed to complement architecture and interior design. Men like William Kent and Robert Adam, architects first and foremost, also saw to the design of the furniture for the great houses that were built under their direction.

The 18th century saw a succession and an admixture of styles, notably rococo, *chinoiserie*, Gothic and neo-classicism. While in the earlier Georgian period (1714–60) the baroque style was gradually superseded by the lighter rococo, the later Georgian period (1760–1820) is characterized by the arrival of the neo-classical style. The greatest designers and cabinet-makers of the Georgian period were William Kent, Thomas Chippendale, Robert Adam, George Hepplewhite and Thomas Sheraton, and it is usually after these men rather than reigning monarchs that styles in 18th century English furniture are named.

William Kent

William Kent (1684–1748) was the first architect to use furniture in his schemes. Kent used mainly gilt soft-woods but also some parcel-gilt mahogany. His lavish marble-top side tables, with elaborate carving and gilding below, have an Italian baroque flavour; prominent female masks decorate much of his work and the shell motif appears in his desks. Kent also made elaborate chairs for wealthy clients, with scroll legs and flower, fruit and mask ornament.

Kent, an architect-decorator working in the style of the 18th-century Palladian revival, attempted to re-create the magnificence of Greece and Rome, which he combined with a taste for the Baroque. But Palladianism was not the only style; Giles Grendey (1693–1780), a prominent cabinet-maker, retained a contrasting, simpler style similar to that of the preceding Queen Anne period.

Thomas Chippendale

The name of Thomas Chippendale (1718–79) is associated with furniture in rococo, *chinoiserie* and Gothic styles. His fame rests on a book of designs for furniture entitled *The Gentleman and Cabinet-Maker's Director*, the first edition of which he published in 1754. A second edition appeared in 1756 and a third in 1762. To paraphrase Chippendale's own words, the aim of the *Director* was to assist the gentleman in the choice, and the cabinet-maker in the execution, of the various designs presented in the book. As he had intended, the *Director* brought Chippendale many clients among the English aristocracy. For example, it was Chippendale who furnished Nostell Priory and Harewood House, both in Yorkshire, attending not only to the furniture but to the wallpapers and curtains as well. The publication of the book also meant that the designs which it contained were copied everywhere. By means of excellent engravings the *Director* illustrated all kinds of furniture, in a range of designs from Classical to rococo, *chinoiserie* to Gothic. But the *Director* was not a feat of innovation; Chippendale was merely following the fashions of the age. Chippendale's workshops in St Martin's Lane, London, produced a range of furniture, most of it in mahogany, but the proportion of furniture produced at his workshops was far smaller than that made by other craftsmen copying his style. Chairs in the Chippendale style were well-proportioned, with back legs curving away and elaborate splat-work. The chairs are of four kinds: ladder-back, rococo, Chinese and Gothic. The simplest were the

Chippendale used fretwork extensively. In the Director, *he illustrated over twenty different patterns, samples of which are shown right. Below them is a print of the title page of his* Director, *which was first published in 1754.*

Below: *a basic design for a bureau bookcase from the* Director. *Note that many different details are shown on the piece, for the customer to choose from.*

ladder-back chairs, of traditional country design. Chippendale chairs in the rococo style usually have a pierced back splat, cabriole legs and claw-and-ball feet. Ribbon-back chairs, the most ornate, fall into the rococo category. Chinese Chippendale chairs, which also sometimes show touches of rococo, have geometric designs to their backs and the legs are usually of square section. Chippendale Gothic chairs have backs carved with arches and quatrefoils derived from Gothic architecture. Other notable pieces in the Chippendale style include pedestal desks and tall, elegant break-front bookcases.

After the mid-18th century, the fussiness of the rococo was beginning to pall. A return to a more disciplined style was about to take place. Chippendale's style gradually changed, moving from rococo to neo-classicism.

*These three mahogany chairs are either by Chippendale himself or inspired by his designs. **Above left:** shows rococo motifs to the carved back (c. 1760). **Above:** note the lyre back, in severely classical style (c. 1770). **Left:** illustrates typical Chinese Chippendale with fretwork (c. 1765).*

*__Far left:__ the saloon at Nostell Priory, in North Yorkshire, for which Chippendale was commissioned to make furniture. The Priory was also decorated to designs by Robert Adam and contains fine examples of his furniture as well. **Left:** a detail of the inlay on the commode in the saloon.*

*Slender proportions and symmetrical decoration – hallmarks of the Adam style – are evident in this late 18th-century giltwood pier table (**above right**). Pier tables were often designed with pier glasses, or tall mirrors, that hung above them, usually between the tall windows of grand rooms.*

*The painted decoration on this dressing room chair (**right**) is in Robert Adam's Etruscan style. Ancient Greco-Italian pottery, mistakenly believed to be Etruscan, inspired the black, white and terra cotta colour scheme.*

Robert Adam

Discipline, in contrast to rococo frivolity, was found in neo-classicism, the style based on what were seen as true Greek and Roman ideals, which was sweeping Europe in the second half of the 18th century.

It was the architect Robert Adam (1728–92) who, in about 1760, brought neo-classical ideals to bear on the design of furniture. From 1754 to 1758, Adam had studied in Italy, where excavations on sites in Rome, Pompeii and Herculaneum were inspiring the classical revival. On his return to England, Adam was soon in demand among the educated aristocracy. Neo-classicism was soon to make the rococo, *chinoiserie* and Gothic styles of the previous decades seem outmoded. Adam's neo-classical style dominated design in England until the last years of the 18th century.

Adam saw furniture as a complement to his interiors, which were light and elegant, with classical mouldings in low relief. As well as making patterns for carpets and ceilings, Adam designed furniture to complement them. His designs for furniture are characterized by fluting, classical motifs such as urns, medallions and rams' heads, and fine inlays. His dining rooms were often graced by a sideboard flanked by a pair of urns on pedestals. Chairs in the Adam style are light, with oval or lyre-shaped backs and straight legs.

ROBERT ADAM 1728–1792

Robert Adam was the second, and most famous, of four architect brothers. Ambitious, and an arrogant social climber, he was a friend at university of David Hume, and Adam Smith, the economist. Adam worked on many projects with his brothers, such as Kenwood House, and Landsdowne House in Berkeley Square. Their business acumen was not always as sound as their designs, however, and the Adelphi, in London, was a commercial disaster.

Adam's neo-classical style was far from being severe. The surfaces of this satinwood and marquetry commode are packed with interesting motifs.

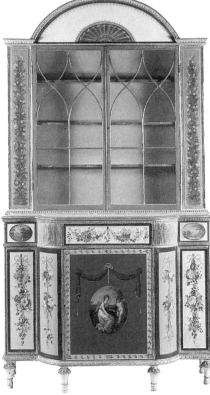

The interior of Osterley Park, Surrey (**above**) – once an Elizabethan mansion – was transformed by the neo-classical designs of Robert Adam. The mouldings on walls and ceiling, the pier glass, pier tables, urns and classical landscape all lend a sense of well ordered grandeur.

Far left: a late 18th-century secretaire cabinet painted in the style of Angelica Kauffmann. Painted decoration on furniture well suited the needs of Robert Adam. Artists employed to paint ceilings and walls were now being commissioned to decorate the furniture as well. The inlaid decoration in the late 18th-century (**left**) secretaire bookcase shows a more discreet use of neo-classical motifs.

Cornices for Beds or Windows

Subtly different usage of the straight-lined elegance of the neo-classical style advocated by Hepplewhite and Sheraton may be seen in these chairs. they span the last four decades of the 18th century. **Left to right:** a painted chair, c. 1760–1800; two designs from Hepplewhite's Guide, c. 1788; an armchair, c. 1795, after a design by Sheraton; another Sheraton design for a parlour chair from his Drawing Book; and a mahogany dining chair with x-frame back, c. 1800. The progression shows an increasingly subtle use of decoration as fashion moves towards Regency.

A design for a cornice from Hepplewhite's Guide. Symmetry was essential to his style.

Right: the clean lines of this late 18-century Pembroke table, with relatively simple inlay, is in keeping with the neo-classical tendency towards a simpler elegance.

George Hepplewhite and Thomas Sheraton

George Hepplewhite (d. 1786) and Thomas Sheraton (1751–1806) were two important cabinet-makers and designers who followed the neo-classical style developed by Adam. Like Chippendale, they were born in the provinces and later came to London, where Hepplewhite set up a workshop but Sheraton lived mostly in poverty.

Hepplewhite's *Cabinet-Maker's and Upholsterer's Guide* was published in 1788, two years after his death, with two further editions appearing subsequently. The *Guide* interpreted the new style for craftsmen, often recommending mahogany. Hepplewhite is also known for his shield-back chairs, although he also used heart motifs, ovals and lyres. For splats, Hepplewhite favoured the wheat-ear motif or the Prince of Wales feathers.

Left: a design for a library table from Sheraton's Drawing Book. *The lion-mask handles and paw feet are features which often appear in neo-classical pieces.*

Right: restrained ornamentation and sparing use of inlay classify this mahogany secretaire chiffonier – in the manner of George Smith – as being in Regency style.

Sheraton's *The Cabinet-Maker's and Upholsterer's Drawing Book* bridges the gap between neo-classicism and Regency. Sheraton is thought to have made no furniture, but pieces made after his designs are light, delicate and straight-lined. Sheraton chairs have rectangular backs with upright splats, and were sometimes of painted beech rather than mahogany or satinwood. Carving was replaced by straight-lined inlay on the top rail, and striped material, matching the straight lines of the chair, was used for the upholstery. Sheraton is also associated with the bow-fronted chest of drawers, although he made designs in a variety of other shapes. He also designed many delicate small tables, including ladies' work tables with ingenious drawer arrangements. And it was Sheraton who popularized the Pembroke table, a narrow table with two folding side flaps on hinges. Like Hepplewhite, Sheraton designed elegant sideboards which often have a brass rail at the back to hold plates.

The Regency style

Although the years of the Regency were 1810 to 1820, the Regency style in furniture dominated from 1795 to 1830. Two new strains are apparent in Regency furniture: French taste and a new desire to imitate accurately Greek and Roman styles. English Regency is the equivalent of the French Empire style and was partly inspired by it.

French taste was favoured by the Regent himself, and by his architect, Henry Holland, who designed in the neo-classical, Louis XVI style. The fashion for the accurate imitation of the "antique" (Greek and Roman styles) was promoted by Thomas Hope, a millionaire who designed his own furniture, adapting ancient models. Hope liked furniture with expanses of flat veneer and small ormolu ornaments and discreet ebony inlay. He

also favoured vase stands (*torchères*), in the shape of Greek or Roman tripods, and simple couches with scrolled ends. Hope's *Household Furniture and Interior Decoration*, published in 1807, presented a selection of his designs, but it was George Smith's *A Collection of Designs for Household Furniture and Interior Decoration*, of 1808, which popularized Hope's scholarly ideas.

The Regency style, however, was not entirely based on the scholarly, archaeological approach. Regency had its 'pop' side, well illustrated in Rudolf Ackermann's *Repository of Arts* (1809–28). Napoleon's campaigns in Syria and Egypt had already inspired the Egyptian style. But Nelson's victory over Napoleon at the Battle of the Nile and a growing awareness of Ancient Egypt itself further encouraged the use of the Egyptian style and Egyptian motifs. For example, there was the

Top, left and right: two examples of the simple elegance of Regency furniture. The sabre legs in both the table and the chair are also typical of the style.

Above and above right: a mahogany pedestral desk by Thomas Chippendale the Younger, and a mahogany drum-top table: further examples of the Regency style. The reeding on the table's sabre legs echoes that on the pilasters of the desk.

Right: an illustration from Thomas Hope's Household Furniture and Interior Decoration, *showing his rather academic, stilted approach.*

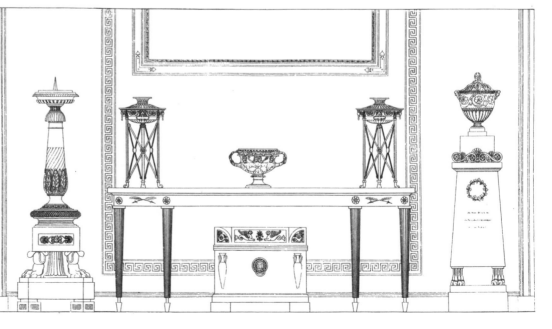

Trafalgar chair, with "scimitar" legs and a turned rope motif in the centre of the top rail.

Other distinctive Regency pieces included the sofa or couch, the drum table with tripod support, and the *chiffonier*, a low cupboard with shelves for books. The most popular form of sideboard was a table between flanking cupboards. Rosewood was preferred, and brass inlay work, lion-mask handles and reeded corner columns were common. Thomas Chippendale the Younger worked in the Regency style; his mahogany and gilt furniture is dignified and well proportioned.

From 1811, with the end of wartime austerity, tastes were changing. Furniture became less refined; the "scimitar" legs of the Trafalgar chair, for instance, were replaced by turned legs, and simple Doric and Tuscan capitals used in furniture were replaced by florid Corinthian capitals.

THOMAS HOPE 1770–1831

The eldest son of a rich Amsterdam merchant, Thomas Hope spent his youth studying architecture and sketching architectural remains in Europe and the Middle East. Settling down in England in his mid twenties, he devoted his considerable wealth to collecting ancient vases, sculptures and works of art. He also bought houses in London, and one, Deepdene, in Surrey, whose rooms he designed and furnished in Regency style to display them in. He published several works on architecture and interior decorating, promoting neo-classical ideas, which had some effect on public taste. His chief interest was, however, literature, and Byron, who despised him as a mere "house-furnisher", is said to have wept on reading Hope's Anastasius *because he had not written it himself.*

The Victorian Age

By 1830, furniture design no longer followed a single style. The dictates of the Regency period were cast off and furniture was made in a variety of past styles. Revivals of "Renaissance", "Gothic", "Elizabethan" and "rococo" styles played a central part and were often freely interpreted.

Most early Victorian furniture is of mahogany, rosewood or oak. Large mirrors were often incorporated into sideboards and cabinets. Comfort had also become the main criterion in popular furniture so that deep all-over upholstery was especially common in the 1840s and 1850s. As the Victorian period progressed, so furniture became more flamboyant. Upholstery declined in favour of more angular lines and a greater degree of surface decoration; marquetry and ormolu were much used and china plaques were incorporated.

While mahogany, oak and rosewood continued to be used for the more imposing items of Victorian furniture, other materials were employed for the more informal pieces. There were attempts at making furniture out of papier mâché, but although some chairs and a limited amount of case furniture have survived, the brittle nature of the material made it more suitable for smaller objects such as firescreens, trays and boxes. Cast and wrought iron was fashioned into hat-stands, chairs and furniture for the conservatory. Bentwood, bamboo and cane were used in the last quarter of the 19th century.

A papier mâché work table, c. 1850, with mother-of-pearl inlay. Highly decorated and difficult to classify, pieces of this kind came as a complete contrast to the ordered style of the Regency period.

The extreme fineness of the carving on this marquetry side cabinet was made possible by machine-assisted methods of production; Thomas Jordan's woodcarving machine was introduced in 1845.

The Victorian era was also the age of the first factory-made furniture. It was modern machinery rather than manual labour that catered for the needs of a growing and prosperous middle class, allowing them to fill their homes with furniture machine-made to a range of past styles. Leading London furniture-making concerns included Gillow, Trollope, Howard & Sons, Thomas Fox and Johnstone & Jeanes.

Right: a painted and rosewood-veneered dining chair of about 1890. It is an , example of Victorian re-interpretation of earlier styles (including Regency and neo-classical) with the addition of decoration wholly of the period.

This was the popular, unadventurous side of Victorian furniture. The other side was "progressive", the result of dissatisfaction with the low standards of factory-made furniture. The first of the great reformers of Victorian design was A. W. N. Pugin (1812–52). Pugin's aim was to revive the "honesty" of Gothic furniture, making it more authentic by allowing joints to show on the surface of the piece.

Continuing Pugin's work, William Morris (1834–96) set up the firm of Morris & Co. in 1861. Morris himself was not involved in the design of furniture; this was done by his collaborators, Philip Webb, William Burges and J. P. Seddon. Their products include bedroom furniture, simple country-style rush-seated chairs, drawing-room easy chairs with adjustable backs, and monumental case furniture with Pre-Raphaelite painted decoration. One of the Morris school's principal aims was to direct popular taste away from mass-produced furniture towards the individually made, artistically produced and hand-crafted. In this it was only partly successful because being hand-made the furniture of Morris & Co. remained out of the reach of the poor, yet it failed, through its plainness and apparent lack of sophistication, to appeal to the rich.

Thus, mass-production in the furniture industry continued. Nevertheless, the Victorian obsession with past styles gradually weakened. Bruce Talbert (1838–81) broke away from the Gothic revival

WILLIAM MORRIS 1834–1896

Designer, artist, poet and social reformer, William Morris had, from his earliest years a strong love for all things Mediaeval, and it was a somewhat free interpretation of this period that was the motivation of the firm of Morris, Marshall, Faulkner and Co. that he set up in 1861. Working in stained glass, textiles, furniture, carpets and wallpaper, Morris and his followers tried to stem the tide of machine development by concentrating on simple naturalistic forms and designs. Morris also founded and led both the Art and Crafts Movement, and the Society for the Preservation of Ancient Buildings, which still exists today.

with his sternly rectilinear furniture with geometric decoration. A bigger break with past styles came with the Japanese-inspired furniture of E. W. Godwin in the 1870s and 1880s.

Next came the establishment of the Arts and Crafts Movement, which aimed to offer an alternative to low commercial standards. The Arts and Crafts Movement, inspired by William Morris but founded by later craftsmen, stressed the beauty of hand-made furniture. Important followers of the movement included C. F. A. Voysey (1857–1941), C. R. Ashbee (1863–1942), A. H. Mackmurdo (1851–1942) and Charles Rennie Mackintosh (1868–1928).

Although trade manufacturers at first ignored the developments of "progressive" furniture, some, towards the end of the 19th century, began to incorporate into their products the more obvious features of the new style. Only at the turn of the century were the principles of the Arts and Crafts Movement adopted by such firms as Heal and Son, J. S. Henry and Wylie and Lockheed.

*Charles Rennie Mackintosh was one of the most important followers of the Arts and Crafts Movement. His "Design for Dining Room for House of Art Lover" (**below**) dates from 1901–2.*

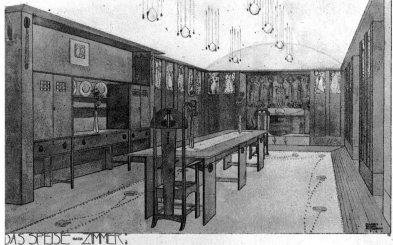

*Left: two examples of the "progressive" furniture, resulting from dissatisfaction with low standards of factory-made pieces: a "Sussex" rush-seated armchair from Morris & Co (**far left**) and a more formal ebonized square occasional table with gilt decoration, by E. W. Godwin (**left**).*

FRANCE

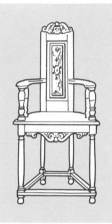

Above: *a* caquetoire *chair.*

*Italian Renaissance influence is seen on this carved walnut double-decker cabinet (**left**) of the mid-16th century decorated with marble panels and gilt.*

Louis XIV fauteuil (***above***) *shows how designs evolved between the 17th and 18th centuries. The curves of top rail, arms and legs are more pronounced than formerly.*

The 16th and 17th centuries

Very little French furniture of the 16th century has come down to us. However, apart from the relatively small number of surviving pieces, furniture types can be seen in French paintings of the period and in drawings and designs. As always, only the nobility and the upper classes owned fine furniture and it was for them that the best pieces were made. More lowly, utilitarian furniture remained plain and changed little.

Walnut was the most frequently used wood in France in the 16th century, and the most common surviving piece of furniture is the dresser, sometimes with carved decoration and panels of Romayne work. Renaissance ideas, from Italy, made themselves felt in France from the early decades of the 16th century and Italian Renaissance styles were eagerly sought at the French Court and among the nobility. Reliefs on chairs, dresser panels and double-decker cupboards (known as *armoires à deux corps*) show obvious Italian influence. An exaggerated form of Renaissance decoration, known as Mannerism, was most common in the south of France, in Burgundy and in western Switzerland; Hugues Sabin, of Dijon in Burgundy, made cabinets and dressers with grotesque carved ornament, and in 1572 issued his own set of designs for furniture. Another French 16th century maker, du Cerceau, favoured architectural motifs in his designs.

Chairs and tables tended to be large and robust. Upholstered chairs were also used, and armchairs appeared later in the century. The *caquetoire* chair is characteristic of the period; it was designed for women, and the shape of the seat, narrow at the back and wide at the front, was developed to take the generous skirts that were fashionable at the time.

Between the mid-16th and mid-17th centuries, French furniture underwent little change. But from the mid-17th century, France took the lead in the arts. Moreover, the accession to the throne of Louis XIV, the Sun King, in 1643, brought a new demand for splendour; the King's palaces had to be furnished, and furnished magnificently. Rich tapestries were in use on furniture as well as on walls. The luxury pieces that survive were, initially, almost entirely made by foreign craftsmen, especially Italians, working in France. The later 17th century was a period of expansion and wealth in France, and besides encouraging splendour, Louis XIV, the Sun King, was also a patron of the arts. Under him a new importance was placed on French manufacture. In 1663, a centre controlling the design and quality of French furniture – the *Manufacture Royale des Meubles de la Couronne* was set up by Colbert, chief minister to Louis XIV. There, under strict state control, French makers took the lead in satisfying the opulent tastes of the court and aristocracy. The first director of the *Manufacture* was Charles le Brun, whose first task was to decorate and furnish the new palace of Versailles.

The most celebrated cabinet-maker of the period was André-Charles Boulle (1642–1732). Boulle created the bombé commode, a concave-fronted chest of drawers. Boulle is also known for his fine wood marquetry, but he is most famous for intricate inlays of tortoiseshell and brass, a technique now known as Boulle-work (or buhl-work). Much of Boulle's work, such as tables and commodes, was made for the Court. Few pieces by Boulle survive today, and many that are attributed to him were in fact by later makers.

In the 17th century, veneers on luxury furniture were usually of light sculpted ebony and this was the origin of the name *ébéniste*, to describe a French cabinet-maker. Precious metals and semi-precious stones were also used on furniture and turned decoration was popular. The commode, a chest of drawers, was introduced in about 1700; it was probably the most important innovation in French furniture. A form of bureau or desk was also made, with two sets of drawers flanking the knee-hole. Tall wardrobes appeared in the late 17th century. Armchairs were often throne-like, sometimes with extravagantly arched stretchers.

*This Louis XIV marquetry bureau mazarin, possibly by Boulle, is inlaid with engraved brass on a scarlet tortoiseshell ground. Its ormolu-moulded top (**below**) is intricately inlaid with a central design of figures from the fashionable* Commedia dell 'Arte *beneath a festooned arbour and flanked by lappets, caryatids, masks, putti, monkeys and urns with interlacing engraved brass scrollwork.*

The 18th and 19th centuries

France led furniture fashion through the 18th century and into the early 19th century. The furniture produced during this time is divided into five periods: Régence (*c.* 1715–30); Louis XV (*c.* 1730–74); Louis XVI (*c.* 1774–85); Directoire (*c.* 1785–1810); and Empire (*c.* 1810–30).

During the 18th century, there were interesting centres of furniture-making in France such as Grenoble, Lyons and Normandy, but Paris was supreme. The Parisian guild system rigorously enforced a division of labour. The joiners (*menuisiers*) produced everything made of wood, while the main job of the cabinet-makers (*ébénistes*) was to enrich furniture with veneers and marquetry. From 1745 to 1790 members of the Paris guild were obliged to stamp their names on their furniture.

Régence

The death of Louis XIV in 1715 put an end to the glorious court life of the Age of the Sun King. Louis XIV was succeeded by a small boy, the future Louis XV, controlled by a pleasure-loving Regent. This was the Régence period, during which apartments became smaller, thus creating a need for smaller furniture, elegant rather than monumental. Boulle marquetry passed temporarily out of fashion. The new taste was for elaborate wood marquetry with ormolu mounts. Lines became more curved and decoration often took precedence over function.

Above right: one of a pair of highly ornamented marble-topped encoignures, or corner cupboards, dating from the mid-18th century. The marquetry and the extravagantly curving ormolu decoration was inspired by a taste for the rococo in mid-18th-century France.

Right: a Régence ebonized bureau plat, or writing table, dating from about 1725-50 and pre-dating the craze for the rococo. The relatively restrained use of ormolu and gently curving cabriole legs give this piece a refined appearance.

Louis XV (1723–74)

In Louis XV's reign, the rococo was born. This was a style of shell motifs, calculated asymmetry and writhing, interlaced curves. In addition to the new rococo decoration, the typical Louis XV commode had two or four drawers in two layers, with legs longer than the Régence type. Another type of furniture at this time was the *encoignure*, an elegant corner cupboard, usually supplied in pairs. From the middle of the century, the *commode à vantaux*, a chest of drawers with doors enclosing the front was made. Also at this time, the writing table (*bureau plat*) became popular, and sometimes a cabinet or set of pigeon-holes for papers, known as a *cartonnier*, was placed on top. The drop-front writing cabinet (*secrétaire à abattant*) became popular from the 1750s. After about 1750, there was a vogue for the *bonheur du jour*, a lady's small writing table on tall legs, with drawers in a raised part at the back. (The *bonheur du jour* was frequently imitated in 19th-century England). Another type of writing desk was the *bureau-toilette*, which also doubled as a toilet table.

Chairs during the period included the *marquise* (a double armchair), the *bergère* (an armchair with closed upholstered sides and back), and the *voyeuse* (with a padded rail for spectators at card games to lean on).

The rococo style persisted, but the opening of

These four examples of Louis XV furniture show function and decoration skilfully combined. **Above left:** a parquetry commode possibly made by Charles Cressent, whose work was much admired at the French court. This sumptuous serpentine-fronted piece has a marble top and rich ormolu decoration in the rococo style.

Above: a secretaire à abattant, or drop-fronted cabinet. Like many pieces of this period, it has marquetry and ormolu decoration and a marble top. **Left:** a beechwood bergère chair. Though of relatively simple form, the serpentine seat, cabriole legs and scrolled arms and feet are all characteristic of the period, and give it a subtle elegance. **Below left:** a tulipwood and marquetry table de toilette, or dressing table — a decorative yet functional adjunct to a lady's boudoir; the hinged top conceals a dressing mirror and wells for bottles, and the front has four drawers and a writing slide.

trade routes with the Far East brought Oriental goods to France. Among the wealthy, the novelty of the Far East created a taste for lacquer and a demand for Oriental woods for use as inlays. Some of the most attractive pieces of French furniture of the time were decorated with *Vernis Martin*, a lustrous imitation lacquer, often in blues, reds or greens, developed by the four Martin brothers and first patented by them in 1730.

Among the leading cabinet-makers of the 18th century were Charles Cressent (1685–1758), Antoine-Robert Gaudreau (*c.* 1680–1751) and Bernard II van Risenburgh. The two supreme Louis XV *ébénistes* were Jean François Oeben and Jean-Henri Riesener. Both were German by birth and masters of the rococo style, though Oeben also produced Boulle-work and later progressed to the transitional style.

The transitional style, coming between the exuberance of the rococo and the sobriety of classicism, combined rococo and neo-classical features, and long before the accession of Louis XVI in 1774, a reaction had begun against the extreme excesses of the rococo. Outlines became rectangular again, the legs of chairs and tables lost their scrolls and became straight, tapering and fluted, and the asymmetry of the rococo was replaced by the symmetrical use of neo-classical motifs. And porcelain (including Sèvres) was set into furniture.

The 1780s in France saw a fashion for all things English. Wedgwood jasperware plaques were used in furniture, and solid mahogany chairs were introduced to France, from England, by Georges Jacob.

Georges Jacob was the greatest joiner (*menuisier*) of late 18th- and early 19th century France. Jean-Henri Riesener, meanwhile, was the greatest cabinet-maker (*ébéniste*), who had also been important during the preceding Louis XV period.

*These four early neo-classical pieces show a return to straighter lines characteristic of the late 18th century. Among their neo-classical features are the tapering, fluted legs of the commode (**above left**) and of the sewing table (**left**), the urn motif of the fall-front desk (**above**) and the more restrained use of ormolu on the chest (**far left**). Decoration remained important, as the vernis martin flowers (**above left**) and Boulle marquetry (**far left**) show.*

*The move away from rococo curves and scrolls is seen in these two mid to late 18th-century pieces. The tulipwood bureau à cylindre, or roll-top desk, (**left**), c. 1765, is an example of Jean-François Oeben's work in the Transitional style; although Oeben has retained scrolls on the feet, he has given the desk a plainer outline which, with the Greek key pattern of the gallery, clearly looks forward to neo-classical ideas.*

The Directoire and Empire styles

The French Revolution (1789) ended the guild system, but some workshops continued production, among them Georges Jacob and his sons. The keynote of the Directoire period (named after the government of 1795–99) was a classical style known as "Etruscan"; for Jacques-Louis David, artist and revolutionary leader, Jacob had made furniture with red and black upholstery from "Etruscan" designs supplied by David himself. Egyptian ideas were also used at this time. Furniture typical of the period included the *méridienne* (a day-bed with either one or two curl-over arm ends), the *athénienne* (a three-legged washstand) and the vase-stand. The first gondola-shaped beds, enveloped in draperies, date from the end of the century.

French industry recovered from the effect of the Revolution under the firm rule of Napoleon Bonaparte's First Consulate (1799–1804). The Empire style (1804–15) was Napoleon's propaganda vehicle, created for him to give an illusion of

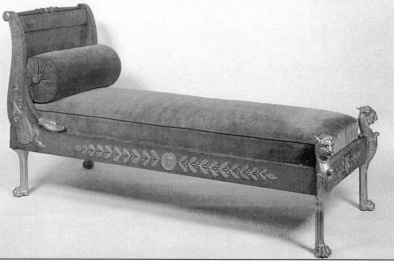

*A more fully developed neo-classical style is seen in the day bed (**above**). The straight lines, paw feet, lion's heads and symmetrical band of leaves are all taken from Ancient Egyptian, Greek and Roman designs.*

Right: *an Empire ormolu-
and bronze-mounted burr
yew console table which was
made around 1805 probably
by Jacob Desmalter.*

Below: *an early 19th
century tôle peinte centre
table. The circular tray top is
decorated in colours and gilt
in a design of chimerae,
scrolls and vines. The heads
and delightfully sandled feet
of the square tapering legs
reflect the Empire style's love
of classical motifs.*

Two fauteuils *showing the
evolution of taste in the early
19th century. The giltwood
example on the* **right** *– part
of a set supplied to Napoleon
by Jacob Desmalter in 1810
– has a scroll back.
Generally much lighter in
appearance, the
white-painted and gilded
chair (1814–20)* **(far right)**
has a rectangular back.

authority and grandeur, and it spread throughout Europe with his conquests, and also through engravings. The Empire style made free use of styles and motifs from Ancient Greece and Rome. The finest work was by Jacob Desmalter et Cie. From 1806, imports of maghogany from the English colonies were halted by the Continental blockade. This made mahogany even more valuable – Napoleon therefore had his palaces furnished with it – but also increased the use of native, French woods. Furniture became increasingly heavy and bronze mounts coarser, and draperies were used in abundance. Rectangular-backed chairs replaced scroll-backed ones, and console tables often had animal supports. Egyptian motifs were added to the Empire style after Napoleon's campaigns on the Nile.

Towards the middle of the 19th century, furniture began to be made in large quantities. Manufacturers were now engaged not only in making luxury pieces but also in producing less expensive, more ordinary items of furniture that were also of a poorer quality. While walnut, the abundant native wood, was used for these cheaper pieces, rosewood, mahogany and veneering were used for fine furniture.

The Empire style finally died out in the late 1830s, to be replaced by a discreet use of Gothic, rococo and, later, Renaissance styles. In the Second Empire (1848–70), various upholstered seats were made. These included *pouffes*, low, soft seats, and *crapauds*, low armchairs, and various types of settee. One of the best furniture makers of the time was L. E. Lamarchand, who imitated the style of the late 17th and early 18th-century maker Boulle, and copied 18th-century lacquer pieces. Oriental styles and motifs, which had been used from the early 19th century, became especially popular with forward-looking designers of the 1860s. Their free use of Oriental forms contrasted refreshingly with the rather formal styles of most other 19th-century furniture. Japanese artifacts – paintings, ceramics and glass, as well as furniture – were to be seen in Paris in the shop of a German dealer, Samuel Bing. Bing named his shop "L'Art Nouveau", and it was this name that was conferred on the new, naturalistic style of design, with its asymmetry and plant-like forms. Meanwhile, however, conventional furniture firms continued to produce furniture in the old, revivalist styles.

Left: this mahogany bureau aux orchidées *with ormolu mounts by Louis Majorelle is a good example of Art Nouveau furniture. However, by the time this was made in 1907, the popularity of the style was on the wane.*

GERMANY

Right: a heavily carved 17th century oak buffet. Renaissance influence can be seen in some of the motifs, in particular the flowers, foliage and cherub-heads of the frieze.

*Much South German furniture of the 16th and 17th centuries was decorated with marquetry. This late 17th-century walnut example (**far right**) is inlaid on every part, except the spirally turned legs, which are ebonized.*

Augsburg was an important centre for the making of cabinets, cupboards and desks. Augsburg's specialities were intarsia work and the use of precious stones and metals for extravagant inlays. Nuremberg was also famous for its furniture, and especially its cupboards, which were profusely decorated. By the early 18th century, however, there was a preference for plain walnut furniture.

In north Germany, oak remained the favoured wood until well into the 18th century. Cologne was noted for its intarsia and the use of different coloured woods. Eger, in Bohemia, produced cabinets with intricately sculpted intarsia panels. From the Trier region came large fruitwood cupboards, and in Berlin Gerard Dagly made superb lacquered furniture for Frederick of Prussia. Italian baroque influence in Munich gave rise to marble-mosaic tables with caryatid legs.

The 16th and 17th centuries

Renaissance ideas reached Germany later than they did France. German cabinet-makers clung to the Gothic style, mixing it with the new Italian ideas. Peter Flötner (1485–1546) designed cupboards with Renaissance touches such as putti and foliage. Flötner, and another cabinet-maker known only by his initials H. S., published wood-cuts of furniture designs in the Renaissance style, with classical columns for example, which had overtaken the Gothic mode with pinnacles and tracery.

In the 16th century, a popular piece of furniture in southern Germany was the "façade cupboard"; its design was inspired by architectural ideas and it was often overcrowded with mouldings. Other south German furniture, much of it made of softwood, was decorated with marquetry and painting. By contrast, north German furniture was more severe, and most of it was of carved oak.

The 18th and 19th centuries

Although it maintained its Teutonic character, some 18th-century German furniture was subject to the tastes and fashions of other European countries. The French tradition, for example, with ornate tendencies, was strong in Munich; and pieces by leading French cabinet-makers were imported and copied. Another influence was the decorative designs of François Cuvilliés (1695–1768), a Flemish architect, whose furniture combined the delicate French style with the more flowery Bavarian rococo. For the Würzburg court, the sculptor Wolfgang van der Auvers (1708–56) made magnificent carved console tables. Other important mid-18th-century cabinet-makers include Johan Georg Nestfell (1694–1762), a master of marquetry, and Carl Maximilian Mattern, who specialized in ivory and coloured woods.

In Dresden and its environs, the Electors of Saxony established a furniture centre, which flourished from 1670 to 1763. Typical products of this centre were writing cabinets with looking glasses in their upper doors. The finest pieces were the lacquered furniture made by Martin Schnell.

In Berlin, the best 18th-century furniture was made under Frederick the Great (1740–86). Some of it was designed by Johan August Nahl (1710–85), who worked in an exuberant rococo style, and Johann Melchior Kambli, whose speciality included magnificent ormolu against tortoiseshell.

The Rhenish cabinet-maker Abraham Roentgen (1711–93) and his son David were perhaps the most successful 18th-century designer-craftsmen in the German tradition. Both travelled widely, in England, Belgium and France. David Roentgen is considered to be the greatest German furniture maker; he favoured *trompe l'œil* intarsia and

*This highly decorated mid-18th-century kingwood parquetry commode (**above**) is thought to have been made for the Elector of Saxony. The piece has a marble top and ormolu mounts.*

ingenious mechanical devices, particularly for writing desks.

But the age of rococo was drawing to a close in Germany and by the early 19th century, German cabinet-makers had rejected extravagant decoration in favour of more restrained Napoleonic Empire style. After 1815, this then gave way to a more informal, middle-class style known as Biedermeier. Biedermeier furniture is plain and functional, with simple surfaces and few gilt-bronze mounts. Josef Danhauser, of Vienna, who produced his best pieces from 1804 to 1830, was the most accomplished craftsman in the Biedermeier style.

Above: this walnut marquetry and parquetry commode of the third quarter of the 18th century has pictorial panels in stained and engraved wood.

*The restrained lines of the fruitwood chair made around 1820 (**far left**) are typical of the Biedermeier style. It contrasts sharply with the opulent neo-classical giltwood side chair (**above left**) made half a century earlier.*

ITALY

An Italian walnut table of about 1550 (**right**). Its rectangular top has three trestle supports with acanthus leaves carved on the feet.

Below: the cassone (chest) is one of the basic pieces of Italian Renaissance furniture.

Right: this elaborately decorated cabinet was made around the middle of the 17th century. The panels illustrate fables from folklore.
Far right: a closer view of one of the panels.

The 15th and 16th centuries

Italian Renaissance furniture is highly prized today. Little has survived, and almost all of it, from Renaissance times up until the 18th century, was made for a wealthy, powerful aristocracy.

Basic types of Italian Renaissance furniture are the *cassone*, a chest, sometimes richly decorated with painted panels; the *cassapanca*, a bench which doubled as a chest; the *armadio*, a large cupboard; the *credenza*, a side table or serving table; and the X-shaped chair. This furniture was relatively simple in design, with classical decoration in the form of columns, leaves, scrolls and human figures. From the 16th century, inlays of semi-precious stones were sometimes applied to table tops.

The 17th century

Just as Italy had been the birthplace of the Renaissance, so Italy was the fountainhead of the baroque style. The baroque, which was applied to furniture from about 1670, is a style of extravagant curves and outlandish motifs designed to create an impression of overwhelming energy and fruitfulness. Motifs connected with the sea were often employed; shells, sea-horses, river gods and imaginary sea monsters enjoyed prominence in the baroque style. Not surprisingly, Italian baroque furniture tended to be made by sculptors rather than cabinet-makers; Andrea Brustolon made fantastic chairs supported by carved blackamoors, and Antonio Corradini, a Venetian sculptor, produced chairs swarming with cherubs. Other impressive pieces in the Italian baroque style were console tables, which now became purely decorative.

The 18th and 19th centuries

Italian furniture became less interesting in the 18th century as French influence took over. This was the age of the rococo, though Italian rococo is often simply an overblown version of French rococo.

The best early 18th-century furniture came from Venice; it included bombé commodes and extended sofas. Because of that city's trading links with the East, Venice also produced attractive lacquered and painted furniture. Superior lacquerwork was also produced in Rome and Piedmont.

By the 19th century, cabinet-makers were turning their attention to the neo-classical style. And although the remarkable excavations at the ancient cities of Pompeii and Herculaneum stimulated a renewed interest in classical motifs, the French influence still dominated. Napoleon's conquest of Italy brought with it a taste of the Empire style, characterized by a sense of grandeur and a combination of classical and Egyptian styles and motifs. From the middle of the century, however, the Empire style was overtaken by the "Dantesque" Renaissance revival.

Overall, in Italian furniture of all periods, functionalism takes second place beside a delight in form and decoration. Splendour and liveliness of design also seem to have meant more to Italian makers than the exact finish typical of a Chippendale, for example.

Left: this late baroque parcel-gilt and ebonized cabinet-on-stand was made around 1700. Marine motifs are typical of the style.

Below: a painted and gilt Venetian bombé commode of the mid-18th century. The charming floral decoration is typical of Venetian cabinet-making.

Left: a parcel-gilt walnut and fruitwood marquetry commode in the neo-classical style of the late 18th and early 19th centuries.

THE NETHERLANDS

Before the late 16th century, furniture design in the Netherlands was entrenched in the Gothic tradition. By 1580, however, Hans Vredeman de Vries had brought classical motifs, such as chimerae, figures and garlands, to furniture. He also developed a form of decoration known as strapwork. Hans Vredeman de Vries' innovations, continued in the 17th century by his son Paul, spread to England, Scandinavia and Germany.

It was early in the 17th century that Netherlandish furniture began to develop a national style. In 1579, the northern, Protestant states of the Netherlands had split from the southern, Catholic ones; furniture from the northern states tended to be more restrained than that from the south, where connections with Spain and Italy were reflected in Moorish and Italian influences.

The most notable form of 17th-century Netherlandish furniture was the Antwerp cabinet. This was a cabinet on a stand, the cabinet fitted with numerous small drawers, often flanking a small central cupboard. Antwerp cabinets were also highly decorative. They were usually veneered in ebony and tortoiseshell, and sometimes further embellished with ivory or semi-precious stones. As their name implies, these pieces were made chiefly in Antwerp, and it was from Antwerp that they were exported world-wide.

Another important type of furniture produced in the Netherlands in the 17th century was the *Beeldenkast,* a cupboard with upper and lower sections, decorated with carved caryatids and human figures. *Beeldenkasts* from the northern provinces of the Netherlands were usually less highly ornamented than those from the southern provinces. After the middle of the century, the *Beeldenkast* was largely replaced by two-door cupboards with baroque ornamentation.

With the arrival of the baroque in the mid-17th century, all forms of Netherlandish furniture underwent a dramatic change. Gilded tables, with extravagantly carved supports, were typical of the baroque period. Antwerp now specialized in elaborate many-drawered cabinets.

In the 17th century, Netherlandish chairs became generally rectangular. They now had vase-shaped legs and the back uprights were topped with lion heads or shield-bearing lions. These chairs are usually of walnut and were upholstered in leather, velvet or cloth, attached by large brass studs.

After 1685, Huguenot refugees from France added their talents. Among them was the influential Daniel Marot, who, today, is associated with an ornate type of chair, with low upholstered seat and slender tall back. He also cleverly used drapery with furniture, such as velvets and rich hangings with four-poster beds. William of Orange's accession to the English throne in 1695 brought some

This Antwerp cabinet on stand, dating from the late 17th century, is a classic example of its kind; it is veneered in tortoiseshell, ebony and silver and has an arrangement of small drawers either side of a cupboard.

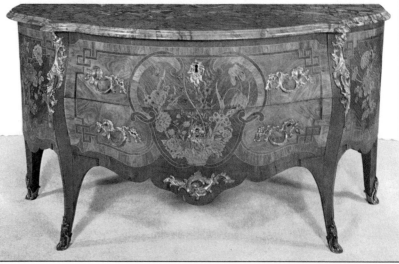

Far left: though this late 17th-century oak press cupboard is an example of plainer Netherlandish furniture, it is nevertheless not without discreet decorative curves.

Above: an exquisite inlay of tulips and roses set off by rococo scrolls embellishes this late 18th-century kingwood "bombe" commode, inspired by French models.

Left: Netherlandish floral marquetry at its most spectacular covers this mid-18th-century walnut press cupboard. The applied rococo decoration adds further interest to this graceful piece.

English influences to the Netherlands, particularly in chairs, which acquired pierced splats and cabriole legs.

By the mid-18th century, the rococo style, more delicate than the baroque, was coming in. English influence continued, for example, in the form of the claw and ball foot at the end of cabriole legs. Netherlandish commodes were made on the French model, though they were more bombé (swirlingly convex). By the late 18th century, the classical, rectilinear style had arrived.

The best furniture in this new, plainer style had accomplished marquetry and showed a masterly use of veneers. In the southern states of the Netherlands, oak wardrobes were decorated with scrolls and flowers asymmetrically carved.

The use of marquetry is characteristic of 18th-century Netherlandish furniture as a whole. Motifs in Netherlandish marquetry usually consist of naturalistic birds, flowers and foliage, the rich brown tones of the veneers sometimes embellished further with pieces of bone or ebony. Marquetry, copied from the Netherlands, was also used to good effect in England in the late 17th century and early 18th century.

The early decades of the 19th century saw the arrival of the Empire style, which was also sweeping the rest of Europe. Classical and Egyptian motifs and a sense of grandeur were the main tenets of the style. Carel Breyspraak made Empire furniture for the royal palace in Amsterdam, and an Empire flavour persisted in the work of G. Nordanus, a cabinet-maker from The Hague, but in the mid-19th century, a form of the Biedermeier style, which evolved from the Empire style in Germany, was dominant.

SCANDINAVIA

Above: an 18th-century Swedish chair with cane back in the English style.

*The pine chest-of-drawers (**below**), veneered with elm, elm-root and plumwood, was made in Stockholm in the mid-18th century. This "foreign" style was more or less confined to court furniture.*

Because of the absence of hardwoods in Scandinavia, most early Scandinavian furniture was made of deal or pine – soft woods which grow abundantly in northern regions. But, because of the less hard-wearing nature of these softwoods, very little Scandinavian furniture has survived from before the 17th century. Harder woods, like oak and walnut, reached Scandinavia later on as trade increased with countries such as England.

Furniture produced in Denmark and Sweden in the later 17th century shows a mix of English, Dutch and German influences, which came largely as the result of trade. Trade with England, for instance, was boosted by the Great Fire of London in 1666, when huge quantities of timber were suddenly needed to rebuild the capital. In return, English furniture was imported to Scandinavia.

The English-style high-backed chair, with cane seating or leather upholstery, was eagerly adopted by Danish and Norwegian makers. This type of chair, often with elaborately carved stretchers, continued to be made in Scandinavia well into the 18th century and well beyond the time it fell from fashion in England.

Other English influences that continued in Scandinavia in the 18th century were the claw and ball foot and the cabriole leg, which Scandinavian makers incongruously combined with stretchers in the earlier manner.

Dutch influence in Scandinavian furniture was strongest in the 17th century when Holland was a major sea power and the Dutch styles were seen in floral marquetry and in the bombé shapes of case furniture.

In the second half of the 18th century, French styles came in. French-inspired marquetry, depicting musical instruments, books and human figures, rivalled the Dutch floral motifs. It was also in the 18th century that French rococo became the court style in Scandinavia. Furniture was imported from France and some Swedish cabinet-makers went to Paris to study. These foreign-ideas, however, were mostly confined to court furniture; Scandinavia's comparatively wealthy peasantry continued with simple deal or pine furniture, often painted, of a style which was probably little changed since the 16th century.

Neo-classicism, reaching Scandinavia from France and England in the later 18th century, had a wider effect on furniture both within and beyond the court. Georg Haupt worked in Paris and brought back a fully developed Louis XVI (French neo-classical) style to Sweden in 1769.

In Denmark, German influence was particularly strong, as much of the Danish aristocracy was of German origin. Mathias Ortmann was an important 18th-century Danish maker in the German tradition. German influence was also brought to Denmark by Georg Roentgen, a German cabinet-maker who worked at the Royal Furniture Emporium which was set up in Copenhagen in 1777. But in 1871, Carsten Anker became director of the Emporium. His preference was for the English Hepplewhite/Sheraton taste.

Norwegian furniture followed Danish developments, though with less elegance. On late 18th-century chairs, a distinctly Norwegian feature is a band of fluting along the lower edge of the front seat rail. English influence waned in the 19th century, to be replaced in the early years of the century by the French Empire style, which was particularly strong in Sweden.

SPAIN AND PORTUGAL

armchair, with a fretted and carved front stretcher. It was upholstered in velvet or leather and could be hinged for folding. The *vargueño* was another 16th-century Spanish invention; this was a drop-leaf cabinet, resting on either a panelled chest or a trestle stand, and often decorated with *mudéjar* (geometric) marquetry. Romayne work, carved roundels depicting profile heads, was another form of decoration on 16th-century Spanish furniture.

The 17th century

In the 17th century, *vargueños* continued to be made, though they were now highly decorated in the baroque style. Another type of cabinet developed; unlike the *vargueño*, it had no fall front, and was topped by a gilt gallery. In Portugal, the

Far left: a 16th-century Spanish vargueño *with geometric (*mudéjar*) decoration.*

*The late 17th-century Portuguese stained chestnut chair (**left**), has a back and seat of embossed and incised leather.*

The 16th century

In Spain and Portugal, as in France and Germany, Gothic and Renaissance styles were combined at the beginning of the 16th century. Renaissance styles dominated eventually, but Moorish influences remained strong. In furniture, the Moorish legacy is seen in fine leatherwork and intricate geometric patterns. Walnut was the commonest wood for furniture in 16th-century Spain and Portugal. Chairs replaced benches at this time. The X-frame chair (*sillón de cadera*) arrived from Italy early in the 16th century. A little later the most characteristic Spanish chair appeared; this was the *sillón de fraileros*, or monk's chair, a framed

recapture of Brazil from the Dutch in 1654 led to the use of Brazilian woods, such as jacaranda, for furniture. The Portuguese elaborated on the *sillón de fraileros*, producing chairs with high, arched backs, turned legs and tooled leatherwork. Inventive turning was a characteristic of Portuguese furniture being particularly applied to the headpiece of a distinctive type of bed. Tables were of simple trestle construction, sometimes with the addition of decorative wrought-iron stretchers.

The 18th century

From the beginning of the 18th century, French influence affected furniture-making in Spain. This was largely due to the fall of the Spanish royal house in 1770 and the accession of the French house of Bourbon in Spain. French influence showed itself in gilding and rococo curves, and the ornate *vargueño* was replaced by the French-inspired commode, with early examples made of solid carved wood. 18th-century Spanish chairs, as in the rest of Europe at that time, were often basically English in form, though with gilt decoration. The Portuguese developed their own distinctive form of "Queen Anne style" chairs, using Brazilian hardwoods and adopting a more florid style.

The 19th century

In the early 19th century, the fashion for the neo-classical style affected furniture design in Spain as it did the rest of Europe. Spanish neo-classical furniture is usually of mahogany with bronze mounts, and is heavier than the French designs that inspired it. Gothic forms were also revived; a popular style was "Isabellino", a Spanish version of Louis Philippe and Second Empire periods. There was, also, an accent on comfortable upholstery and neo-rococo decoration.

*Above: a painted and gilded chair in the "English" style of the 18th century. Although the shape is similar to a Queen Anne chair, the style of decoration is very much that of Spain. This gilded stool with bronze mounts (**left**) is in the neo-classical style popular in the early years of the 19th century.*

MIRRORS

From ancient times right up to the 15th century, mirrors took the form of highly polished sheets of gold, silver or bronze. Such mirrors were small and were intended for use as hand mirrors rather than as objects to be hung on the wall.

The process of silvering glass was not unknown before the 15th century, but glass mirrors had been impracticable because glass made before that time was still too opaque to reflect an image.

Plates of mirror glass were first made on a commercial basis in Murano, in the republic of Venice, from about 1500. For a time, the Venetians enjoyed a monopoly in the production of looking-glasses, although Flanders and Germany were among the first countries to follow the Venetian model. By the 17th century, mirror glass was also being made commercially in England, notably at the famous glassworks established by the Duke of Buckingham at Vauxhall, in London.

The main challenge to the successful manufacture of mirror glass was in obtaining a smooth, level surface of an even thickness. It was first made by blowing a large bubble of glass, then cutting and flattening it and then, when it was cool, grinding and polishing it. There were two problems with this method; it was difficult to blow the glass to an even thickness and impossible to produce an expanse of glass beyond a certain size.

Glass casting, invented by the French in the late 17th century, solved the problem. This method involved pouring molten glass into a metal plate and quickly rolling it flat. Not only were finer mirrors produced in this way, but larger ones could also be made.

Mirrors were silvered not, at first, with silver but with tin foil and mercury. It was not until about 1840 that real silver was used for mirrors, following a discovery made by J. von Liebig, a German chemist, involving a method of chemically depositing silver onto glass.

If the manufacture of mirror glass and methods of silvering changed relatively little between the mid-17th and the mid-19th century, mirror frames were the subject of a remarkable evolution and have frequently outshone the mirrors themselves.

Left: a mid-18th-century giltwood pier glass with two separate mirror plates.

America

The 17th century

Being highly prized, the first American mirrors acted as a focal point in the home, and were often hung in a prominent position in the hall or parlour. These early mirrors were rectangular and simply framed in cove-moulded oak or pine, which was sometimes painted or, later in the 17th century, veneered in walnut. From the late 17th century, additional embellishment took the form of a crest, often elaborately carved like the cresting rails on William and Mary chairs.

The 18th century

As mirrors become more commonplace, so their position in the household was no longer confined to the hall or parlour. They were now hung above fireplaces, when they are known as chimney glasses, or between two windows, when they are known as pier glasses. The frames became more elaborate, with channelled rather than cove moulding, and crests, now usually scrolled, were sometimes balanced by a skirt, or scrollwork on the mirror's lower edge.

Mirrors now were often as much as five feet high, but the glass, being costly in large sheets, was usually in two pieces. The upper portion, too high to be of use in reflecting an image, was sometimes decorated with engravings.

Towards the middle of the 18th century, mirrors decorated with japanning became increasingly fashionable. All manner of Oriental and European motifs were depicted on the frame in gilt on a dark ground. Mirrors "new Silvered and the Frames plaine, japand or Flowered" were among the items offered by Gerardus Duyckinck, of New York, in the mid-18th century. Japanning continued to be a popular style of decoration on mirror frames into the 19th century.

By the middle of the 18th century, frames in mahogany were favoured above pine and walnut, and they became even more elaborate, developing a carved and gilt inner border, and crests were further embellished with a shell motif, symmetrical at first but becoming more fanciful as rococo tastes encouraged greater frivolity in design.

This period also saw the rise in popularity of the architectural style of frame, surmounted by a broken pediment and eagle and phoenix finial. To the basic architectural outlines were added symmetrical swags of leaves and flowers, rosettes, or streamers and scrolls. Carried along by the spirit of

Right: this elegant pine mirror, with pierced crest, made in about 1716, is an early forerunner of the tall pier glass made to hang between two windows.

Below: with the candles in its sconces burning, this chimney glass, made in about 1720–30, would have made a homely sight above the fireplace. Large sheets of glass were precious in the 18th century; here, two smaller pieces flank a larger central panel.

Crests also adorned another type of mirror, known today as a courting mirror. These mirrors had wide moulded frames incorporating glass painted with flowers and foliage, and were topped with a stepped crest.

In the 17th century, mirror glass, which was still being imported from England, was a precious and expensive material. Old mirrors were frequently re-framed, a practice which continued into the late 18th century.

the rococo, such decoration became increasingly exaggerated, and extreme examples sported free-standing flowers and papier mâché figures. Makers of mirrors in the rococo style include John Elliott and James Reynolds, both of Philadelphia.

The Federal period

Towards the late 18th century, the sobriety of the classical style began to challenge the exuberance of the rococo. New, oval-shaped mirrors were at first set into essentially rococo frames. But by the early 19th century, the Federal style was seen in delicate inlay, veneers, swags, beading, cornucopias and classical urns. Oval mirrors thus framed were used as dressing mirrors and also hung for purely decorative effect. It was also around this time that the

cheval glass appeared. This was a tall, tiltable dressing glass mounted on pins set into two uprights. Notable makers working at this time include Stephen Badlam Jr (1751–1815), of Dorchester, Massachusetts, John Doggett (1780–1857), of Roxbury, Massachusetts, and Peter Grinnel & Son, of Providence, Rhode Island.

A further development in the Federal period was the appearance of round, convex mirrors, surrounded by heavy carved frames and surmounted by an eagle. With the addition of candle-holders, they are sometimes referred to as girandoles. The architectural frame still persisted, but the broken-arch pediment of the mid-18th century was gradually replaced by a flat cornice. These mirrors, with their Classical columned frames, are sometimes called tabernacle mirrors. The upper portion was usually decorated with painting, gilded plaster or *verre églomisé* (glass decorated with a painted design and backed with gold or silver leaf).

Left: Rococo exuberance transforms the frame of this mirror, made in Philadelphia in 1770, into a riot of curves, scrolls and flowers. By the end of the 18th century, however, such excesses had gone out of fashion, to be replaced by a more sober style.

Top: this overmantel mirror, made in New York in about 1805, is a grand example of the Federal style. The verre églomisé panels that surround the mirror glass are pale blue, gold and white. The general effect is highly decorative.

Above: gilding and verre églomisé, together with an elaborate crest and skirt, embellish this Federal period mirror, dating from the early 19th century. The oval panel in the crest bears the words "To The Memory of His Excellency Genl George Washington" and "Liberty".

England

The 17th century

Because of the restraints of manufacture, early English mirrors were small. Up until the later half of the century they did not exceed 45 cm by 30 cm (18 in by 12 in) and most were smaller. By contrast, their frames – usually of wood at this stage – were proportionately large. They were also elaborate, being decorated with all manner of finery, such as tortoiseshell, stumpwork, beads and pieces of silver. Frames in the style of Grinling Gibbons, consisting of a mass of carved figures, foliage, fruit and flowers, also mark this early period. It was also towards the late 17th century that mirrors began to be referred to as "looking-glasses".

From about 1675, the cushion type of mirror appeared, with a plainer, rectangular frame, sometimes with marquetry veneer or incised lacquerwork. *Verre églomisé* was sometimes used for decorative borders.

Above: a Charles II limewood mirror carved in the style of Grinling Gibbons. The central motif – the royal arms – is flanked by cherubs climbing up through fruit and flowers from sea creatures below.

Right: an example of a cushion-frame mirror in ebony of the William and Mary period (late 17th century). The marquetry inlay consists of various woods and stained ivory.

*A Charles II mirror in a limewood frame with naturalistic carving, (**far right**). The frame was originally intended for a picture.*

By the early 18th century larger mirrors were made. **Left:** *the tall mirror in a giltwood frame is decorated with leaves and birds' heads.*

Below: *an overmantel mirror has a large central plate. The frame is giltwood and blue and gold* verre églomisé *(glass decorated on the back).*

Bottom: *two Georgian mirrors. An example (**left**) of a walnut veneered frame topped by a broken pediment. William Kent was instrumental in introducing the classical style to England. The giltwood mirror (**right**) is in the chinoiserie style which was very fashionable in the mid-18th century.*

The 18th century

By the 18th century, mirrors of modest size had become cheaper and more commonplace in the homes of the wealthy. Many consisted of a single vertical plate within a flat, walnut-veneered frame, with decoration often taking the form of carvings and gilt pendant husks, and a scrolled pediment.

As techniques for making larger sheets of glass advanced, so the decorative possibilities of frames began to be explored. No longer were mirrors used primarily for satisfying personal vanity; they began to assume the status of important pieces of furniture and to play a central role in interior decoration.

Large mirrors remained expensive and were placed in a prominent position in the most important rooms of the house or they were used in a lavish manner to create an air of wealth and enhanced space. Overmantel mirrors – wide mirrors sometimes consisting of two smaller plates flanking a large, central one – were hung over the fireplace. Their frames were sometimes designed in

Top left: a late-Georgian giltwood mirror reflecting the exuberance of the rococo. Asymmetry is a feature of this style.

Left: a design by Hepplewhite for a pier glass and girandoles. The carving on one of the latter practically obscures the glass.

More restrained decoration returned in the late-18th century with Robert Adam's neo-classical style. This Adam pier glass (**above**) is surmounted by delicate swagging and a classical urn, flanked by draped figures and sphinxes. The commode, designed to go with it, has similar motifs.

combination with the fireplace itself, sometimes incorporating flowers and landscapes. Pier glasses – mirrors hung between tall windows – started to appear in elegant interiors and were increasingly used to dramatic effect between windows and at the far end of suites of rooms to create the illusion of even greater space.

Fashions in mirrors, as with other furniture, changed rapidly in the 18th century. Generally speaking, the period had seen an increase in the size of the mirror glass and a corresponding reduction in the size of the frame. Gilding was also widely used, and the baroque classicism of William Kent was reflected in architectural frames with pediments and gilt decoration. From about 1750, and responding to the fashion for the rococo, frames became more elaborate, with gilding on carved gesso. Frames in the Chippendale style were modelled with a range of lively motifs such as rocks and shells, birds, goats, sheep, flowers and Chinamen. Girandoles, small wall mirrors with candle-holders, were often embellished with rococo carvings that all but obscured the glass itself. This exuberant style persisted until the 1770s, when Robert Adam's neo-classical style encouraged the more restrained use of decoration which, in mirrors, consisted of Classical columns, urns, rams' heads, sphinxes and swags. Shapes were now frequently oval or circular as well as rectangular.

Toilet mirrors, mounted on a miniature chest of drawers and, as their name implies, intended for personal use, generally escaped the excesses of elaboration seen in large examples. Mahogany was frequently used for the frames and bases of toilet mirrors, and the shapes were generally rectangular, oval or shield-like. The cheval mirror, popularized by Sheraton, consisted of a rectangular glass standing between two uprights, and sometimes having painted, inlaid or fretted headpieces.

The 19th century

The Regency period (1800–30) saw a return to more severe frames with sober embellishment in the form of Egyptian motifs and mythological Greek figures. The use of *verre églomisé,* first seen in the 17th century, returned but it was now used chiefly for panels above overmantel mirrors rather than for borders.

Convex mirrors, introduced from France, were made in England from about 1800. Many examples were surmounted by an eagle which, like the deep frame, was gilt. Some convex mirrors were also fitted with arms for candles.

In the Victorian period, mirrors were widely used in the bedroom. A long plate of mirror glass was sometimes set into the door of a wardrobe and flanked by two blank panels. Dressing mirrors – revived in a number of earlier styles – were also popular. They consisted of a framed mirror swinging between two ornate uprights, but, unlike earlier dressing mirrors, Victorian examples tended not to have drawers in the base below the glass.

CERAMICS

The term "ceramics" embraces two basic categories – pottery and porcelain – though both of these may be subdivided. Under pottery come stoneware, redware, slipware and faience, and under porcelain the earlier soft-paste and later hard-paste varieties. Country by country, this section traces the development of ceramics, from the simple forms of early pottery to the sophisticated achievements of hard-paste porcelain, not forgetting the ancient but advanced products of China which stunned the western world.

AMERICA

New England potters kept to simple forms glazed in rich colours and seldom decorated. In Pennsylvania, by contrast, the Swiss Mennonites and Germans from the Palatinate produced lively pie dishes, butter pots, money boxes and puzzle jugs. *Sgraffito* decoration, in which the design was incised through the slip, was a speciality of Pennsylvania potters.

In the 19th century, the Shenandoah Valley, in Maryland and Virginia, was notable for its potters. Foremost among them was the Bell family, who decorated their wares with flowing designs in slip.

Fears that lead-glazed pottery could be poisonous led to the development of salt-glaze stoneware. The earliest stoneware kilns, probably in New York and Philadelphia, started production around 1730, and redware potters also turned their hands to stoneware. Most stoneware was grey,

Right: a simple earthenware jug that was made in Massachusetts 1690–1730. Coloured glazes applied to such wares included brownish black, brown, yellow, orange, pink and green.

Pottery

Above: a figure of a lion by John Bell in lead-glazed earthenware, made in 1840–65. It was probably used as a doorstop.

In terms of natural resources, America was well suited to pottery. Common red-burning clay, as well as buff-burning and white-burning clays, were abundant and there was no lack of wood with which to fire the kilns. Stoneware clays were brought by boat to New England from New Jersey and Staten Island.

The first pottery made by European colonists was coarse redware, produced from the late 1600s until well into the 19th century. The simple forms of early redware were intended for domestic use. Irregularities of the manufacturing process often caused attractive mottling, but for more controlled effects coloured glazes or slip were used; tones included brownish black, brown, yellow, orange, pink and green.

In keeping with their Puritan ethics, the early

although different clays and variations in kiln temperature could produce a buff, cream or dark brown body. After about 1800, vessels were generally coated inside with brown slip. Decoration was often in cobalt blue, or very rarely brown. Important centres of stoneware production were northern New Jersey (the "Staffordshire of America") and East Liverpool, Ohio.

Creamware, invented in England by Josiah Wedgwood in about 1760, inspired many imitators in America. Creamware was especially desirable because of its fine grain, which made it similar to porcelain, and from around 1790, Philadelphia was the major centre of creamware production. After about 1838, however, very little creamware was made in America, although attempts at an inferior cream-coloured ware were made at the Shaker colony in Amana, Iowa, in the second half of the 19th century.

Printed pottery was not made in any significant quantities in America until the middle of the 19th century. This was probably because English potters, notably those of Staffordshire and Liverpool, already supplied America with an ample range of wares printed with a variety of patterns in different colours. American-made printed pottery was not properly launched until 1839 with the work of the American Pottery Company, of Jersey City. Motifs included the American eagle and scenes and motifs relating to American history.

Another kind of pottery made in the second half of the 19th century was Rockingham ware, a yellow ware decorated with a lustrous brown glaze. Rockingham, widely made from the 1840s until 1900, was an everyday ware that took many forms, from pudding pans and jugs to doorknobs and picture frames.

Virtually simultaneously, majolica started to be made by American potters. Majolica, an earthenware decorated with polychrome lead glazes, had been exhibited in England at the Great Exhibition of 1851. In 1853, it was being made by Edwin Bennett in Baltimore and Carr & Morrison in New York, and by the last decades of the 19th century majolica was made everywhere; the best known late 19th-century producer was Griffen, Smith & Hill, of Phoenixville, Pennsylvania.

Other types of late 19th-century American wares included those made at the Rookwood Pottery, founded in Cincinnati in 1880. The Rookwood Pottery concentrated on vases and ornamental jugs of simple shapes covered in a rich green or brown glaze and painted with motifs which were sometimes Japanese inspired.

A vase from the Rookwood Pottery, one of a growing number of art potteries which began to appear in different parts of the United States from the middle of the 19th century.

In the 19th century the Shenandoah Valley was noted for its potters. The pair of earthenware jars (left) are by Solomon Bell.

Above: *a plate dated 1804 with the sgraffito decoration favoured by Pennsylvania potters; the slip was cut through to the body underneath.*

Above: this early soft-paste porcelain basket is decorated in underglaze blue and comes from the factory of Bonnin & Morris of Philadelphia.

The porcelain ewer with gilt decoration (above, right) exhibits the rather heavy taste of the mid to late 19th century.

Right: a Parian ware figure from the Bennington factory. This was one of the most important factories of the mid-19th century.

Porcelain

In America, as in Europe, Chinese porcelain had been enjoyed by the fashionable and well-to-do long before the ingredients of true, or hard-paste, porcelain were discovered in the Western world.

A pioneer in the quest for hard-paste porcelain was Andrew Duché, of Savannah, Georgia, son of the stoneware potter, Antoine Duché. Although, in 1738, Andrew Duché discovered deposits of the two constituents of hard-paste porcelain – china clay in Virginia and a stone, possibly petuntse, near Ebenezer – his products apparently remained at the experimental stage. Duché's work was continued at the same pottery by Samuel Bowen.

The earliest surviving American soft-paste porcelain was made by the firm of Bonnin & Morris at Southwark, Philadelphia, between 1769 and 1772. It consists of a group of tablewares decorated in underglaze blue similar to the products of the Bow soft-paste factory in London. It appears that hard-paste porcelain was being made from about 1826 at the Jersey Porcelain & Earthenware Company, in Jersey City.

The first truly successful porcelain factory in America was that established by William Ellis Tucker in Philadelphia in 1826. Tucker made hard-paste porcelain in a French Empire style, and decoration took the form of effective landscapes painted in sepia monochrome combined with simple gilding.

This group of hard-paste porcelain wares by William Ellis Tucker of Philadelphia (left). His was the first really successful American porcelain factory. Sepia monochrome landscape decoration on the pieces, often combined with simple gilding, was typical.

Products included vases, tea-sets and other table wares. Although the enterprise enjoyed success, winning a silver medal at the American Institute in 1831, it was relatively shortlived, closing in 1838.

Another noteworthy 19th-century porcelain factory was in Bennington, Vermont. Here, John Harrison, who had worked at the Copeland factory, in England, introduced a formula for biscuit porcelain, used for figures and relief-decorated jugs. The Bennington factory also produced white wares, including Parian, blue and white porcelain, and tea and dinner services with heavy gilt decoration.

Parian ware was also made by the Etruria Pottery, owned by the firm of Ott & Brewer, in Trenton, New Jersey. The Etruria Pottery's Parian ware, dating from about 1875, included portrait busts of figures such as Washington and Franklin. However, Ott & Brewer is most famous for its Belleek wares, which it produced from 1882. Belleek, a thin, translucent porcelain with a pearly glaze, invented in about 1860 in England and improved in Ireland, caught the imagination of American potters when it was shown at the Centennial Exhibition in 1876. Belleek was also made by Knowles, Taylor & Knowles, of East Liverpool, where it was known as "Lotus ware", and by the Ceramic Art Company, at Trenton, which became the Lenox Company in 1906.

Belleek, developed in England and Ireland, became popular in America in the late 19th century. The creamer, cup and saucer (above) are by Ott & Brewer. "Lotus ware" (left) is the name given to the same type of thin, translucent porcelain by Knowles, Taylor & Knowles, who made it in East Liverpool.

BRITISH POTTERY

Slipwares

Above: a charming example of trailed slip decoration on an early Staffordshire baking dish c. 1720–30.

Above right: one of John Dwight's Fulham stoneware figures. This one represents his daughter Lydia, who died in 1674.

Slipware consists of red earthenware decorated with a diluted clay. The earliest commonly surviving English slipware dates from the 17th century. Most examples were made in Staffordshire, London and Wrotham in Kent. Slipware generally takes the form of simple pots, beakers, jugs and dishes. Designs on dishes include lions, mermaids, Adam and Eve, and Charles II in the oak tree. Decoration was at first applied by means of a slip, freely trailed to form the design. By the 1720s wares were press-moulded and coloured slip was poured into a recessed design. "Marbled" and "feathered" slipwares also became common.

Stonewares

Stoneware, consisting of clay and fusible stone, is midway between earthenware and porcelain. Partial vitrification, which occurs during firing makes it non-porous. Salt-glazed stoneware was especially popular and relatively easy to produce; salt was shovelled into the kiln at the hottest point in firing, and, when it had cooled, produced a brown glassy covering.

At a time when true porcelain was being made only in China, John Dwight experimented with porcellaneous stoneware at his factory in Fulham, London, which was founded about 1672. Dwight's main output, however, was red unglazed and grey salt-glazed stoneware. He made wine bottles, bellarmines (pear shaped wine jugs with a moulded mask on the neck) and some excellent figures.

Potters in Staffordshire produced brown-glazed stoneware from the end of the 17th century, and white salt-glazed stoneware mainly in the period 1740–60. Early wares are often decorated with stamped reliefs. A simple incised decoration was sometimes also used, and the incisions were filled in with blue pigment to create a type of decoration known as "scratch-blue". Some relief-decorated stonewares in eccentric shapes (e.g. camel teapots) were produced by slip casting in plaster moulds. A brilliant palette of colours was available for additional embellishment.

Nottingham was another important centre of stoneware production from the late 17th century when James Morley made vessels of a rich russet colour with a particularly smooth finish and with incised decoration. This Nottingham ware, as it is known, was also made at Chesterfield, Swinton, Derby and Crick.

Elers, Astbury and Whieldon wares

Elers redware, a fine red stoneware, is named after the brothers John Philip and David Elers, who came to England from Holland in 1686. They worked at Bradwell Wood, Staffordshire, from about 1694 to 1700. Elers redware is thinly potted and can vary in colour from buff, through red, to brown, and generally takes the form of mugs, cups and teapots with applied relief decoration.

John Astbury (1686–1743), also working in Staffordshire, made wares similar to that of the Elers. Astbury ware consists mostly of teapots and jugs in red, buff or black clay ornamented with applied white sprigs and then lead-glazed. Astbury also produced figures in which different coloured clays were often used in the decoration.

The variegated wares usually called "Whieldon" were made by Thomas Whieldon, of Fenton (active 1740–80) and by numerous imitators. Whieldon's products included marbled "agateware" teapots, milk jugs and cow creamers, and "tortoiseshell" plates and dishes, as well as groups of figures, few of which have survived. From 1754 to 1759, Josiah Wedgwood partnered Whieldon and revived the use of a brilliant green glaze. This was used for the foliage on "pineapple" and "cauliflower" pieces, vessels such as tureens and teapots modelled as pineapples or cauliflowers.

Mellow colours and a sense of fun characterize much early British pottery. **From top to bottom:** *a Staffordshire salt-glazed teapot, c. 1760; an Elers redware beaker, c. 1690, and an 18th-century Whieldon plate; a group of mid-18th century Whieldon-type wares; and a Staffordshire "agate-ware" cat, c. 1745.*

Josiah Wedgwood

Josiah Wedgwood (1730–95) revolutionized the manufacture of English ceramics. First, he wholeheartedly embraced neo-classicism as a new mode of decorating ceramics, and secondly he developed stonewares of a finer grain than had been known before. These fine-grain stonewares, which Wedgwood left unglazed, could be coloured by metallic stains.

Wedgwood is best known for the "jasper" stonewares, in which neo-classical motifs are applied to a blue, lilac, sage green, yellow or black body. Wedgwood also made "black basaltes" (unglazed black stoneware) and "Etruscan" wares,

Neo-classical elegance in a group of fine "jasper" relief stonewares, the first of Josiah Wedgwood's achievements.

which were painted with red figures on a black ground.

By 1760, Wedgwood had perfected his creamware, a creamy white earthenware with a transparent glaze. It was an immediate success, and Wedgwood re-named it "Queen's ware" as the result of an order for a tea-service from Queen Charlotte. Creamware was decorated with transfer-printing and later with enamelling. Creamware rivalled tin-enamel wares so much that it sounded the death-knell of the tin-enamel industry.

Most Wedgwood pieces are plainly marked. "Wedgwood & Bentley" was used on many ornamental wares from 1769 to 1780, while other pieces were marked simply "Wedgwood". "England" or "Made in England" appears on pieces after 1891.

Above: *a jug, cup and saucer, c. 1770 – handsome examples of Wedgwood's black basalt ware.*

*The pierced plate (**right**) and coffee pot (**far right**), both with transfer-printed decoration, are examples of cream-ware, Wedgwood's second great innovation. More extravagant pieces included this épergne (**below**), from a catalogue of 1790–93. Specific types of decoration could also be selected from the Wedgwood factory's pattern books; this page (**below right**) shows a range of border patterns.*

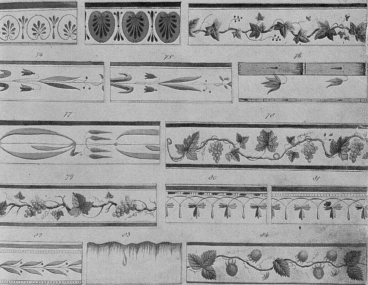

*Rustic pursuits animate
many of the figures made by
Ralph Wood – father and
son – and their imitators.
This late 18th-century spill
vase (**below**) is in the
manner of Ralph Wood the
younger.*

*A taste of Regency grandeur
combined with typically
naïve modelling and painting
is displayed in this
Staffordshire plaque made in
1811.*

The Wood family and Prattware

The Wood family of Burslem, Staffordshire, are
famous for their figures. Most desirable are those of
Ralph Wood (1717–72), covered with lead glazes
in a way that resembles enamelling. His son, also
Ralph (1748–95), actually used enamels instead of
glazes. Enoch Wood (1759–1840) produced portrait busts of the famous, and also made basaltes,
blue-printed earthenware for America, and figures
decorated in enamels.

The name of Felix Pratt, of Fenton, is associated,
often inaccurately, with many attractive figures,
jugs, Toby jugs and other wares decorated in high-
temperature underglaze enamels. Prattware was
produced from about 1780 to 1820.

Leeds, Liverpool and Bristol

The Leeds Pottery is best known for its creamware,
although it also produced a variety of other
earthenwares and stonewares. Much enamelling on
early Leeds pottery was done by David Rhodes
from about 1760 to 1768. From 1790 to 1800,
many figures were produced, mostly in pearlware,
a form of creamware with a bluish glaze. Transfer-

printing was in use by 1780. The factory also made
elaborately pierced wares, including épergnes.

Creamware was also manufactured at Liverpool,
where the Herculaneum factory was set up in 1796.
Bristol produced creamware from about 1785.
Liverpool and Bristol also made delftware.

English delft

English delft, earthenware with a white opaque tin
glaze, was produced in England long before similar
wares were made in the Dutch town of Delft. The
earliest English use of tin-enamel is known from a
group of jugs ("Malling jugs") dating from the
middle of the 16th century. Some, in a Rhenish
style, have a blue ground flecked with orange, and
are known as "Tygerware".

The delft industry proper seems to have been
started at Norwich in 1567 by two Flemish potters,
Jacob Jansen and Jasper Andries. The Norwich
pottery continued until 1696 or later. In about
1571, Jansen moved to Aldgate, London, and by
about 1620 there is evidence of other Flemish
potters active in this area. The earliest specimen of
this group of wares is a dish dated 1600 and decorated with blue dashes round the rim; it is the first
known example of the so-called "blue-dash
chargers".

About 1620–25, production of a different kind of delftware began at Southwark, London. Small barrel-shaped jugs, posset pots, wine bottles and dishes were decorated in blue and manganese (variable in colour from purple to rich brown) in imitation of Ming porcelain. The Southwark potteries and the one at Aldgate, gave rise to later factories at Lambeth, Bristol and Liverpool. Common London products of the 17th century are white-glazed wine bottles inscribed with their contents in blue. Puzzle jugs with perforated necks were also made, as were mugs, wine cups, bleeding bowls, apothecaries' jars and barbers' bowls.

As cultural links between England and Holland increased in the late 17th century, Dutch delft influenced English. As with Dutch wares, a strong influence was Chinese porcelain. Polychrome decoration, as well as blue and white, was used in imitation of Chinese *famille verte* to render both Chinese and European themes. The early 18th-century tea-drinking vogue spawned teapots, cups and sugar bowls, sometimes following silver forms. A popular form of English delftware at the time was the flower brick, a low rectangular vase.

Painting on Bristol delftware is sometimes complemented by *bianco sopra bianco* borders, decoration in white on a pale grey or lavender glaze. Transfer-printing on delftware was a development of the Liverpool potteries. Production of delftware ceased by about 1790.

Chinese porcelain inspired the decoration on this Bristol delftware bowl, c. 1735.

Nineteenth-century pottery

The early 19th century was the great period of blue and white transfer-printed earthenware from Staffordshire, much of it depicting topographical views or architectural fantasies. Josiah Spode's factory at Stoke-on-Trent was notable for this type of ware. During the partnership there of Copeland and Garrett (1833–47), many pieces were decorated with Italian scenes. Multicolour transfer-printing was introduced by F. & R. Pratt of Fenton.

A popular 19th-century medium was white stoneware protected with a smear of lead-glaze. Another commonly used technique was slip-casting, in which slip was poured into plaster moulds. Slip-casting allowed intricately modelled pieces to be made. From the early years of the century, lustre wares, glazed with gold and platinum to create a metallic lustrous effect, were produced at a number of factories in England and Wales. In Sunderland, County Durham, which is especially associated with pink lustre, pieces were transfer-printed with views of the famous iron bridge over the river Wear.

The "Rockingham" glaze, a deep brown containing manganese, probably originated at the Rockingham factory, Swinton, Yorkshire, but was extensively used elsewhere. In the 1840s,

F. & R. Pratt, and Dillwyn & Co. of Swansea, made wares in imitation of red-figure Greek pottery (which they called "Etruscan"). Wedgwood continued to make neo-classical jasperware with white decoration, although products were now of slightly cruder workmanship than the 18th-century examples. From 1858 to 1875, Wedgwood employed the Frenchman Emile Lessore as decorator. Lessore decorated creamware in a distinctive style, often depicting figures in soft colours. His pieces are always signed.

The 1860s vogue for neo-Renaissance motifs was particularly in evidence at Minton's. Here products of inlaid coloured clays were made in imitation of earthenware made in France under Henri II (1547–59). Maiolica (or "majolica" as the Victorians called it) was also imitated, notably by Minton under the direction of Leon Arnoux. "Majolica" was used to refer to earthenware decorated with coloured glazes. Vegetable dishes, fruit stands, umbrella stands and countless other objects come under the heading of "majolica".

Doulton & Watts, at Lambeth, London, founded in 1815, concentrated in their early years on modest salt-glazed stoneware and terracotta pieces.

The firm was run by John Doulton and John Watts. It was very successful and by the mid-19th century was the largest producer of stoneware in Europe. The factory's main products were functional items such as pipes, chimney pots and water filters, though there were also decorative jugs and other vessels. Decorative wares became a more important part of the factory's output when Henry Doulton, John Doulton's son, became interested in the Lambeth School of Art. In 1867, with the help of the school's principal and a group of its students, Henry Doulton set up the Lambeth Pottery, which specialized in wares made by individual potters following their own ideas.

Shortly afterwards, George Tinworth joined the Lambeth Pottery and contributed considerably to its success. Tinworth specialized in figures and amusing groups of frogs or mice, usually engaged in a range of human activities.

Around the middle of the 19th century, flat-backed Staffordshire figures began to be made. Being press-moulded, flat-backed figures could be made in large quantities. They have a naïve appearance and were either purely ornamental or portrayed famous figures of the time, such as Queen Victoria, Prince Albert, Garibaldi and Dick Turpin. Typical animal subjects included sentimental figures of dogs.

Vivid glazes on Minton majolica were highly popular when they were first introduced in 1851. Here they enliven a teapot of 1874, imaginatively modelled as a monkey grasping a fruit.

Top left: *with its browns and ochres, this ewer, c. 1878, is typical of the "Henri II" ware which Minton made in imitation of 16th-century French earthenware.*

Top: *an example of Emile Lessore's figure painting on a pair of Wedgwood creamware plates.*

Left: *the decorative stoneware made at Doulton & Watts included items such as this salt-glazed figure-tankard, c. 1821–30, in the shape of a bust of Lord Nelson.*

Above: *a large Minton majolica horse, made in 1873, is a further example of the wide range of glazed earthenware made at Minton.*

Above: this stoneware spoon warmer is an unusual example of the Martin brothers' grotesque wares.

Right: George Tinworth, of the Lambeth Pottery, was as much at home with serious commissions, as here, as he was producing his humorous models of animals.

Far right: freely applied floral decoration on a Doulton vase.

Below: part of panel of tiles by William de Morgan, among the most outstanding artist potters.

Art pottery

An artist potter was one who followed his own bent, free of commercial considerations and the dictates of the factory system. The first English art pottery was salt-glazed stoneware decorated in the Doulton factory in Lambeth by students of the Lambeth School of Art from 1871. From about the same time, the Martin brothers started making their extraordinary wares. Martinware is ususlly mottled and often takes grotesque forms; some of the more remarkable pieces include fish, goblins, armadillos and birds with shifty expressions.

William Morris's disciple, William de Morgan, made highly inventive lustre wares, usually in red and turquoise blue. The Robbia Pottery at Birkenhead, Cheshire (1894–1901) specialized in painted and *sgraffito* decoration in the Art Nouveau style. Artist potters also experimented with glazes, and W. Howson Taylor's "Ruskin" pottery, made near Birmingham (1898–1935), was decorated in brilliant hues, even or shaded colours and mottled glazes. James Macintyre & Co., of Burslem, made art pottery known as "Florian ware" under the direction of William Moorcroft.

BRITISH PORCELAIN

These figures, with detailed modelling and bright colours highlighted with gilding, typify the rococo style of the Chelsea factory's Gold Anchor period.

Porcelain was unknown in the West until the first imports from China started to arrive in the 17th century. By comparison to the thick-set European earthenware and stoneware, Chinese porcelain appeared remarkably thin and white. For obvious reasons, it remained rare and expensive.

The nearest approximation to Chinese porcelain was first made with powdered glass and clay; it is known as artificial, or soft-paste, porcelain and was unfortunately prone to collapsing during firing. Not until after 1700 were the real constituents of true, or hard-paste, porcelain – kaolin and feldspar, a natural fusible rock – discovered and the Chinese secret revealed. This momentous discovery was made by Johann Friedrich Boettger, an alchemist working in Saxony.

Chelsea

The first English porcelain factory was probably the Chelsea Works, set up in about 1745 by Nicholas Sprimont, a silversmith from Flanders. A fine soft-paste body was used, at first very glassy.

The first four years of production at the Chelsea Works are known as the Triangle Period (*c.* 1745–49), when an incised triangle was the mark. Not surprisingly, early Chelsea porcelain imitates forms of silverware. Among these early products was the goat and bee jug, possibly based on a silver prototype and incorporating moulded decoration in the form of two goats and a bee on foliage below the

Below right: a hibiscus sprig with butterflies realistically painted on this dish, dating from about 1755, exemplify the high standard of flower painting achieved during the Chelsea factory's Red Anchor period.

Below: one of the earliest pieces of British porcelain, a Chelsea "goat and bee" jug, c. 1745, dating from the factory's Triangle Period.

lip. Modelling was initially rather coarse. Occasionally, decoration in the Meissen style was applied. The translucent body of Triangle Period porcelain shows "pin-hole" imperfections when held to the light.

In the Raised Anchor Period (1749–53), when the anchor mark was embossed, the glaze was cloudier and "pin-holes" disappeared, to be replaced by "moons" (translucent patches), common until about 1755. Wares of the Raised Anchor Period were mostly of simple form, with decoration often based on Japanese Kakiemon designs with their clean red, green, yellow and blue colours. Joseph Willems modelled Chelsea figures from about 1749, many copied from Meissen figures.

In the Red Anchor Period (1753–58), when the anchor mark was painted in red instead of being embossed, the glaze became whiter. Decoration took the form of flower painting based on Meissen designs, but some original botanical designs were

also used. In 1755–56, the influence of the French factory at Sèvres began to make itself felt; among Sèvres influences are crimson monochrome landscapes. Tureens were realistically modelled as vegetables, animals, fish and birds.

French styles predominated in the Gold Anchor Period (1758–70). Bone-ash was added to the paste, reducing its translucency. The glaze was thick but clear, giving a "wet-look" and having a tendency to craze. The Gold Anchor Period was one of rococo excess, with elaborate gilding. New colours included a rich underglaze blue and the "claret" ground imitating the *rose Pompadour* of Sèvres. Figures, surrounded by *bocage*, a mass of flowers and leaves, stood on scrolled rococo bases. Many delightful miniatures (for example, scent bottles) were produced. The Chelsea factory changed hands in 1769 and again in 1770, when it passed to William Duesbury, of Derby. This period until the factory's closure in 1784 is the Chelsea-Derby period, when Derby styles were followed.

Aesop was a lively source of themes. This Red Anchor sauceboat is in the style of Jeffryes Hamett O'Neale.

Inspired by Japanese porcelain, the bright colours of the Kakiemon palette decorate a tureen made around 1750, during the early years of the Bow factory.

Bow

The Bow factory, founded in about 1746, produced the first "bone China", containing the ash of burnt bones. The presence of bone in the paste helped to prevent pieces from collapsing during firing, a problem frequently encountered with soft-paste porcelain.

Bow porcelain is creamy-white. Some of the earliest wares, dating from 1750–51, are inscribed "Made at New Canton". The factory used a bewildering variety of marks, including simulated Chinese characters.

The output of the Bow factory consisted largely of tableware and figures. Oriental-style tableware in underglaze blue was made in quantity but brilliant enamels were also used. A popular enamel pattern was the "Quail" or "Partridge" pattern, based on the Japanese Kakiemon manner. From the factory's earliest years, the *blanc de Chine* style, exemplified by unpainted figures and dishes, was practised. Typical decoration on *blanc de Chine* dishes took the form of applied prunus blossoms on a white ground. Other *chinoiserie* designs on Bow wares include the peony and fence, and the cross-legged Chinaman. From about 1759, some wares had a powder-blue ground decorated with scenes or motifs in a round or fan-shaped panel. From about 1756, some Bow wares were decorated with transfer printing by Robert Hancock, an engraver.

Above: *the inscription on this inkpot refers to the name, "New Canton", by which the Bow factory was also known.*

Top: *blue, pink, green and yellow, highlighted with gold, animate this pair of Bow figures of "a sportsman and his companion", made in about 1760.*

Left: *a covered cup with an amusing dog-shaped finial, is a good example of the tableware produced at Bow.*

Early Bow figures are generally left white, in the manner of *blanc de Chine* employed for other wares, and represent the Muses and popular actors and actresses. In their greatest period (1755–60) Bow figures show lively modelling and colouring, often imitating Meissen. Some figures have a square hole at the back, intended to receive a candle-sconce or a *bocage* of porcelain flowers. Bases to figures became increasingly rococo and by about 1760 had acquired four feet. Little is known about Bow after 1763. The factory had closed by 1776, when Derby acquired the moulds.

Derby

Porcelain was made at Derby in the early 1750s. Andrew Planché may have been the first maker there; Planché figures have an unglazed band round the base, which is funnel-shaped inside.

The Derby Porcelain Manufactory was established in 1756 by William Duesbury and John Heath. The factory's first products were pale-coloured figures with a bluish glaze, intended to resemble Meissen. More successful were the useful wares, some of which featured dishevelled birds in the decoration. From about 1758, Meissen imitations were abandoned in favour of figures copied from the Chelsea factory. Colours became stronger and gilding was added to the decoration. In the period 1755–70, three or four unglazed patches are often found under the base. The simpler types of Chelsea tableware were copied from 1756 to 1760. Decoration often took the form of flowers, birds and moths. The products of the Derby factory's early period bear no regular mark.

In 1770, William Duesbury acquired the Chelsea factory. During the Chelsea-Derby phase (1770–84), the usual mark, shared by the two factories, was a gilt anchor and a D. The first of the famous Derby marks of a crown, crossed batons and D was adopted about 1782; after 1800 it was generally painted in red.

Derby porcelain of the Chelsea-Derby phase reflects the neo-classical tastes of the time. Finely potted tablewares were decorated with neo-classical swags and festoons. Products of the Derby factory's neo-classical period included pieces decorated with fine flower painting and with landscapes and Classical subjects on coloured and striped grounds. Sèvres influence was also strong, encouraging the neo-classical style and giving rise to biscuit porcelain figures. The main modellers

Two figures made during the Derby factory's early years: (above) "Winter", from a set of the four seasons, made by Andrew Planché in about 1750–55, and (right) "Jupiter", made in 1760.

Marks on Derby porcelain

Chelsea-Derby (1770–84)

Left: *Derby (1784–1810) Bloor period (1811–48)*

The rich flower painting on this pair of chocolate cups demonstrates the talent of William Billingsley, for 21 years a flower painter at Derby.

were Pierre Stéphan and J. J. Spängler.

William Duesbury died in 1786. He was succeeded by his son (who died in 1796 or 1797) and Michael Kean, who controlled the factory until 1811. The period 1786 to 1811 is the Crown Derby period. Figures continued to be produced and much use was made of "biscuit", porcelain deliberately left unglazed. Tablewares were decorated with figures and landscapes. Naturalistic flower-painting was introduced by William Billingsley, the Derby factory's most important flower painter.

In 1811, the factory was leased to Robert Bloor. Although Bloor went mad in 1826, the term "Bloor Derby" is used for wares up to 1848. Bloor favoured showy "Japan" patterns, which replaced the neo-classical wares of the previous phase in the factory's history.

In 1877, the company became the Derby Crown Porcelain Company. The factory's products then tended to consist of gilded wares and pieces decorated with printed rather than hand-painted scenes. In 1900 the factory became the Royal Crown Derby Company and is still in existence.

Sensitive modelling has been achieved in this biscuit group of two lovers, inspired by a similar model from Sèvres. It is just one of many biscuit figures produced during the Crown Derby period.

Above: *a Crown Derby tea service for two, perhaps intended for lovers of the great outdoors. The finely depicted animals and insects were painted by John Brewer, who is also thought to have decorated the Bloor Derby vase (**Left**).*

Longton Hall

The Longton Hall porcelain factory was established in 1749–50, but continued only until 1760. It effectively introduced porcelain manufacture into Staffordshire.

Much Longton Hall porcelain is quite heavy although surprisingly translucent. Items produced at the factory included leaf-shaped dishes, tureens, sauceboats, and teapots modelled as a fruit or vegetable. Handles were generally rather inelegant and decoration was often in bright colours. The Longton Hall factory also made finer porcelain in the Meissen style. Other pieces were transfer-printed at the Liverpool factory and underglaze blue decoration was also used. On Longton Hall wares, the mark of a crossed L was sometimes applied, usually in blue.

Other products thought to be typical of Longton Hall are lumpy figures known as "snowmen" and made in the factory's early period. "Snowmen", in which the glaze partially obscures the modelling, include animal as well as human figures. Later Longton Hall figures have scrolled bases picked out in red.

Below: these covered tureens – one with stand – and the rose box are modelled on petals and vegetables and exemplify one aspect of the Longton Hall products.

Bottom: these two sauceboats, made in about 1750, are either the rare products of Benjamin Lund's short-lived porcelain factory or among the first pieces made by the Worcester Porcelain Company.

Far right: a Chamberlain's Worcester jug, made in 1798. Profuse gilding was often used by Robert Chamberlain, who left the Worcester factory in 1873 to work as a decorator.

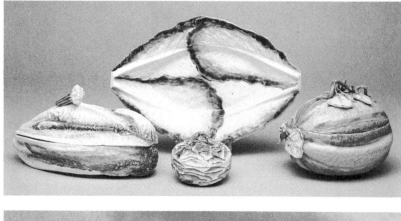

Lund's Bristol and Worcester

From about 1748, Benjamin Lund's factory in Bristol started using soaprock porcelain, a soft-paste porcelain in which ground glass was replaced by soaprock (or soapstone). Soaprock porcelain was superior to the soft-paste porcelain used at Chelsea, Bow and Derby because it could hold hot liquids without cracking and could be moulded with greater precision. The few pieces of Lund's Bristol porcelain that survive are Chinese-style figures and a handful of sauceboats and creamboats. In 1752 the factory was absorbed by the Worcester Porcelain Co. which took over the Bristol moulds.

The early phase at Worcester (1751–76) is referred to as "First Period" or "Dr Wall Period", after Dr John Wall, a leading partner. As at Lund's Bristol factory, soapstone was used in the porcelain. Most pieces dating from this early phase were based on silver or on Chinese porcelain. Decoration in enamels was practised, but the most popular decoration for Chinese-style wares was painting in underglaze blue. Pseudo-Chinese marks were sometimes used. A Worcester version of the Chinese *famille rose* was adopted by 1760. Transfer-printed wares, dating from 1757, became very popular. In Worcester porcelain, the fashion for rococo is seen in leaf-form dishes, "cabbage-

Left: *a most attractive combination of moulded and painted flowers, fruit and insects on a Worcester dish decorated in the workshop of James Giles in about 1770.*

Below: *a more informal use of moulding and painting, on a Worcester dish c. 1765.*

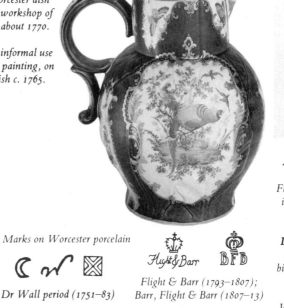

Above: *in this Worcester vase c. 1810 of the Barr, Flight & Barr period, gilding is combined with a striking rendering of feathers.*

Marks on Worcester porcelain

Dr Wall period (1751–83)

Flight & Barr (1793–1807); Barr, Flight & Barr (1807–13)

Left: *this jug, richly gilded and ornately painted with birds and butterflies on a blue ground, is typical of the elaborate pieces made at Worcester between 1770 and 1785.*

leaf" jugs and "cauliflower" tureens. In the early 1760s, some elaborate painting was done in London in the workshop of James Giles, where fruit, ruffled birds and dishevelled tulips were painted on. This decoration was applied to blank panels on wares already partly decorated in underglaze blue. These predecorated areas were commonly given an effect of overlapping scales (known as "scale blue"). The influence of Sèvres, strongest from 1770 to 1784, led to the use of rich and various ground colours and elaborate gilding. Topographical decoration is typical of the late 18th century at Worcester. Worcester figures are extremely rare; among known examples are a Turk, a gardener and a nurse and child.

Until 1783, Worcester porcelain was thinly potted, with a glaze that suffered from crazing. Illuminated by transmitted light, the porcelain appears greenish, sometimes orange and later sometimes grey.

Although Dr Wall died in 1776, the period 1751 to 1783, as already mentioned, is referred to as the Dr Wall period. In 1783, the factory was bought by Thomas Flight and managed by his two sons. In 1793, Martin Barr joined the factory, which was then known as Flight & Barr. An incised "B" mark was sometimes used. The impressed mark "B.F.B." (for Barr, Flight & Barr) under a crown was used from 1807 to 1813. The final period in the factory's history was Flight, Barr & Barr, which ran from 1813 to 1840, when Robert Chamber-

lain, a former decorator at Worcester who had set up a rival establishment in about 1786, took over. In 1801, a third Worcester factory was established by Thomas Grainger, a relative of Robert Chamberlain, but its products were unremarkable. From 1852 to 1862, the original Worcester factory was run by Kerr & Binns. Fine decoration was carried out at this time by Thomas Bott, who imitated Limoges enamels.

Liverpool

Blue and white soft-paste porcelain was among the main products of Liverpool during the 18th century. Liverpool wares have a characteristic bluish glaze which, forming a pool on the underside of the base, produced a "thundercloud" effect. Foot rims on Liverpool porcelain are generally vertical, and areas of blue are sometimes marbled in gold.

Many porcelain factories are known to have existed in Liverpool. The largest was Richard Chaffers' factory, which was founded in 1756 and made a soaprock porcelain similar to that produced at Worcester. Most typical of Chaffers' wares was a bulbous mug enamelled with a Chinese scene. The factory passed to Philip Christian in 1769.

Other Liverpool makers included James, John and Seth Pennington, who made bowls and other wares painted in a bright blue, and Zachariah

The mug (above) with a Chinese scene painted in enamels, is an example of the porcelain made in Liverpool by Richard Chaffers.

Barnes, who is thought to have made pieces printed in smudgy blue. By 1756, W. Reid was making porcelain, and, from at least 1762, so was Samuel Gilbody.

Transfer-printing, discovered independently by Sadler & Green of Liverpool, is often found on Liverpool wares in a dark shade of red. Some Liverpool decorated in this way is signed "Sadler Liverpool", though Sadler & Green were not porcelain manufacturers.

Caughley and Coalport

The Caughley Works, in Shropshire, started producing soft-paste porcelain in 1772, when Thomas Turner bought the factory. Most of the wares made at Caughley from this date were blue and white, in rather poor imitation of Worcester. Two shades of blue are typical, one greyish, the other mauvish. Under Turner's proprietorship the Willow Pattern and the Brosely Blue Dragon were introduced, both based on Chinese models. The Caughley mark was most often a C, frequently drawn to look like the Worcester crescent. The word "Salopian", impressed into the paste, was also used.

In 1799, John Rose bought the Coalport Works and used the factory to supply his factory at Coalport, which he had founded in about 1796. Caughley supplied Coalport with biscuit porcelain for glazing and decorating. Coalport styles of decoration imitated Sèvres, Dresden and Chelsea. From about 1830 to 1850, the rococo revival was seen in highly modelled, painted flowers.

Top: three coffee cups, from left to right, made at Lowestoft, Worcester and Liverpool respectively, between about 1750 and 1770. The decorative motifs – groups of flowers and a Chinese scene – are characteristic of the period.

Above: elaborate gilding and rich flower painting on a cup and saucer, examples some of the Coalport factory's more sumptuous products and the result of Continental influences.

Right: the Caughley factory's adaptation of Oriental patterns is seen in this late 18th-century dish.

Below right: these four Lowestoft "trifles" were made in the late 18th century for the souvenir trade.

Lowestoft

Porcelain containing bone-ash was made at Lowestoft, in East Anglia, from 1757 until 1799. The paste was similar to that of Bow, where the first bone china was made, although the glaze was thinner. Lowestoft ware was at first decorated only in underglaze blue. Enamel colours became more common from about 1770. Decoration on many pieces took the form of initials and dates, and sometimes the words "A Trifle from Lowestoft". Oriental designs and marine views were also much used.

Lowestoft specialized in table and tea wares. The range included tea caddies, globular teapots, minia-

The marks of three lesser porcelain factories:

Caughley

Coalport (Coalbrookdale)

Plymouth

ture tea-services, cabbage-leaf jugs, mugs with double-twisted handles, openwork baskets, and commemorative jugs, punch bowls and plaques. Cream jugs with "sparrow beak" spouts have a curved "tail" at the base of the handle and a mound in the centre of the inside base. Very few figures were made; known forms include cats, swans, sheep and putti.

Plymouth and Bristol

New Hall, Plymouth and Bristol were the first three factories in England to make hard-paste porcelain.

William Cookworthy discovered the raw materials of true porcelain – clay and feldspar – in the late 1740s. He took out a patent for his Coxside factory, near Plymouth, in 1768. Then the factory was moved further north to the busy port of Bristol in 1770.

Mugs are among the best-known products of the Plymouth factory. Moulded sauceboats, many based on rococo silverware, were also made. Other types include vases (some hexagonal), pieces in the form of shells, tea and coffee pots, and leaf-shaped pickle trays. There were also a few figures, mostly imitating those made at Bow and Longton Hall. Plymouth plates and saucers are rare.

Decoration on Plymouth wares frequently took the form of an underglaze blue which tended to have a greyish, or even blackish, tinge, probably the result of firing at too high a temperature. Decoration in enamels, again often having a dirty tone, was also practised.

The Bristol factory's output consisted mainly of domestic wares, the most frequently surviving pieces being cups and saucers. "Wreathing", a spiral effect in the paste, is common. Decoration was in underglaze blue or overglaze enamel in colours which included red, clear yellow and the distinctive, bright "Bristol" green. Gilding on Bristol wares was outstanding. Flowers were the favourite ornamental motif and teapots commonly took the form of an inverted pear. Figures, often with a rockwork base, were an important part of the factory's output. Biscuitware in the form of presentation plaques, for example, were rare and are now greatly prized.

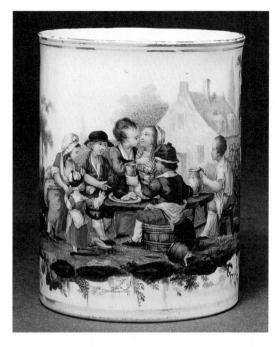

Right: this mug, painted with a rustic scene of conviviality, is one of the New Hall factory's more unusual products.

Above: many products of Nantgarw travelled to London for further, more sophisticated decoration. The ice-pail, here, received the gilding in London, but the plate was decorated locally.

Right: this plate is from the dessert service that the Rockingham factory made for William IV in 1832. Elaborate gilding, a masterful example of which is seen here, was a speciality of the factory.

New Hall

In 1772, William Cookworthy retired from the Bristol factory and assigned the rights of his hard-paste porcelain manufacture to Richard Champion, who for a time continued at Bristol. In 1781, Champion sold his patent to a group of Staffordshire potters. Some of these withdrew and, after a false start, operations were moved to Shelton in the Potteries. Here, at the New Hall factory, hard-paste porcelain was made until about 1810, when bone china was made instead.

The New Hall paste is similar to Bristol's and also subject to "wreathing", but the glaze – soft, oily and gathering in hollows – is quite different. The New Hall factory's output consists largely of useful wares. Flowers were the most common form of decoration but pseudo-Oriental patterns were also used. The hard-paste porcelain bears a pattern number, while the bone china commonly has the mark "New Hall" in a double circle.

Nantgarw and Swansea

The Nantgarw factory, in Cardiff, Wales, was founded by William Billingsley in 1813. The paste developed by Billingsley was white and translucent, and comparable to that of Sèvres, which was a major influence. While some of the factory's products were simply decorated with flowers and birds in the manner of William Billingsley, many were sent to London for elaborate decoration.

Although Billingsley's soft-paste porcelain was of superb quality, it was very difficult to fire successfully and the disproportionate amount of kiln wastage threatened the factory's existence. The factory was later transferred to Swansea, where, under Lewis Dillwyn, who owned the Cambrian Pottery there, efforts to make Billingsley's porcelain commercially viable were also unsuccessful. Billingsley returned to Nantgarw in 1816, where he stayed until 1820.

After the transfer of the Nantgarw factory to Swansea, porcelain was made there for a few years only. The Nantgarw porcelain was initially altered to a body with a greenish tinge, some exquisitely painted with flowers by Billingsley and probably also by other artists working in his style. After 1817, Swansea produced an inferior porcelain with tiny depressions in the glaze. Pieces made to this formula were often marked with crossed tridents.

Rockingham

A pottery had existed on the site of the Rockingham works, at Swinton, Yorkshire, from about 1750. Porcelain was made there between 1820 and 1842, during which time the factory was owned by Thomas Brameld and his two brothers. From 1826, the factory was subsidized by Earl Fitzwilliam, whose crest, a griffin passant, was used as a mark. The name "Rockingham" which was henceforth adopted, referred to the late Marquis from whom the Earl had inherited his estate.

Under the Brameld brothers, excellent porcelain was made, using bone-ash paste. The decoration, often very ambitious, was in a revived rococo style, with a lot of elaborate gilding. A favourite Rockingham theme was the use of named views of castles and country seats for decoration; a great dessert service made for William IV is a fine example of this genre.

Coloured grounds, usually blue, green or grey, were also used for dinner, dessert and tea services. Tablewares were also often decorated with flowers on a pale green ground. Rockingham figures, made between 1826 and 1830, are rare. Other decorative wares, also relatively rare, include models, cottages and castles.

Other 19th-century porcelain

The 19th century saw three main developments in the use and decoration of porcelain. First, *pâte-sur-pâte* decoration, achieved by building up layers of white slip on a dark ground, was introduced by Marc-Louis Solon at Minton. Secondly, the neo-rococo style was widely adopted, notably at Coalport. Thirdly, "Parian" ware, a white biscuit resembling marble, was introduced by Copeland's and was used a lot for small-scale statuary at Copeland's, Minton's and elsewhere. Belleek, in County Fermanagh, Northern Ireland, produced an inferior version of Parian ware with an iridescent glaze.

The most significant stylistic innovation of the second half of the 19th century was brought on by Japanese exhibits at the 1862 Exhibition in London. The Royal Worcester factory responded to this new influence by producing pieces made in an ivory-tinted body to resemble Japanese Satsuma ware.

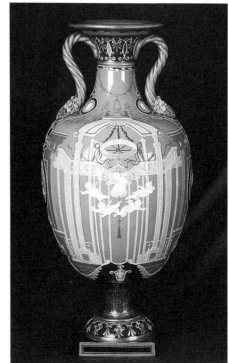

Top left: *"Miranda", a classic example of the simple parian ware – Minton, 1866.*

Top right: *the complex pâte-sur-pâte decoration on this vase was executed at Minton by Marc Louis Solon – one of the best-known practitioners.*

The Minton mark

Above: *naturalistic scenes inside ornate borders were fashionable in the mid-19th century. This dessert plate, seen here with the pattern book for the service, was made at Minton in 1867.*

Left: *too much decoration and the conflict of styles sometimes unbalanced late 19th-century porcelain, as this Coalport vase illustrates.*

CHINA

The tradition of potting in China, stretching back from the present day to before the 2nd millenium BC, is the longest in the world. The Chinese potter had an important position in society, and the products of the kiln were valued above precious metals. The earliest Chinese pottery took the form of unglazed utilitarian earthenwares, and the first glazed wares appeared around 1000 BC. The first translucent white porcelain, an important development, was produced by the end of the 10th century AD. All the methods of manufacture and decoration known today had been mastered in China by the end of the 14th century.

That the arrival, in the 16th century of the first shiploads of Chinese porcelain in Holland started a complete revolution in European ceramic manufacture is a measure of the advanced state of Chinese potting. Porcelain, as opposed to coarser pottery, was until then quite unknown in Europe. The translucence, the wholly novel shapes and the stunning decoration of Chinese porcelain was highly prized against the crude European pottery.

With the exception of familiar geographical names, the Pinyin system of romanization is followed here. To aid cross-reference to books which follow the old Wade–Giles system, conversions of the most frequently encountered terms and place names are also given. Terms romanized in Pinyin are given first. In the list of dynasties and reigns, names romanized by the Wade–Giles system are shown in brackets.

Terms and places

Cizhou *Tz'u chou*	Jian *Chien*
Dehua *Te Hua*	Jingdezhen *Ching-te Chen*
Ding *Ting*	jue *chueh*
doucai *tou ts'ai*	Jun *Jun*
gu *ku*	Longquan *Lung-ch'uan*
Guan *Kuan*	Ru *Ju*
gui *kuei*	Yixing *I Hsing*

Dynasties and reigns

Han (Han)	206 BC–AD 220
Six Dynasties	AD 221–AD 581
Sui (Sui)	581–618
Tang (T'ang)	618–906
Five Dynasties	907–960
Song (Sung)	960–1279
Yuan (Yüan)	1280–1368
Ming (Ming)	1368–1644
Hongwu (Hung Wu)	1368–1398
Jianwen (Chien Wên)	1399–1402
Yongle (Yung Lo)	1403–1424
Xuande (Hsüan Tê)	1426–1435
Zhengtong (Chêng T'ung)	1436–1449
Jingtai (Ching T'ai)	1450–1457
Tianshun (T'ien Shun)	1457–1464
Chenghua (Ch'êng Hua)	1465–1487
Hongzhi (Hung Chih)	1488–1505
Zhengde (Chêng Tê)	1506–1521
Jiajing (Chia Ching)	1522–1566
Longqing (Lung Ch'ing)	1567–1572
Wanli (Wan Li)	1573–1619
Taichang (T'ai Ch'ang)	1620
Tianqi (T'ien Ch'i)	1621–1627
Chongzheng (Ch'ung Chêng)	1628–1644
Qing (Ch'ing)	1644–1912
Shunzhi (Shun Chih)	1644–1661
Kangxi (K'ang Hsi)	1662–1722
Yongzheng (Yung Chêng)	1723–1735
Qianlong (Chi'en Lung)	1736–1795
Jiaqing (Chia Chi'ing)	1796–1821
Daoguang (Tao Kuang)	1822–1850
Xianfeng (Hsien Fêng)	1851–1861
Tongzhi (T'ung Chih)	1862–1874
Guangxu (Kuang Hsü)	1875–1908
Xuantong (Hsüan T'ung)	1909–1912
Chinese Republic	1912–

The Han dynasty

Although pottery had been made in China from about 2000 BC, it was not until the Han dynasty (206 BC–AD 220) that techniques had developed sufficiently to allow significant artistic advances to be made.

The Han dynasty is associated mainly with red earthenwares. An important innovation of the time was the use of glazes; lead glazes on the red earthenware gave a green colour similar to well-patinated bronze. Forms continued to be modelled after bronze prototypes and were often decorated with bands of relief modelling depicting figures or animals. Grey earthenwares tended to be left unglazed, decorated with unfired painting. In pottery that accompanied the dead, scenes from contemporary life were re-created in miniature with models of watch-towers, farmhouses, animals, cooking pots and figures.

Left: though it is functional, this Han dynasty granary jar has been enlivened by a realistic "roof" and amusing feet in the form of seated figures. It is also a good example of lead-glazed red earthenware.

Below left: like many such figures of the period, this Han dynasty court lady is painted but has been left unglazed.

Below: this appealing little dog and model of a stove are among the rich variety of everyday objects placed in the tombs of the dead.

Early stonewares

In the politically disunited Six Dynasties period (AD 221–581), great technical advances were made in ceramics. Lead glazes were superseded by a kind probably made from finely crushed feldspar, and high temperatures were attained in the kiln to produce a dense, heavy stoneware sometimes called "proto-porcelain". As in the Han dynasty, forms continued to reflect bronze prototypes, but heavy wheel-thrown stoneware jars with glazed upper parts were now a more typical form.

This figure of a "seated" ram, from the Six Dynasties period, is an example of stoneware sometimes described as "proto-porcelain".

Yue wares

The Yue wares are in important group of glazed stonewares made in Chekiang province, in south-eastern China. Their manufacture flourished by early Tang times (618–906). Although the body was grey, it often oxidized red, and the glaze varied from brownish-yellow to grey-green. Ewers, jars, dishes and bowls were produced with sparse decoration in the form of birds and flora.

The Tang dynasty

Below: a Tang dynasty green-glazed pottery drinking cup. This little vessel is an unusual example of the use of animal forms in Tang times.

Below right: a Tang brown-glazed stoneware pilgrim flask. The flask's moulded, rather than carved decoration is uncommon for this dynasty.

The Tang dynasty (618–906), China's golden age, saw a remarkable flowering of lead-glazed earthenware manufacture. Forms assumed refinement and pleasing proportions and lead glazes, taken up once again after their abandonment from the Six Dynasties period, appear in rich colours. Copper, cobalt and iron pigments were added to the glaze to colour it green, blue and amber. Colours were mostly applied freehand but were sometimes prevented from running by the use of unglazed engraved lines. The glaze on Tang vases usually stops short of the base. Figures made for tombs included horses, camels, musicians and monsters.

Far left: *a Tang pottery figure of an attendant wearing an official hat and a gentle expression. Until the end of the dynasty, these figures were placed in the tombs of noblemen. The straw-coloured glaze, first seen in the 6th century, was perfected in early Tang times. The superb horse (**left**) would also have been intended for a tomb. As with most Tang horses, the head is turned slightly to the left, and the rich cream, green and brown glazes are typical Tang colours.*

*This set of Tang dynasty wine cups (**left**) were for ritual use. The mixed glazes are known as Sancai ("three colours").*

*With random splashes of cobalt over a chocolate brown glaze, this Tang stoneware jar (**above**) has a remarkably modern appearance.*

Celadons are characterized by pleasing shapes and restful greenish blue colours, as the hexagonal plate (**above**), octagonal bowl (**above right**) and rare vase (**right**) all show. All three, from Longquan, are southern celadons; they have typically cold bluish glazes. By contrast, the northern celadons are generally olive green; the rare jar (**below**) is characteristic of this northern group.

The Song dynasty

The Song dynasty (960–1279) is characterized by excellent stonewares, fine shapes and beautiful glazes. Some of the products of kilns in the north are regarded as classic examples of Chinese ceramics. These include the beautiful Ding wares made at Ding Zhou, in Hopei province, until about 1300. The porcellaneous body of Ding wares was decorated with either incised or moulded designs brought out by the application of an ivory-white glaze. Rims were often protected by a copper band.

The celadons – stonewares with a feldspathic usually green-coloured glaze – constitute another important group of Song-dynasty pottery. Celadons were especially prized in the Near East because they were thought to change colour or break on contact with poison. The northern type, made in Henan province, was olive-green. The type made at Longquan, in southern Chekiang, had a glaze which varied from leaf green to cold blue-green; the greyish body, fired to a reddish brown where it was left unglazed, was sometimes used decoratively.

Jun ware, another constituent of Song-dynasty

Right: this circular pillow is a classic example of Cizhou domestic stoneware. The typical Cizhou leaf and flower pattern has been incised by sgraffito (carved through the glaze).

pottery, was made at Jun Zhou, in Henan. The glaze, thick and opalescent, is most commonly a lavender blue. It contains a mass of air bubbles and, sometimes, irregular grooves known as "earthworm" marks. Splashes of red and purple were often added to the lavender ground. Other classic Song-dynasty wares include the rare Ru and Guan types, manufactured in the 12th century to serve the Imperial households in Kaifeng and Hangchow respectively.

A wide variety of stonewares with black or deep brown glazes was also produced in this period. Best known is the grey-bodied Jian ware made in Fukien. Its high iron content produced the streaky "hare's fur" effect especially admired by the Japanese.

Cizhou wares

The name "Cizhou" covers a variety of domestic stonewares made in northern China from late Tang times until the 14th century. The glaze in Cizhou wares, usually transparent and sometimes with a blue or turquoise hue, was applied over a covering of slip. Decoration often featured leaf and flower patterns and was applied in an amazingly varied range of techniques, among them carving, incising, *sgraffito* with one or two slips, and slip-painting.

Qingpai wares

Qingpai is a thin translucent porcelain which fires to a reddish colour when unglazed. An alternative name is Yingqing, meaning literally "shadowy blue" and referring to the tinge of the glaze. Qingpai wares were made from Tang times onwards.

The Yuan dynasty

The Yuan dynasty (1280–1368) saw the introduction of cobalt as an underglaze decoration. Porcelain factories were established at Ching-te-chen and taste now shifted away from stoneware to porcelain decorated in underglaze blue. Porcelain in this style dating from the 14th century includes pieces decorated with ducks, water and vegetation.

*Above: two examples of Qingpai or Yingquing "shadowy blue" wares. These dishes, with their scalloped edges and chrysanthemum centres, are further illustration of the delicacy of which the Song dynasty potter was capable. By contrast, in the Yuan dynasty jar (**left**) and Song dynasty dish (**below left**) restraint and precision are less evident. While the bowl is covered in a thick blue glaze, the dish is decorated with blue with random splashes of red.*

Above: a Ming dynasty jar, dating from about 1500, decorated by the fahua technique of painting straight on to the unglazed body – here moulded and pierced. The turquoise background is very typical.

Left: this Ming jar, from the reign of Jiajing, is decorated with dragons chasing a pearl and is rendered in wucai, or contrasting colours.

This delicately painted ewer is typical of the blue and white wares made from the beginning of the Ming dynasty; it dates from the reign of Yongle. The scrolling peonies are a recurrent motif in Chinese porcelain.

Ming dynasty reign marks

Hongwu 1368–1398	Yongle 1403–1424	Xuande 1426–1435	Chenghua 1465–1487

Hongzhi 1488–1505	Zhengde 1506–1521	Jiajing 1522–1566	Longqing 1567–1572	Wanli 1573–1619	Tianqi 1621–1627	Chongzhen 1628–1644

The Ming dynasty

The Ming dynasty (1368–1644) patronized the porcelain industry. The variety of wares and glazes of earlier times was replaced by a more standardized body. Ming porcelain is white and translucent and is generally tinged with buff on the underside of the footring. Most glazes of the early period are thick and uneven, with a bluish tinge.

Superb blue and white wares were made in the reign of Xuande (1426–35). The blue was blackish, with points of especially dense colouring. Motifs included lotus flowers amid scrollwork, and aquatic birds. Xuande's reign also saw the perfection of underglaze red, seen at its best on delicate cups ornamented with three red fishes. The Xuande reign-mark often reappears on admirable 18th-century copies of the ware. Indeed, the practice of using reign marks on vessels of a later period is common in Chinese ceramics, and the copying of earlier styles was inspired not by a desire to deceive but to venerate ancestors.

Coloured enamels, often used with underglaze blue, were introduced in the reign of Chenghua (1465–87). The combination of enamels and underglaze blue, called the *wucai* technique (meaning "contrasting colours", was particularly favoured at court. *Sancai*, or "three-coloured, wares, both in stoneware and porcelain, were made from the late 15th to the 16th century. Turquoise, purple and blue enamels were separated by lines of clay, in the *fahua* technique, in a way that suggests

cloisonné work. Nevertheless, much Imperial ware was plain, decorated in a single colour; yellow and copper red were particularly favoured.

An innovation of the Zhengde period (1506–21) was a decoration of incised dragons coloured green on a yellow ground. The manufacture of blue and white wares was also revived, and reached heights of excellence in the reign of Jiajing (1522–66). Further mid-16th-century developments were the introduction of an overglaze iron red and the rise to popularity of fine monochrome porcelain.

Although the Ming dynasty is famous for its painted wares, celadons continued to be made up until the 14th century. These three plates are late examples.

Above left: this Ming dish, decorated with an energetic dragon, is a fine example of the revival of blue and white decoration which occurred in the reign of Jiajing.

Above: this Ming jar is a classic example of decoration using green dragons on a yellow ground – a new development introduced during the reign of Zhengde.

Left: a large jardinière is another example of blue and white Ming of the reign of Jiajing, whose reign mark appears in the rim above the dragon's head. Reign marks are more usually found on the base of vessels.

Above: this Qing dynasty dish is an exquisite example of Kangxi famille verte decoration. Like much Kangxi porcelain, it was made for export to Europe, and the arms of the client for whom it was made appears on the rim above the figures.

The baluster vase (**right**) and octagonal plate (**far right**) are further examples of Kangxi famille verte. Lively decoration, often incorporating birds, insects, flowers and trees, is characteristic of famille verte and famille rose wares.

The Qing dynasty

During the early years of the Qing dynasty (1644–1912), Jingdezhen, centre of the Chinese porcelain industry, was destroyed by rebels. After its reconstruction, exquisite porcelain was made there in the reigns of the emperors Kangxi (1662–1722), Yongzheng (1723–35) and Qianlong (1736–95).

Porcelain of the Kangxi period is characterized by fine underglaze painting. Many pieces were made for export to Europe. Such export wares were not always in authentic Chinese taste, as the Chinese, believing Europeans to be barbarians, often sent them grossly over-decorated pieces.

The best-known motif on Kangxi wares is the early flowering prunus depicted on a blue ground intended to suggest cracked ice.

The enamalled wares of the Qing dynasty fall largely into two categories, *famille verte* and *famille rose*. In the *famille verte* a brilliant green predominates; in the *famille rose*, a rose-pink. The *famille rose*, which reached China in about 1720, was Europe's one contribution to Chinese ceramics; this opaque enamel colour, which ranges from pink to purplish, was derived from colloidal gold. The finest *famille rose* pieces were made during the reign of Yongzheng.

As well as decorating vessels, enamels were also applied to figures from the late 18th century until modern times. In order to retain the fine modelling of the figures, enamels were applied directly onto the biscuit porcelain. The reign of Qianlong was marked by an important achievement in glazing, as

Qing dynasty reign marks

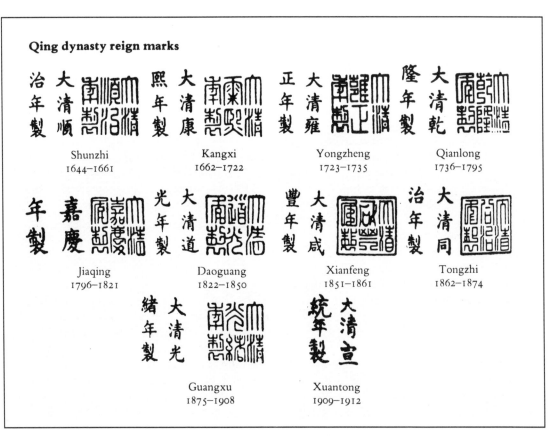

Shunzhi
1644–1661

Kangxi
1662–1722

Yongzheng
1723–1735

Qianlong
1736–1795

Jiaqing
1796–1821

Daoguang
1822–1850

Xianfeng
1851–1861

Tongzhi
1862–1874

Guangxu
1875–1908

Xuantong
1909–1912

Famille rose enamels pick out the clothing on these charming Qing figures (**left**) dating from the reign of Yongzheng. Each carries a vase designed to hold a real candle.

Brilliant famille rose colours depict the familiar Chinese peonies and chrysanthemums, complemented by grasshoppers and butterflies, on this Qing dynasty jardinière (**above**) from the reign of Yongzheng.

potters now reintroduced copper red often combining it with cobalt blue; the resultant glazes, characterized by turquoise splashes, are known as *flambés*. One variant is known as *sang de boeuf*, from its similarity to ox-blood. A delicate "peach-bloom" – pink mottled with red – was used on small pieces. Glazes often took the form of soft, low-temperature enamels applied in monochrome.

By the early 18th century, large quantities of porcelain were being made for export to the West. They included not only pieces with European-style decoration, such as biblical scenes, but also vessels made to European shapes ornamented in blue and white, or in *famille verte* or *famille rose* enamels. European armorial bearings were sometimes also added. This traffic in European-style porcelain decorated by Chinese hands did not, however, proceed without misunderstandings; it was not unknown, for example, for the instruction "our coat of arms here" to be literally interpreted by the Chinese painters who would carefully ornament the centre of a plate not with the relevant coat of arms but with those very words! Chinese porcelain for the American market included wares decorated with ships flying the American flag.

Dehua porcelain

From Dehua, in Funkien, came a fine porcelain which became popular from the 17th century. The glaze produced a milkier look than on Jingdezhen wares and the potting tended to be heavy. In Europe, the term *blanc de Chine* was applied to this type of porcelain. *Blanc de Chine*, especially the kind decorated in relief with prunus blossom, was often copied by European factories.

Yixing ware

Brown or red stoneware was made at Yixing, in Kiangsi province, from the mid-17th century. The well-known Yixing teapots were reputed to make tea taste nicer than any other wares. They were a favourite export and were decorated with designs in low relief or with incised inscriptions. Some 19th-century examples of Yixing stonewares are covered with exaggerated enamel decoration.

This Qing dynasty vase painted with flowers and leaves shows the effective use of copper-red rediscovered during the Qianlong period. Energetic all-over decoration was usual in the Qing dynasty.

Below: *a Qing dynasty cockerel which dates from the reign of Jiaqing, and is an attractive example of* blanc de chine. *The absence of painted decoration, highlights the sensitive modelling and brings these graceful all-white figures to life.*

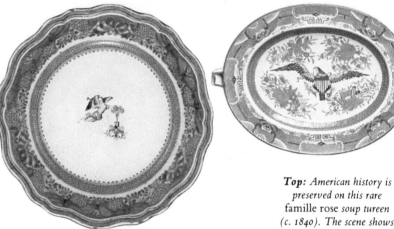

Top: *American history is preserved on this rare* famille rose *soup tureen (c. 1840). The scene shows the surrender of General Burgoyne to General Gates after the Battle of Saratoga, with the American eagle presiding.*

*The warming dish (**above**) and plate (**left**) show that, as exports continued standards declined. On the dish the eagle is just squeezed in, while the motif is almost lost on the plate. The plate is from George Washington's Order of Cincinnati service.*

Left: *a selection of 18th and early 19th-century "tobacco-leaf" export porcelain. Over-decorated by Chinese standards it was thought suitable for European "barbarians"!*

FRENCH FAIENCE

joint influence came from baroque silverware and Chinese porcelain. From that time also decoration on Nevers faience was applied in colours that included pale blue, orange and yellow. Red was never used. One well-known style of decoration was *bleu persan*, consisting of a cobalt blue ground decorated with orientalized birds, flowers and figures in white, or sometimes white, orange and yellow. Nevers faience reached its peak in the early 18th century. By the late 18th century, only cheap, popular wares were produced, some decorated with Revolutionary slogans. In 1647, Edmé Poterat's factory was granted a fifty-year monopoly controlling the manufacture of faience throughout Normandy. When that period expired, the number of factories increased to eighteen. Few of the wares made in Rouen were pictorial in the Nevers manner. Poterat's famous contribution was blue and white ware decorated with rich borders and ornament in the *style rayonnant*. It was in Rouen that the *style rayonnant* originated; this manner of decoration, developed from *lambrequins* (baroque border patterns), consists of a radiating pattern of symmetrical motifs.

Polychrome faience, popular from about 1720 to 1750, was also made in Rouen. A yellow ochre was developed in 1725. Polychrome Rouen faience often featured flower painting and naïve *chinoiseries*. Rouen faience was often imitated at other French factories, among them Sinceny, Quimper, St Cloud and Lille.

Nevers and Rouen

Most early decorative French pottery takes the form of faience, tin-glazed earthenware. The best-known maker of faience during the early period was Masseot Abaquesne, of Rouen. Abaquesne worked in the Italianate style, from about 1530 producing paving tiles for château-owners and drug jars decorated in cool blues and yellows. Faience was also made in Lyons in the late 16th century, and products of that city bear a confusing similarity to Urbino maiolica.

Italian influence remained strong. Only at Nevers was it translated into something distinctively French. The pictorial style of Urbino was continued there until about 1650 but after that a

Moustiers and Marseilles

In southern France, the important faience factories were at Moustiers and Marseilles. The first factory at Moustiers was established by Pierre Clérissy in about 1679. Early products of that factory include wares decorated in blue and the decorative repertoire featured borders in which hunting scenes were depicted. The later blue and white pieces, dating from between about 1710 and 1740, are often based on the delicate, fantastical engravings

Above: a fine example of Nevers faience in the baroque style of the mid-17th century. The centre of this huge dish is decorated with a hunting scene adapted from two prints by the Florentine engraver Antonio Tempesta; the border continues the theme. Colour – green, orange, manganese purple and pale blue – has been used daringly.

by Jean Bérain. Such decoration, consisting of mythological and grotesque figures, vases, drapes and urns, became known as the *style Bérain*.

Polychrome faience was also made at another factory in Moustiers set up in 1739 by Jean-Baptiste Laugier and Joseph Olerys. Here, designs were in the *style Bérain* at first, but later progressed to a style in which human or animal figures are loosely disposed among flowers and foliage.

The first faience factory in Marseilles was established in 1679 in the suburbs of St-Jean-du-Désert by Joseph Clérissy, brother of Pierre, who had set up the first Moustiers concern. Wares from the first Marseilles factory were often similar to those made at Moustiers and Nevers. At another factory in Marseilles, Joseph Fauchier II introduced the idea of painting sparse flowers in high temperature colours on a soft yellow ground. The most famous product of the Marseilles factories, however, was the beautiful work decorated in low-temperature enamels, dating from after about 1750. The most striking examples were executed by the Veuve (Widow) Perrin, who depicted flowers, fish and seaweed in a free, unacademic style.

Strasbourg, Niderville and Sceaux

The faience factories at Strasbourg, founded in 1721, and other locations near the German frontier, produced wares that were more strongly affected by the rococo style than were those of Moustiers and Marseilles. In the early Strasbourg period, the *style rayonnant* was imitated, with the addition of some polychrome and gilding, but in 1748, decorators from Meissen joined the factory, bringing with them the techniques of painting in overglaze enamels and a range of robust rococo shapes. A common form of flower painting in the later Strasbourg period was *fleurs des Indes*, based on the Chinese *famille rose*.

At Niderville, in Lorraine, where faience was produced as well as porcelain, the rococo took a less extreme form than at Strasbourg. Another important faience manufactory of the late 18th century was at Sceaux, near Paris. Sceaux faience veered from a civilized form of rococo to neo-classicism. The flower painting there was excellent. Much Sceaux faience was intentionally decorated in the manner of the porcelain made at nearby Sèvres.

*This mid 18th-century pot-pourri vase (**below**) has all the robust vigour of the rococo. Polychrome relief decoration is typical of the style.*

Above: work from southern factories which produced similar wares. The plate on the right is by Veuve Perrin, about 1770; the other plate is from Moustiers, around 1750; the tureen, made about 1765, is from Montpellier.

*The Strasbourg faience partridge tureen (**left**) was made between 1748 and 1754.*

Far left: a naturalistically modelled Lille faience chinoiserie polychrome figure, about 1750.

FRENCH PORCELAIN

St Cloud

The St Cloud soft-paste porcelain factory was established in about 1700. The period of its greatest achievement was between about 1725 and 1750. Early products of the St Cloud factory have a greenish glaze. Decoration, often in blue, was frequently in the *style rayonnant* introduced by the Rouen faience makers. Other decorative forms were applied prunus blossom, as on Chinese *blanc de Chine* and a scaled pattern suggestive of the French artichoke.

Many of the shapes, including those of bowls, covered jars and cachepots, were based on silver originals. Tea wares included *trembleuse* cups and saucers – cups which fitted into saucers with deep rings to prevent spillage by users with an unsteady hand. Teapots often had spouts and handles modelled in the form of amusing animal and bird heads. St Cloud wares also included spice boxes and unpainted "Chinese" figures. Figures of Europeans are rare.

18th-century blue and white porcelain from the St Cloud factory and a late 17th-century Rouen vase, (above). All these pieces have border decorations in the style known as Bérainesque.

Right: St Cloud unpainted soft-paste porcelain of the mid-18th century. Chinese-style figures are more usual than European ones from this factory.

Chantilly

Louis-Henri of Bourbon, Prince de Condé, had a large collection of Japanese porcelain in his château at Chantilly. He succeeded in his ambition to own a porcelain factory when Ciquaire Cirou brought to him the St Cloud factory's secret porcelain formula. The Chantilly factory was established in 1725.

Not surprisingly, Japanese porcelain exercised a strong influence over the factory's products. Many motifs, including the "Partridge", "Banded Hedge" and "Squirrel", were taken from the Kakiemon style. Tea wares and snuff boxes, for example, thus decorated, reflected the playfulness of French rococo. This Japanese phase ended around 1740, when Meissen became the main source of decorative inspiration.

Chantilly suffered a blow when the royal Vincennes factory, set up in 1738, was granted a monopoly over porcelain production. The Chantilly factory did not fully obey the edict but reverted to monochrome decoration. Underglaze decoration in the form of small blue flower sprays, known as "Chantilly sprig", became popular, especially on plates with moulded basketwork borders.

Above: a Chantilly drug jar and a silver-mounted jug, both made in about 1735 when Japanese influence was strongest. The jug is typical of the Kakiemon style and the reverse of the drug jar and its lid are decorated in this way.

This figure of a Chinese girl with nodding head (above) is also from the Chantilly factory. She wears a dress decorated with Kakiemon motifs.

Mennecy

The Mennecy soft-paste porcelain factory was founded in 1734. Its early wares resemble those of the St Cloud factory, though the glaze on Mennecy ware is smoother and wet-looking and the body a darker ivory. Mennecy's mature style was chiefly inspired by the products of the Vincennes factory.

The commonest surviving type made at Mennecy are small custard cups and covers painted with flower sprays and small boxes, sometimes modelled as animals. Figures, both glazed and in biscuit, were also made, some of the finest by Nicolas-François Gauron.

Vincennes-Sèvres

In 1738 two brothers, Gilles and Robert Dubois, arrived in Vincennes from Chantilly and set up a factory in an abandoned royal palace. Their venture was unsuccessful, but in 1745 a new company was established and was granted a twenty-year monopoly over porcelain production. In 1735, the enterprise was renamed "Manufacture Royale" and five years later became the sole property of Louis XV. A factory mark of two interlaced Ls

Sèvres marks

The enclosed letter indicates the date – 1754 and 1778

Marks for 1793–1800 (left) and 1852–70

A Sèvres rose Pompadour pear-shaped milk jug (**top right**); the colour was named after the King's mistress. Smaller milk jugs of this shape were usually sold as part of a service, but larger ones were sold separately.

Right: this large Vincennes tankard, c. 1753, has a cylindrical body and domed cover. The gilt border and decoration of flying and walking birds among bulrushes is set against a bleu lapis *ground*.

was introduced, supplemented by a date letter (A for 1735, B for 1754, etc.; AA for 1778, BB for 1779, etc.). In 1756, the site was moved to Sèvres.

Although Vincennes set out initially to rival Meissen, the factory did not produce hard-paste porcelain for many years. The secret formula was still unknown in France and it was not until 1769 that the right clay was discovered near Limoges. At its new location at Sèvres, the factory made both the new hard-paste porcelain (named "Porcelaine Royale") and soft-paste (named "Porcelaine de France").

Vincennes' early speciality was exquisitely moulded porcelain flowers. These were used for bocages and as parts of candelabra, clocks and other decorative objects. Whole bouquets were occasionally constructed. Other products included jardinières, jugs, ice pails and trays. From 1752, production changed towards wares based on silver prototypes, with continuing influence from Chantilly.

The first of Vincennes-Sèvres' many famous ground colours was a slightly uneven blue, known as *bleu lapis* or *gros bleu*. Additional decoration took the form of gilding and reserved panels painted with figures and birds in landscapes, or birds silhouetted against blossoms.

The factory's spectacular range of ground colours expanded with the addition of *bleu céleste*, a turquoise, from 1752, yellow from 1753, and violet and green from 1756, when the concern moved to Sèvres. *Rose Pompadour* was introduced in 1757 and *bleu de roi*, a strong, even blue, in 1763. *Bleu de roi* was sometimes embellished with *oeil de perdrix*, an all-over pattern of gilt dots within circles. The paintings enclosed in panels on these coloured

Right: The Sèvres jardinières in bleu de roi (also known as bleu nouveau) flank a Vincennes white tureen and plate with gilt decoration. The royal factory moved from Vincennes to Sèvres in 1756.

as internal problems, threatened the prosperity of Sèvres. Towards the middle of the 19th century, however, production, both in terms of quantity and quality, improved. An innovation of the period was the *pâte-sur-pâte* method of decoration, in which layers of white slip are built up to form a design in low relief. This technique, introduced at Sèvres by Robert, head of the painting department, was subsequently taken to England by Marc-Louis Solon, who left Sèvres to work at Minton's, and to Meissen, where it was perfected.

Nineteenth-century porcelain

In 1830, Jacob and Mardochée Petit bought a hard-paste factory at Fontainebleau, which had been set up in 1795. Under the Petits, the factory produced much decorative porcelain in a neo-rococo style with poor quality gilding. Among its products was the *veilleuse*, or tea-warmer, which at this factory was often made in the shape of a figure.

A baluster-shaped Sèvres blue nouveau vase *(left) with the all-over* œil-de-perdrix *pattern. Part of the ground colour was scraped away to leave space for the coloured decoration of flowers and fruit. This technique was used for a short time around 1770.*

***Below:** a group of Sèvres porcelain pieces of the mid-1750s with rose* Pompadour *and green grounds and a Vincennes blue lapis* cup and saucer of *about 1750.*

grounds are generally richer during the Sèvres period than in the early days at Vincennes. More elaborate painting in the later period included Meissen-inspired shipping and harbour scenes. The Sèvres range included complete services, tea-sets, potpourri vases, toilet ware and clock cases.

The factory also produced figures. While the earliest Vincennes figures were glazed, most figures made after 1751 were left in biscuit. The influence of Boucher affected the early biscuit groups of children and pastorals until 1757, when the sculptor E. M. Falconet arrived at the factory. Falconet looked back to the masters of the baroque; the models which he produced are among the factory's best. By 1780, pastoral themes were abandoned in favour of mythological and contemporary literary themes rendered in a neo-classical manner.

Sèvres introduced the newly-discovered hard-paste porcelain in 1770. New ground colours – brown, black and dark blue – were devised. In the 1780s, a further innovation was the fusing of translucent enamels over silver gilt or foil. Decoration was by this time purely neo-classical. From about 1785, biscuit reliefs were moulded in the Wedgwood style. During the First Republic, Revolutionary emblems became a popular form of ornament.

Between the late 18th century and early 19th century, competition from other factories, as well

Art Nouveau

Among the leading potters of the late 19th and early 20th centuries were Ernest Chaplet, based at Choisy-le-Roi, Auguste Delaherche at Armentières, Albert Dammouse at Sèvres, Jean Carriés at St-Armand-en-Puisaye in the Nièvre, and Adrian Dalpeyrat at Bourg-la-Reine. Artists such as these drew inspiration from Japanese artifacts exhibited in Paris, as did so many exponents of Art Nouveau.

There was, however, more Art Nouveau feeling in the wares of the two big French porcelain factories than those of the studio potters. Taxile Doat's design for Sèvres and Georges de Fleure's for Limoges are excellent examples.

***Below:** a vase by Ernest Chaplet, one of the leading studio potters working in France around the turn of this century.*

GERMAN POTTERY

Above: a very early, unglazed Jakobakannen jug made around 1400.

The salt-glazed stoneware jug (right) bears the date 1594. It has moulded decoration – three medallions (one with the arms of Queen Elizabeth I, the others with those of the Holy Roman Empire) and a bearded mask.

Far right: a polished red stoneware coffee pot of about 1715 made by Johann Böttger. Porcellaneous stoneware was an approximation of the porcelain imported from China.

Hafner ware

Hafner ware, lead-glazed pottery, was produced in Germany from the 16th to the early 17th century. *"Hafner"* means "stove-maker" but the word refers to a class of lead-glazed pottery including not only stove tiles but vessels made in a similar way. Hafner ware vessels include dishes and round-bellied jugs on which an ornamental pattern of raised lines kept the coloured glazes from merging. Decorative subjects were often biblical, historical and mythological.

Stoneware

An early Germanic contribution to ceramics was the invention of salt-glazed stoneware, stoneware fired with common salt to produce a thin glassy glaze. At the Rhineland town of Sieburg, *Jakobakannen*, tall slender jugs, were made as early as 1400. Other distinctive types were the *Schellen*, tall, cone-like tankards, and the *Schnabelkannen*, long-spouted jugs, both with elaborate relief decoration.

Underglaze blue decoration was especially common in the Westerwald potteries. Westerwald ware consists generally of jugs, mugs and chamber pots with stamped or incised decoration picked out in blue or mauve.

From the 16th century, stonewares were also made by the Vest family at Kreussen, in Franconia. Whereas Kreussen stoneware had a brown or black slip beneath the glaze, in Freiburg and other centres in Saxony this was absent. In the earliest period at Meissen, a fine red stoneware was made.

German faience

Hamburg became a well-known centre for the production of faience in the middle of the 17th century. A factory at Frankfurt had its heyday from about 1667 to 1723, producing Chinese-style pieces in the manner of Dutch delftware. Faience was also made at Stockelsdorff near Lübeck, and at Kellinghusen in Holstein.

GERMAN PORCELAIN

Böttger discovered the secret of making white hard-paste porcelain in 1708. This coffee pot (**far left**) was made by him in 1720.

Left: a small Meissen beaker vase of about 1730 with Imperial yellow ground and shaped panels painted with Chinese figures.

Below: examples of Meissen coloured-ground wares: a lime-green oval quatrefoil tea caddy, and a flax-blue teapot. Both had panels painted with landscapes.

Meissen

From the time that Oriental porcelain first reached Europe, potters in France and Germany had imitated it using soft-paste, or artificial, porcelain. The ingredients of true, or hard-paste, porcelain remained a mystery.

In 1708, an alchemist named J. F. Böttger achieved a superb white porcelain like the Chinese. Augustus the Strong, his patron, was delighted, and in 1710 founded the Meissen factory, near Dresden, which produced the first hard-paste porcelain in Europe. The Meissen factory's earliest work was based on silver forms. Decoration, often floral, was rendered in primitive enamel colours, gilding or a purplish lustre. At the end of the Böttger period (before 1719), the first *chinoiseries*, in gilt silhouette, were applied.

From 1720 to about 1735, the factory benefited from the services of a brilliant artist, J. G. Höroldt, whose *chinoiserie* decorations on porcelain established a fashion. Höroldt also perfected a clear yellow ground which invited comparison with the Imperial colour of China. The Japanese Kakiemon

style was an important influence at this time, and the well-known *indianische Blumen* ("Indian flowers"), introduced by Höroldt, were based on Japanese flower painting. Topographical painting appeared in the 1720s. Harbour scenes with figures enjoyed a vogue in the 1730s, followed by battles and *commedia dell'arte* scenes in the 1740s, and pastoral subjects in the 1750s. *Deutsche Blumen*, a type of floral decoration based on botanical illustration, were popular after about 1735.

The great period of figure production at Meissen began in 1727, when J. G. Kirchner became the factory's first great modeller. By 1733, Kirchner was replaced by an even finer modeller, J. J.

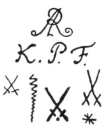

*Marks on Meissen porcelain **Top:** the monogram of Augustus the Strong, 1723–36. **Centre:** initials standing for "Koenigliche Porzellan Fabrik", used until 1724. **Bottom row:** three examples of the crossed swords, used from 1724 onwards, and the caduceus mark, used on early Meissen porcelain.*

*J. J. Kändler was Meissen's greatest modeller. The crinoline group (**left**) of a lady with a pug-dog and a blackamoor illustrates the lightness and vivacity of his work. Stylized indianische Blumen decorate the lady's petticoat.*

Kändler, whose work has a marvellous lightness and vivacity, Kändler's earliest figures were in strong colours, often with *indianische Blumen* on a gold or black ground. By 1750, the palette was becoming paler, and rococo scrollwork on bases was soon introduced. Meissen's so-called "Academic Period", beginning in 1763, was a neoclassical phase, when influences from Sèvres were strong.

The earliest Meissen marks include a pseudo-Chinese square character and the letters "KPM" (for *Koenigliche Porzellan Manufaktur*). In 1724, crossed swords became the standard mark. The debased versions of earlier Meissen wares made in the 19th century are commonly referred to as "Dresden".

Other porcelain factories

C. K. Hunger from Meissen took the porcelain secret in 1719 to Vienna, where Claudius Du Paquier had set up a factory. After the concern was sold to the State in 1744, L. Dannhauser and J. J. Niedermeyer modelled some delightful figures. In the late 18th century Sèvres was copied.

Hard-paste was made at Höchst from 1750 to 1796. Tablewares made here were usually accompanied by fanciful scrollwork. Other centres were Frankenthal (1755–1800), Nymphenburg (from 1753), Ludwigsburg (1759–1824), Fürstenberg (from 1753) and Berlin (from 1761). It is the figure modellers who give this group of factories their main distinction. The greatest was Franz Anton Bustelli of Nymphenburg, famous above all for his *commedia dell'arte* figures. His models usually suggest carved wooden prototypes, and have swivelled hips and thin, flat bases.

J. P. Melchior of Höchst, Frankenthal and Nymphenburg – he was engaged at Höchst in 1767 and made its reputation – is best known for his figures of children.

*These porcelain figures of children in fancy dress (**below**) are from the Höchst factory, which is best known for its statuettes. This pair was modelled by J. P. Melchior, the factory's chief modeller from 1767–79.*

Marks of two German factories

Berlin: Gotzkowsky's factory, 1761–3 and the Royal factory from 1763.

Höchst 1758–65.

Left: *an oval Berlin plate of about 1765. The factory was acquired by Frederick the Great in 1763 and has been state-run ever since.*

KOREA

The best Korean ceramics do not fall far short of the best Chinese. Korean wares fall into three groups, named after dynasties: the Silla (57 BC–AD 936), the Koryo (936–1392) and the Yi (1392–1910).

It was during the Koryo period that Korean ceramics enjoyed a golden age, and celadons of the highest quality were made. These wares were characteristically inlaid with black or white slip, typical forms being ribbed boxes, spouted gourd-like vessels, pierced perfume pots, miniature vases and cups on stands. Lobing, reeding and waved edges were common forms of modelling. Some shapes had a "growing", flower-like character.

Above: a celadon vase of the Koryo period with mishima decoration. This style of ornament involved inlaying black or white slip before applying the celadon glaze. Stars and flowers are the most usual subjects.

JAPAN

Before the 13th century, Japan relied largely on imported Chinese pottery, especially for wares connected with tea-drinking. The earliest native Japanese wares of interest were stoneware bowls made at Seto, in the province of Owari. A low-fired, lead-glazed earthenware known as *raku* became immensely popular; it progressed from black or dark brown to light red, becoming straw-coloured in the 17th century, and finally attaining a polychrome range. *Raku* forms were thick and irregularly shaped.

Beautiful *raku* wares were made by an artist called Kenzan (1660–1743), who also produced finely-painted cream stoneware with a finely crackled glaze. Bizen province is associated with vases, animal figures and other forms made of red or bluish-brown stoneware. Porcelain was first made in Japan in the early years of the 17th century. The secret of porcelain manufacture is said to have been brought from Ching-te Chen to Japan by one Gorodoyu-go Shonzui. The first kilns were set up at Arita, in Hizen province. Underglaze blue was the first decorative technique, but enamelling in colour was introduced in about 1644.

The products of Arita fall into two categories: Kakiemon and Imari. Kakiemon decoration was simple and asymmetrical, balancing white areas against painted areas. Colours included iron-red, bluish-green, light blue and yellow, sometimes with light gilding. Among typical patterns were those now known as the "Quail and Millet" and "Banded Hedge", which were adopted by many European factories.

Decoration in the Imari style was mainly in a blackish underglaze blue and a dark red, often incorporating native brocades as a motif. From the end of the 17th century, Arita produced dishes and vases in the Imari style for export. Imari continued to be made well into the 19th century, but items intended for export became increasingly debased.

Opposite page: a 17th-century jar decorated in Imari style. Imari, the European name given to this type of porcelain, is actually the name of the port from which it was shipped.

Kakiemon figures of the late 17th century (far left). Both Kakiemon and Imari were much copied in the West.

Left: an Imari early 19th century fish plate.

The pot pourri container (below), is an example of "brocaded" Satsuma ware – crackled cream faience richly decorated in enamels and gold – produced from the middle of the 19th century.

Porcelain was also made in the 19th century at Seto, Kyoto, Mikawachi and Shiba. Pieces produced at Kyoto copied Chinese Song-dynasty celadons and Ming porcelains. Satsuma pottery, made from the early 17th century, became heavily decorated towards the late 19th century, when it was produced largely for the Western market.

THE NETHERLANDS

The blue and white decoration on this group of delftware, as well as the shapes of the pieces, show the influence that Oriental porcelain had on Dutch potters from the 17th century This type of delftware is in complete contrast to the earlier style of Dutch delft, which is similar to English delft.

Dutch delft

Delftware, tin-glazed earthenware, takes its name from the Dutch town of Delft. Despite its name it did not originate in Holland; the technique of making tin-glazed earthenware came to the Netherlands from either Spain or Italy.

In 1512, Guido di Savino, from Castel Durante in Italy, set up a pottery in Antwerp. By the third quarter of the 16th century, tin-glaze potteries were established at Middelburg, Rotterdam, Haarlem, Amsterdam and Friesland. In the early years of the 17th century there was also some modest production of tin-glazed pottery at Delft. By the middle of the 17th century, Delft had become an important centre and, from its reputation for producing luxurious and elaborate earthenwares, gave its name to this type of pottery.

In Delft, many potteries took over the premises of breweries that had been driven out of business by competition with English beer. Inheriting the names of the former breweries, these potteries thus became known by such titles at The Three Bells, The White Star, The Peacock and The Greek A. Their best products were made between 1640 and 1740.

Dutch delftware was at first strongly influenced by Italian maiolica. Early forms include "blue-dash" chargers, large dishes with a border of short blue strokes encircling a scene or motif in polychrome. At this stage only the fronts of dishes were covered in tin glaze; the backs had a thin lead glaze.

At the beginning of the 17th century, two shiploads of Chinese porcelain reached Amsterdam. Their arrival caused a revolution in taste. Rejecting the naïve idiom and polychrome palette of the previous century, Dutch potters started to copy the Chinese blue and white wares. Delftware now became finer and designs more sophisticated, and backs as well as fronts of dishes were tin-glazed the better to imitate Chinese porcelain.

During the ascendance of Delft as an important centre for the production of the ware, outlines in manganese purple were added to the blue and white wares. This technique was known as *trek*. A coat of clear lead glaze (*kwaart*) was sometimes superimposed on the tin glaze to produce a high gloss resembling that on porcelain.

Although Chinese influence continued strongly, a nationalistic strain, seen in landscape painting and contemporary scenes, began to appear on delftware. Biblical scenes, executed in manganese purple as well as blue, were common on tiles. These tiles, large quantities of which were made at all the important delftware-producing centres, were not intended for use on floors but as decoration for walls and skirting.

Samuel van Eenhoorn was responsible for the finest wares made in Delft in the late 17th century, most of them fairly accurate copies of Chinese originals. The "Greek A" factory run by van Eenhoorn (where the mark was a capital A with initials) was taken over by Adrianus Kocks, whose "AK" monogram is the most famous (and faked) of all Delft marks. Among the rarest Delft wares are the beautiful pieces made by Rochus Hoppesteyn who worked at the "Young Moor's Head" factory. Hoppesteyn's pieces are similar to those made by van Eenhoorn, but their glaze is bluer and more brilliant, the manganese darker and the drawing surer. Hoppesteyn also embellished his pieces with gold and a brilliant red. The products of the De Roos factory (1662–1775) are also notable; the best known pieces are a series of blue and white plates decorated with biblical scenes.

By the 1690s, Dutch delftware was following European baroque shapes, and continued to be much in demand in the first half of the 18th century, when the rococo style was assimilated. Polychrome decoration was a feature of 18th-century Dutch delftware, and many polychrome imitations of transitional Ming pieces, notably sets of vases, were made.

By the 1770s, loyal tributes to the House of Orange were frequent on Dutch delftware. But from this time, the days of the industry were numbered. Delftware was rivalled not only by continuing, and increasing, imports from China but also by German hard-paste porcelain and Wedgwood's creamware. By the end of the 18th century only ten factories remained in Delft; by the early 19th century, only two.

Above: the decoration on this delftware butter tub, dating from about 1720, is an amusing mixture of Chinese and Dutch motifs.

Both the shape and the chinoiserie decoration on the 18th-century delft jar (*left*) are impressive proof of the Dutch potter's skill in imitating Chinese models.

SCANDINAVIA

Sweden

The faience factory established at Rörstrand, near Stockholm, in 1729 enjoyed its greatest success in the 1750s and 1760s. The earliest Rörstrand faience was decorated in blue with figure subjects or in a kind of *style rayonnant*. The *style rayonnant*, introduced by the faience makers of Rouen, consisted of a central radiating pattern of symmetrical motifs developed from baroque border patterns known as *lambrequins*. By 1745, the Rörstrand factory was producing faience decorated in *bianco sopra bianco*, white over an off-white glaze. Polychrome painting with black outlines was also developed. Painting in enamels was introduced in 1758. In the early period, the factory's products were marked "Stockholm"; after 1758, the mark was "Rörstrand".

From 1759 to 1788, faience was made at another factory, in Marieberg. Its modelling was more accomplished than its painting.

The manufacture of soft-paste porcelain was begun at Marieberg under Pierre Berthevin, the factory's director from 1766 to 1769. Not surprisingly, early Marieberg porcelain shows Mennecy influence, since Berthevin had previously worked at the French factory. Influence from Copenhagen dominated Marieberg in its later period. The factory closed in 1788, having enjoyed but a brief existence, and Marieberg porcelain is therefore rare.

Denmark

In 1722, a faience factory was established in the Store Kogensgade in Copenhagen. The period of the factory's greatest prosperity stretched from 1727 to 1749, the bulk of its output consisting of blue and white wares. Competition, especially from creamware, caused its closure in 1769.

Attempts to make soft-paste porcelain in Denmark began with Louis Fournier in 1759 but lasted only until 1766. Hard-paste porcelain was successfully developed by F. H. Müller, who established a factory in Copenhagen in 1771. In 1780, the factory became Den Kongelige Porcelainfabrik Copenhagen (The Royal Copenhagen Porcelain Manufactory). Royal ownership continued until 1857, although the title has been retained.

In the early years of the factory's existence, Germany was the source both of workmen and styles. Meissen and Fürstenburg influenced both the shapes and decoration (initially in underglaze blue) of Danish porcelain. Well modelled figures formed a large part of the factory's output in the 18th century. From the late 18th century, the Copenhagen factory adopted a classical style and a wider palette. Architectural motifs, historical portraits and landscapes with ruins entered the decorative repertoire. In the late 19th century, some fine biscuit figures, after the neo-classical sculptor Thorwaldsen, were made.

*A range of late 18th-century Royal Copenhagen porcelain. While quiet good taste characterizes the simple blue and white table wares (**above left**), sensitive modelling is seen in this pair of figures – a musician and a lady with her lap dog (**above**). The plate, cup and saucer (**far left**) and the tureen on stand (**left**) form part of the famous "flora Danica" service; the simplicity of the flower painting is somewhat unusual for the period.*

The most famous product of the Copenhagen factory is the "Flora Danica" service, begun in 1789 and probably intended for Catherine II, Empress of Russia. The service, consisting of neo-classical shapes decorated with botanical subjects, was still unfinished when Catherine died in 1796. It is displayed today in Rosenborg Castle, Copenhagen.

Kiel in 1763. Here, the repertoire of the flower painters was wider than anywhere else in northern Europe at the time. The tin-enamel produced at Kiel was remarkably white and the colours with which it was decorated exceptionally brilliant. Shapes included both tablewares and more unusual items such as watch-holders, inkstands and wall-cisterns.

Schleswig-Holstein

Until 1848, Schleswig-Holstein was Danish territory. A faience factory was established at Schleswig in 1755. Decoration on the ware was characteristically in manganese purple, sometimes with the addition of greyish-green. The output of the factory included relief-moulded plates with floral decoration and apple-shaped tureens.

The best of the Holstein factories was founded at

Norway

Peter Hoffnagel found a clay suitable for making faience at Herrebøe, where production started in about 1760, continuing until 1772. The only colours used on Herrebøe faience were blue and manganese, and they were never combined. Designs included various boldly decorated interpretations of the rococo style.

SPAIN AND ITALY

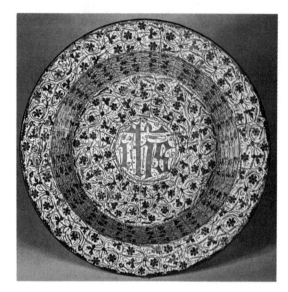

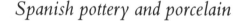

Italian maiolica

The word "maiolica", referring to painted tin-glazed earthenware, is derived from "Majorca", since it was Majorcan traders who first brought the technique from Spain to Italy. Early Italian maiolica is divided into families: in the "green" family, green and purple are the dominant colours, with touches of ochre; the "relief blue" family is based on cobalt blue, usually with some purple. Typical of this latter group are the "oak leaf" drug jars, from Tuscany, decorated with oak leaves in the Gothic style. Yellow, from antimony, was discovered by the middle of the 15th century and was used on some large dishes with borders formed of Gothicized oak leaves.

From about 1475, Faenza became increasingly important as the major centre of the faience industry. (The word "faience" is a French corruption of "Faenza".) Early Faenza plaques, dishes and jugs often bore the sacred initials "IHS". The peacock's feather motif was especially popular. The influence of Chinese porcelain is seen in the *alla porcellana* design, consisting of blue trailing stems on a white ground.

The della Robbia family brought ceramics into the realm of great Renaissance art. Luca della Robbia (1400–89) decorated large architectural reliefs, initially using white over a blue ground but later employing a wider range of colours. Andrea, his

Spanish pottery and porcelain

Tin-glazed earthenware made by the Moors, or made under Moorish influence, was produced at Valencia from the early 15th century. This Spanish pottery is known as the Hispano-Moresque type. Decoration often featured lustre pigment combined with blue; the lustre on the best pieces is generally of a straw colour. Decorative motifs were often based on bryony or vine leaves, and Kufic inscriptions were also incorporated. Gothic gradually replaced Moorish styles, and, after the middle of the 17th century, quality declined.

An important faience factory was founded at Alcora in 1726–27 producing finely painted panels and oval plaques and a number of fine busts.

Porcelain was first made in Spain at Buen Retiro, near Madrid, between 1760 and 1808. The factory was an extension of the Capodimonte works, in Italy, founded in 1743. The Buen Retiro factory's greatest period was between its foundation and 1788. Its products were initially in the rococo and *chinoiserie* style, swiftly changing to embrace the neo-classical influence of Sèvres. Buen Retiro porcelain is very rare.

nephew, and Andrea's son Giovanni, are also well known.

At the beginning of the 16th century, another style of decoration was adopted; this was *istoriato*, or narrative painting, first introduced at Faenza. Subjects were mostly drawn from the scriptures and mythology. By the mid-16th century, the fashion for *istoriato* had begun to decline. Decorators moved towards a freer manner in which sketchy designs were executed with a palette limited to cobalt, yellow and orange. Later in the century, white wares known as *bianchi di Faenza*, often moulded with filigree patterns developed.

Italian porcelain

As Oriental wares reached Europe in greater quantities during the 16th century, they came to be greatly prized by Italian noblemen, though maiolica was more commonly used at their tables.

The first successful attempt at making soft-paste porcelain in Europe occurred in Florence in 1575. The venture, inspired by blue and white Ming ware, was financed by Francesco I de' Medici. Over two hundred years later, hard-paste porcelain was being made in Venice. The first Venetian hard-paste porcelain factory, founded in about 1720 by Francesco Vezzi, produced pieces that rivalled Meissen, but Vezzi's factory had a short existence, closing just seven years later, in 1727.

The best Italian porcelain factories were Doccia, founded in 1735, and Capodimonte, founded in 1743. Doccia's earliest hard-paste ware is easy to identify by its roughness and fire cracks and its dull, sticky looking glaze. The factory's products include tea and coffee wares and brightly enamelled figures with clumsy hands and red-stippled flesh. Most of its wares are in the baroque style; the later fashion for rococo was all but ignored here.

The Capodimonte manufactory was established by Charles of Bourbon in the grounds of his palace near Naples, and moved to Spain in 1759. Both the figures and service ware made at Capodimonte are very rare. Giuseppe Gricci, the chief modeller, made *commedia dell'arte* figures and peasant pieces, which tend to have small heads. Decorative subjects on tablewares include figures, seascapes, landscapes, battle scenes and Oriental designs, often featuring the raised prunus motif of *blanc de Chine*.

Hardpaste porcelain wares decorated with figure subjects in relief and enamelled in polychrome have been wrongly attributed to Capodimonte. They were in fact made by Doccia in the 18th century, and in Naples or in Germany in the 19th century. Other important Italian factories include Le Nove (1762–1825) and Geminiano Cozzi's manufactory in Venice (1765–1812).

Far left: "*The death of the children of Niobe*" *is the subject of this deep majolica bowl. By the late 16th century, yellow had been added to the palette of colours.*

An example of a Capodimonte vase (below); very little porcelain from this factory has survived.

GLASS

To appreciate antique glass, it is important to understand a little about the making of glass. It is made of silica and alkali. The source of silica is commonly sand and occasionally crushed rock; and in old glass the alkali came either from wood ash (producing potash glass) or burnt seaweed (soda glass).

In the 15th century, the Venetians overcame the problem of decolorizing glass when they added manganese. The result was a clear glass which they named "cristallo". Fine quality clear glass has been called crystal ever since. Lead was introduced in the 17th century to produce an imitation rock crystal.

AMERICA

The engraved tumbler, seal bottle, cream basket and taperstick are examples of mid-18th-century clear and coloured glass made at Caspar Wistar's factory. The "Swan finial" on the cream basket is a characteristic decoration on Wistar's glassware.

The 17th and 18th centuries

There were four pioneer glasshouses (or factories) in America: at Jamestown, Virginia, established in 1608; Salem, Massachusetts, established in 1639; New York (when it was still New Amsterdam), established before 1664; and Shackmaxson, established in 1683, now part of Philadelphia.

In 1620 the Jamestown glasshouse began making glass beads for trade with the Indians, and it sur-

vived the massacre of 1622. There was a pressing demand for window glass in the 17th century, and, in Virginia the factories were set up to produce it with bottle-making as a sideline. Indeed, window glass and bottles remained the staple products of American glass factories for over a century.

The first really successful glasshouse in America was established in Salem County, New Jersey, in 1739. Set up by Caspar Wistar (1696–1752), a brass button maker from Philadelphia, this glass-making community came to be known as Wistarburg.

Wistar imported Dutch glass-makers, and

Dutch influence is evident in the factory's later products. Wistar made window glass in five sizes, bottles, "electrofying globes and tubes", drinking-glasses and other table glass. The earliest wares were of plain glass. Coloured glass was successfully introduced later; two-colour work included ruby jugs with dark green wavings, and plain and coloured glass were sometimes used together. Small quantities of a rich, dark-blue glass were made, as well as turquoise, clear green and opalescent glass. Amber and brown were rarer. Some coloured glass was whirled with white in the manner of English Nailsea glass. Balls of glass, often wrongly called "witch-balls" today, were blown in various sizes to serve as covers for bowls and jugs. Another form of decoration, the raised "lily pad" design, is also very characteristic of Wistar's products. It incorporates naturalistic snaking swirls. Another characteristic feature of some of Wistar's glassware is the "swan finial", which in fact resembles a common or garden duck or chicken more closely than it does a swan.

After Caspar Wistar's death in 1752, the factory continued under his son Richard until 1780. Glassware made in the Wistar style, but not assignable to any particular factory or region, is described as being of the "South Jersey" type. South Jersey glass continued to be made until the middle of the 19th century, and the raised "lily pad" design and "swan finial" described above are two characteristics of South Jersey glass.

Other glass factories founded in the 18th century were those of Henry William Stiegel (1729–85), who built two factories in Manheim, Pennsylvania, which were in operation between 1765 and 1774. The wares, of flint glass (lead glass derived from burned flints), were comparatively small and

fragile. Some were engraved with motifs such as tulips, baskets of flowers, sunbursts with birds and borders of intersecting arcs filled with latticework. By contrast to foreign engraving, these designs were executed on thin blown glass and left unpolished, with a "folk art" finish. Typical of Stiegel's wares are pocket flasks, made between 1769 and 1774, patterned with a daisy motif within a diamond or hexagon. Except for these flasks, attributions to Stiegel's glasshouses can only be tentative.

John Frederick Amelung, who founded a factory in Maryland in 1784, was the only American glass-maker of the time to inscribe and date some of his work. Amelung glass, which includes tableware and decanters, is now extremely rare. In Connecticut, the Pitkin family successfully produced glassware from 1783 to 1830. Pitkin glass, which is mainly functional, tends to have vertical or swirled moulded ribbing, most commonly in green or amber. So-called Pitkin flasks are ribbed and are doubly thick in their lower half.

The 19th century

Pittsburg became the centre of American glass manufacture in the early 19th century. The glasshouse established by Thomas Bakewell and Benjamin Page in 1808 was noted for the brilliance of its metal and the quality of its wheel cutting, indistinguishable from contemporaneous Irish work. Bakewell's glasshouse continued until 1882.

The method of pressing molten glass in patterned moulds is said to have originated in America. As with blue transfer-printed pottery,

Examples of later 18th and early 19th-century glassware. The 19th-century amethyst mould-blown bottle (far left) has the "daisy-in-diamond" pattern, clearly declaring it to be a product of one of the Stiegel factories. The ribbed flask (centre), also mould-blown, was probably made by the Pitkin family in the late 18th or early 19th century. The two sketches illustrate (left) an engraved 18th-century wine glass of the type made by Stiegel, and (right) a two-colour Wistarburg glass pitcher.

the most interesting American pressed glass takes the form of commemorative wares showing paddleboats, politicians and military heroes. Pressed glass "cup plates" – used as a rest for the teacup while tea was drunk from the saucer – are also collected today.

The best known manufacturer of pressed glass was the Boston & Sandwich Glass Company, of Massachusetts, which was in operation from 1825 to 1888. The company specialized in objects with an all-over decoration of motifs such as flowers, foliage and rosettes raised against a stippled background, and known today as "lacy glass".

The earliest lacy glass has coarse stippling, which becomes finer in later pieces. Patterns of the early period (c. 1825–50) are so numerous and varied that, when pieces are not marked, their place of manufacture can only be determined by close study. The value of lacy glass, as with paperweights, depends on the rarity of their design and colour. An especially sought-after pattern is one in

Right: this unusual tray, made in New England in the mid-19th century, shows that complicated patterns could be achieved with pressed glass.

Below: a bouquet encased in a New England paperweight; just one of the many patterns created in American paperweights since the mid-19th century.

which an American coin of 1892 was used as part of the mould; lacy glass of this pattern was made for only five months of that year.

About the middle of the century, many kinds of paperweight were made. Patterns included floral bouquets, fruit on a *latticino* base (interlacing strands of opaque and clear glass), *millefiori* ("thousand flowers") and portraits based on coin and medal designs. Realistic fruit-shaped paperweights were made by the New England Glass Company, and in the latter half of the century pressed paperweights sometimes took the form of well-known buildings and of books and animals.

"Opal-decorated" pieces – the contemporary name for opaque white glass – were made in large quantities from about 1855. A popular type of art glass (the products of artists rather than factories) was Pearl Satin Ware, or "satin glass". Late 19th-century American glass, up to the heyday of Tiffany in the first decades of the 20th century, imitated Bohemian wares, followed the revival of Venetian styles and the fashion for ornate shapes, and made use of colour produced by chemical means.

Cut glass, first produced in the late 18th century, continued to be made in the 19th century. Flute cutting was a common decorative technique from about 1830 to 1880. Elegant cased glass (consisting of two or more layers of different coloured glass) was also made, most popularly in ruby and dark blue. "Brilliant-cut" glass of great virtuosity was produced in the 1880s and 1890s.

This commemorative dish, with its portrait bust, inscription and border of leaves, is an example of late 19th-century Pittsburgh pressed glass.

Art Nouveau

Louis Comfort Tiffany (1848–1933) was the giant among Art Nouveau glass designers in America. He founded his own company in 1878, and in 1880 patented a brand of iridescent coloured glass, "Favrile", in which the satin-like finish was produced by means of vaporized metals. Out of Tiffany's early interest in stained glass windows developed the distinctive Tiffany lampshade, which was formed of a colourful glass mosaic with designs often based on plant forms.

Favrile glass was the inspiration behind Steuben's "Aurene" glass, an iridescent blue-gold glass which was first produced in 1904. Other manufacturers also followed the lead of Tiffany; among these were the Quetzal Art Glass and Decorating Company of Brooklyn, New York, and Handel and Co. of Connecticut.

Left: A classic Tiffany lamp in one of the many designs created by Tiffany Studios, New York. This one has a shade made up of glass poinsettia leaves and a twisted, branch-like bronze stand.

Below: the blues, greens and golds of Favrile glass used as a mosaic in a mantel clock also made by Tiffany Studios.

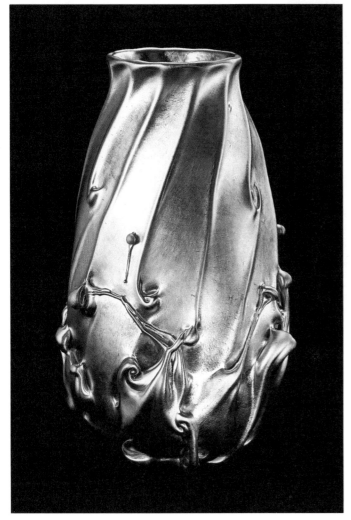

Far left: a surreal effect has been created in this blue-gold Aurene glass vase made by the Steuben Glass Works in 1909.

Left: Tiffany glass took on a wide variety of styles and shapes. This large baluster vase has an almost Oriental shape but the iridescent feathering has a flavour of Art Nouveau.

ENGLAND

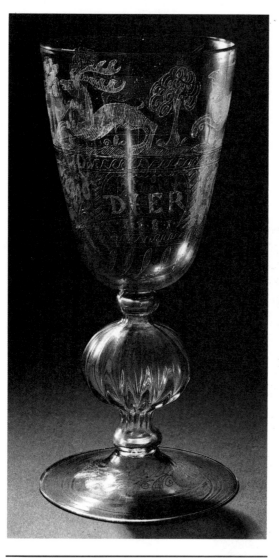

This soda-glass goblet, with diamond-point engraving, is one of only nine surviving glasses made in London by Jacopo Verzelini. Such delicate glassware was a revelation at the time.

Far right: *this ribbed jug, made by George Ravenscroft, is an example of the more robust lead glassware that began to be made in the mid- to late 17th century.*

The 16th and 17th centuries

Although Venetian craftsmen were making glass in England from 1549, the first important figure in English glass-making was Jacopo Verzelini (1523–1606), a Venetian who had arrived in London in 1571. From about 1577, Verzelini's products, fashioned in the fragile Anglo-Venetian soda-glass, included wide-bowled goblets with hollow knopped stems. Inscriptions or scenic decoration were engraved on the bowl.

For most of the 17th century, the English glass industry was dominated by monopolists, who imported Venetian glass, or by Italian craftsmen who could make a fair imitation of it. In the last quarter of the 17th century, however, the new spirit of scientific inquiry and commercial self-sufficiency prompted the English to become independent of the Italians. In 1673, the London Glass Seller's Company engaged George Ravenscroft (1618–81) to undertake researches for them. The company had two factories, one at the Savoy, London, and the other, mainly experimental, in Henley-on-Thames.

By 1674, Ravenscroft had produced a "sort of crystalline glass resembling rock crystal", for which he was granted a patent. The ingredients were flint and potash; the potash produced a defect known as "crisselling" – a network of fine cracks beneath the surface of the glass. In 1676, Ravenscroft solved the problem by adopting a formula which incorporated lead oxide; the result was a denser, heavier glass, strikingly brilliant by comparison with the delicate, slightly dull, soda glass which had been made up until then. Among Ravenscroft's products were jugs, goblets, bowls and tankards. From 1677, he impressed his wares with the seal of a raven's head. By the late 17th century, there were 27 flint-glasshouses in England, the most important in Southwark (London), Stourbridge, Newcastle-upon-Tyne, South Shields and Bristol.

Shapes had at first followed the delicate designs of Venetian glass, and the new flint glass was blown thinly. However, it was soon discovered that flint glass could be blown much more thickly without sacrificing its translucency. Glassware thus became more substantial, losing its delicate Venetian character and assuming more solid and characteristically English forms. Short-stemmed glasses with moulded knops appeared, followed by simpler shapes with longer stems, at first hollow but soon made solid.

The 18th century

By the early 18th century, the distinctive and simpler shapes of Queen Anne silver were also seen in the design of glassware. Stems of glasses were often given discs and knops and sometimes enclosed an air bubble. The shouldered stem (often called a Silesian stem although it was in fact West German) was a reflection of the influence of German glass, imports of which were permitted after the Treaty of Utrecht in 1713.

Until the early 18th century, glasses were given straight-sided funnel-shaped bowls. In the reign of George I (1714–27), they developed a waist and flared outwards. The height of the stem increased and bases simultaneously became thick and solid, their edges often folded under. Jelly, syllabub and custard glasses were characteristic of these years.

From the middle of the 18th century, two independent factors caused glasses to become lighter. The rococo style demanded lightness and frivolity in glassware as in all other adjuncts to luxurious living. On a more sober plane, the Excise Duty levied on glass to finance the wars with France also encouraged glass-makers to reduce the weight of their products.

Interest now shifted from shape to decoration. This took the form of wheel- and diamond-engraving, painting in enamels and air-twist (or "wormed") stems. Engraving on glasses dating

Above: with their fine stems and simple, well-formed bowls, these early 18th-century glasses are among the first examples of characteristically English glassware.

Left: although this goblet is made of lead glass, developed by George Ravenscroft, its shape still imitates the forms of Venetian soda-glass.

from the late 18th century most commonly depicts hops and barley, or vines. Painting in enamels, most commonly in white and more rarely in colours, was most effective. This form of decoration was only attempted in England from the 18th century.

The Beilby family of Newcastle-upon-Tyne – notably William Beilby and his sister Mary – were the best-known practitioners of the art. They worked mainly in bluish-white and turquoise.

Jacobite glasses, engraved with cryptic motifs and inscriptions, were also made in the 18th century. Most date from between about 1745 and 1765. The Jacobites were followers of James Edward Stuart, "The Old Pretender", and Charles Edward Stuart, "The Young Pretender". It was they, so the Jacobites believed, who, as descendants

of James II, should have ruled England rather than the descendants of William of Orange. The Jacobites formed semi-secret clubs and their glasses were used in furtive toasts. Of the various emblems that appear on Jacobite glasses, the most common is a rose, standing for the English crown. One, or sometimes two buds alongside the rose allude to the Pretenders.

The late 18th century also saw a refinement in the finishing of glasses. Most glasses dating from before about 1780 have on their bases a pontil mark – a rough area where the glass was cut or broken off the pontil, a rod on which the glass was held while the bowl was being shaped and the stem and foot added. From about 1780, the pontil mark was usually (though by no means always) ground down to leave a smooth finish.

Right: this bowl, dating from about 1765 and decorated in white and coloured enamels, is an early example of the work of the well-known Beilby family.

Left: the Beilbys' later work, depicting flowers, rustic scenes and landscapes, tends to be more elaborate, as these four examples, dating from about 1770, show. The club-shaped decanter and opaque-twist stems of the glasses are characteristic of the 18th century.

Opaque white glass, imitating porcelain, often took the form of small vessels such as cruet bottles. These three (*above*), painted in enamels, were made in Bristol in about 1800.

In the later 18th century, enamel painting on opaque white glass (which was, incidentally, exampt from the Excise Act) became popular. Opaque white glass is often referred to as "Bristol glass", though it was not all made there. Many forms follow those of Chinese porcelain, while cornucopia-shaped flower holders were made in imitation of Worcester porcelain. Worcester was also the model for finely reeded candlesticks and four-sided tea caddies. The enamel decoration often included pseudo-Chinese figures. White glass was also used for vinaigrettes and snuff bottles, and blue glass for scent bottles. Coloured glass, dark blue in particular, was also used for decanters. By this time, the middle to the end of the 18th century, decanters had become slender and tapered, and most coloured decanters follow this form.

Earlier ones, in clear glass, dating from the first half of the 18th century, are globular, with a rim for tying down the cork. Decanters with glass stoppers appeared from about 1750, and from 1760 spire-shaped stoppers were replaced by flat, two-sided stoppers, some of which were disc-shaped.

Increased duties on glass between 1777 and 1787 caused a considerable migration of glass-makers from England to Ireland. Cut glass was popular by this time, and in the Regency period (1800–30) became so much the rage that Venice was eclipsed as the glass-making centre of Europe. Regency cut glass is generally labelled "Waterford", implying that it was made at the famous Waterford Glass House founded in Ireland in 1784, but the output of lead glass was probably about ten times greater in England and Scotland together than in Ireland.

The 19th century

Despite the Glass Excise laws, the early 19th century produced the weightiest glasses ever made in Britain. Engraving, in the form of diamonds and stars, tended to be more horizontally placed than it had been in the 18th century.

This was the period of the barrel-shaped decanters with rings round the neck and mushroom stoppers. Towards the middle of the 19th century, decoration became more vertical again, often with fluting (vertical cutting down the side of a vessel). Cylindrical and globular decanters replaced barrel-shaped ones in the 1830s and 1840s.

The repeal of the Glass Excise Act in 1845 led to a new freedom in glass-making. Cut glass extravaganzas, for example, showpieces of the glass-maker's art, were displayed by W. H. B. and J. Richardson at the Great Exhibition of 1851. Such virtuosity soon became debased by imitations

Above: a broad-based ship's decanter, dating from 1801, shows the heavier proportions that came into fashion in the early 19th century.

Above, left: this trio of green glass decanters is a handsome example of late 18th-century glassware. The gilt inscriptions indicating shrub (a cordial), brandy and port simulate the silver bottle tickets which became popular around 1760.

in pressed (moulded) glass, and the criticisms of theorists like John Ruskin caused it to decline in popularity for a time. Engraved work, mainly on globular forms, superseded it until the 1880s and 1890s, when cut glass returned to favour.

Coloured glass was much in demand in the early 19th century. Green bottle glass had been made in England since the time of the Venetian supremacy and was exempt from the Excise Act which was enforced from the middle of the 18th century to the middle of the 19th. At Nailsea, near Bristol, where a glass factory was established in 1788 by John Robert Lucas, bottle glass was made in greenish-brown with white spotting and splashing. Wares made in this glass included the distinctive, sturdy Nailsea jugs. The second phase of Nailsea production dates from the management of Robert Lucas Chance (1810–15). From this period come jugs, bowls, pocket flasks and "gimmel flasks" (twin flasks with spouts pointing in opposite directions), decorated with pink and blue loops. "Friggers", trifles made to give as presents or to demonstrate the glass-makers' skills, were also made: friggers take many forms, including pipes, walking sticks and rolling-pins.

Coloured glass in imitation of the Bohemian wares and German Biedermeier pieces of the 1820s was produced in England before 1845 by such makers as Stevens & Williams of Brierley Hill, near Stroud, and Thomas Hawkes of Dudley. Other makers of coloured glass were Benjamin Richardson of Stourbridge, and George Bacchus & Sons, Rice Harris & Son, and Lloyd & Summerfield, all of Birmingham.

Right: the 19th-century fashion for coloured glass resulted in many forms and colours. This pair of green goblets with gilt decoration was made in about 1880 by Richardson's of Stourbridge.

Below: a fine example of cameo glass in the shape of a vase made in about 1885; the figure of Psyche is depicted in opaque white overlaid on deep amethyst-tinted glass.

Below right: "friggers", like this elaborate fountain, were light-hearted tours de force usually made from molten glass remaining at the end of the day. Most friggers take much simpler forms.

Far right: this clear glass bottle, attractively mottled with red and blue, is an unusually colourful example of Nailsea glass.

The Great Exhibition of 1851 saw the culmination of the fashion for coloured glass, a prominent example of its use being layered (or "cased") glass of two or more different colours, with cut decoration, often seen in objects of Gothic form. Opaline glass was made by the Richardsons and J. F. Christy, sometimes in leaf shapes outlined in green. Opaline glass was also used for bulbous jugs with three-lipped mouths in imitation of Greek wares; some were decorated with transfer-printing by J. F. Christy. The designs of historic Venetian glass were also re-created. In 1819, Apsley Pellatt devised a method of embedding white paste figures into clear class. Pellatt also made "Anglo-Venetian" pieces, consisting of frosted glass with incrustations depicting figures. Silvered glass was made by James Powell & Sons in Whitefriars, London. The fashion for colourful *millefiori* ("thousand flowers") paperweights arrived from France. They were sold in stationers' shops and their manufacturers included Bacchus in the late 1840s and Rice Harris at the Islington Glass Works, both of Birmingham.

The mid-19th century saw an influx of engravers from central Europe. Among these immigrants was J. H. B. Millar, who worked in Edinburgh and introduced the popular engraved fern pattern. Paul Oppitz also came to London and worked for Copeland's. Frederick E. Kny and William Fritsche practised their craft at Stourbridge, working for Thomas Webb, and Joseph Kneller worked with Stevens and Williams.

The last decades of the 19th century witnessed a new interest in intaglio engraving, with its deep cutting and polished edges. The firm of Thomas Webb had the highest reputation for this work.

Thomas Webb also made "cameo" glass, glassware with white paste motifs embedded in it after the method devised by Apsley Pellatt, which is also often collected today. Decoration in the 1880s often featured small birds in foliage. In the 1890s, John Northwood (1836–1902) did intaglio work for Stevens and Williams, while Thomas Hawkes of Dudley was the main exponent of acid etching.

In the 1870s and 1880s, the firm of Thomas Webb introduced exotic new colours of glass. The best known is "Burmese", an opaque greenish-yellow glass shading to a deep pink. Also dating from the last decades of the 19th century are the designs in pressed (moulded) glass, often inspired by Japanese designs, made by Sowerby's Ellison Glass Works, Gateshead. Sowerby's also made an opaque marbled glass known as "slag glass", which may easily be dated by its registration marks.

Above: the pale damson of this sugar basin and cream jug, made in about 1820, is an example of the range of coloured glass that was fashionable in the early 19th century.

Left: a fine example of the coloured glass known as "Burmese" is seen in this vase, made in about 1800 by Thomas Webb.

FRANCE

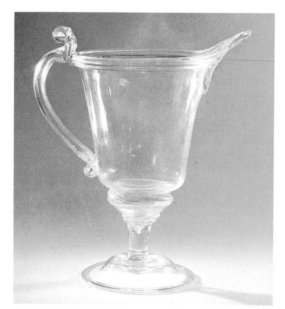

Although, from the Middle Ages, the French were renowned for their outstanding stained glass, their glass-making skills when applied to vessels did not show the same skill and originality. During the Renaissance, Venetian influence took hold in France as it had in the Netherlands, and from the 16th century, French glass factories were run by Italian immigrants. But only one – that established at Nevers – continued to make glass for any length of time; there, the Saroldi family made Italian-style glass for almost 200 years until the 18th century. Their wares included small figures and toys and models fashioned in glass that was sometimes mistaken for enamel, though they were in fact made of glass rods and tubes worked with pincers. Similar figures were later made in Rouen, Bordeaux amd Marseilles, and in Paris by Jacques Roux and Charles-François Hazard.

Right: hints of Italian grace can be seen in this simple but elegant ewer, made in France in the 18th century.

Right: a range of styles and decorative techniques, including cutting, moulding, latticino and overlay, had been mastered in France by the early 19th century, and this is amply shown by this selection of glassware made at the Cristallerie St Louis.

The 18th and 19th centuries

In the 18th century, glass-making in France still lagged behind most of the rest of Europe. In 1760, the Académie des Sciences offered a prize for a report on how to improve the French glass industry. In the subsequent flurry of activity, the Verreries de Ste Anne were founded near Lune-ville; this establishment was later to become the famous Baccarat factory. In 1767, the Cristallerie de St Louis was founded in the Muntzhal, in Lor-raine, and soon earned the Académie's praise for its success in imitating English glass. In 1784, Mayor Oppenheim, from Birmingham, founded a factory at Petit Quevelly, and there, and later in Rouen, he made crystal glass in the English style.

At the end of the 18th century, and indepen-dently of the Englishman Apsley Pellatt, the French invented the method of enclosing white porcellaneous cameos in cut crystal glass. Desprez, of Paris, was one of the early exponents of the craft; his name or that of his sons, and their address in Paris (rue des Recollets du Temple) are some-times impressed as a mark on the reliefs.

The 19th century was a time of experiment and

Above: *this crystal perfume bottle, made in about 1815–20, displays a fine example of enclosed cameos.*

achievement in French glass-making. Although the 18th century traditions of cutting and engraving crystal glass continued throughout the 19th century, there was an emphasis on developing rich colours. Most of the decorative glass of 19th century France came from the factories of Baccarat and St Louis, which were amalgamated in about 1835, and Clichy. Fine lead-crystal vessels were made at Choisy-le-Roi, in subtle colours and decorated with cutting and engraving. Cut crystal pieces were made from the 1820s, and often incorporated cameo portraits. Opaline glass was fashioned into classically simple pieces, most popularly in white up to about 1830, and then in rose-pink, apple-green and turquoise.

Paperweights

With the possible exception of the wares of Emile Gallé and René Lalique, the most desirable of all French glasswares are the 19th-century paperweights made at Baccarat, St Louis and Clichy.

Baccarat produced two main types of paperweights: *millefiori* (meaning "a thousand flowers"), which constituted about two-thirds of the factory's output in paperweights, and examples with flowers, which make up about a third. The balance of the factory's paperweights is made up of examples with butterflies and incrustations (cameos). About half the *millefiori* paperweights are

Above: *this mid-19th-century casket is a remarkable example of the engraved lead crystal produced at the Baccarat factory.*

Left: *the French glass factories produced some of the finest opaline glassware. This candlestick, made at St Louis, is an example of pink opaline glass.*

Right: *a butterfly, a coiled snake and a bouquet are magically enclosed in these three Baccarat paperweights.*

dated between 1846 and 1849; most are dated 1848. Sections of multicoloured rods in star shapes and arrow patterns are characteristic of *millefiori* forms. Flower shapes in paperweights are mostly representations of primroses, pansies and clematis. Cameo incrustations depict figures which include Queen Victoria, Joan of Arc and mythological characters.

The St Louis factory produced fewer *millefiori* paperweights than did Baccarat. About half of St Louis' *millefiori* patterns are known as "*millefiori* mushrooms", as the rods of glass forming the "thousand flowers" spread out from the base in a mushroom shape. Other St Louis *millefiori* paperweights combine green foliage with the flowers to form "bouquets". Most St Louis paperweights, however, enclose representations of flowers, fruit and vegetables, or reptiles. They are also more delicately coloured than those of Baccarat or Clichy. Some St Louis paperweights are dated: the usual dates are 1847 and 1848, though paperweights dating from 1847 are much rarer.

Paperweights were made at Clichy from about 1849, although none are dated and few are signed. Over three quarters of the factory's paperweights are *millefiori*; the most characteristic are those with the "Clichy rose", with its tightly-packed pink and white petals, sometimes also with green and white leaves. Incrustations in Clichy paperweights were similar to those made at Baccarat.

Above: a veritable kaleidoscope of colours and flowers in three Clichy paperweights: two examples of millefiori *work flank a double-clematis weight.*

*Three St Louis paperweights – bright red cherries in an unusual faceted weight (**left**), a large white dahlia (**above**) and six looped garlands of millefiori (**right**).*

Art Nouveau

Emile Gallé (1846–1904) was one of the most outstanding and innovative glass-makers who worked in the Art Nouveau style. Although primarily a glass-maker, Gallé also applied his creative talents to furniture and pottery, and in 1878, established a factory in Nancy. His products were inspired by a range of sources including plant life, English cameo glass, Japanese art and Impressionism. Literary sources, such as the works of Baudelaire and Rimbaud, also influenced Gallé's work.

Gallé's most successful pieces include cased glass vessels, often in grey and amethyst. Pieces produced by the factory after his death were marked "Gallé" with a star beside the name. Gallé's most notable imitators were Auguste and Antonin Daum, who also worked at Nancy. After World War I, Gabriel Argy-Rousseau produced glassware which looked back to the Art Nouveau style, but also worked in new styles.

*This colourful range of vases, bottles and bowls (**right**) demonstrates Emile Gallé's fondness of plant forms and his skill in reproducing them in cameo glass. The greater the number of colours in a single piece, the more time-consuming was the process.*

__Right:__ a striking example of late 19th-century artistry in glass. In this table lamp by Emile Gallé, the motif of oranges among leaves and branches is rendered by means of yellow glass overlaid with orange, lime green and dark green glass. This highly skilled technique produced some of the most exciting designs of the period.

Art Deco

Art Deco glass is dominated by the name of René Lalique (1860–1945). Although he was also a jeweller and also worked in the Art Nouveau style, Lalique excelled as a glass-maker in the Art Deco style.

Lalique is best known for a range of objects in a misty opalescent blue glass, though he also worked in clear glass, with moulded and etched designs. Lalique's main products include lamps, clocks, scent bottles and car mascots. Though it was mass-produced and highly commercial, Lalique's work looks hand-made.

Antonin Daum, who had followed the style of Gallé, also worked in the Art Deco style. Daum's mushroom-shaped lamps display a sense of purist simplicity. The Deco style was also seen in the glass fishes and classic vases of Emile Decorchement.

Taking up the post-Bauhaus concern for "truth to material", Maurice Marinot experimented with new effects in glass, including the myriad air bubbles sometimes known as "caviare". Among Marinot's most gifted imitators were Henri Thuret and Henri Navarre.

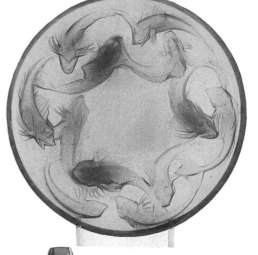

*René Lalique's artistry in glass ranged from boxes (**top**), and bowls (**above**) to vases (**left**), scent bottles (**far left**) and even car mascots. Many of his bowls and vases, like those shown here, were intended for decoration rather than use. His scent bottles, of course, had to be functional as well. Lalique designed bottles for the leading Parisian perfumers, including Coty, Worth, Houbigant, Roger & Gallet and Nina Ricci.*

GERMANY

Above: this 17th-century goblet, with studded stem, is a typical example of the German Römer, or drinking glass.

*Two splendid examples of German enamelled glass. The beaker (**right**), dated 1614 and enamelled with the double-headed eagle of the Holy Roman Empire, is of a type known as "Reichsadlerhumpen". More informal enamelling is seen on the vessel (**far right**), dated 1612 and bearing an armorial and hunting scene, both common decorative devices of the period.*

The precise origin of German glass manufacture is obscure, and much German glass is indiscriminately described as Bohemian. From the 14th century, glass factories were established in forests, near plentiful sources of fuel. For centuries, they produced wares in *Waldglas* (forest glass), which was tinged green, yellow or brown. One of the most popular types of early glassware was the *Römer*, produced from about 1675 to 1825. The *Römer* was a drinking vessel with a near-spherical bowl, a cylindrical stem studded with prunts (tooled or moulded protuberances), and a hollow conical foot. The *Humpen*, the *Wilkommen* and the *Passglas*

were three other popular kinds of drinking vessel. The *Humpen* was a cylindrical glass with a slightly flared foot and often with enamelled decoration. In shape it is identical to the *Wilkommen*, whose distinguishing feature is an inscription. The *Passglas* was a tall, narrow beaker marked with horizontal glass or enamel lines which indicated how much to drink before passing the glass on to the rest of the company. Alongside the native *Waldglas*, clear, Venetian-style *cristallo* glass was imitated by imported artisans working for the royal court.

Enamelled decoration on glass was introduced in about 1575 and initially followed Venetian styles. The most sophisticated motif of the period was that used on vessels known as *Reichsadlerhumpen* (Imperial eagle beakers); this motif consisted of the double-headed eagle of the Holy Roman Empire with shields hanging from its outspread wings. Commoner themes on enamelled pieces included hunting and riding scenes, allegories, inscriptions and coats of arms, generally rendered in a robust, naïve style. Bohemian enamelled glasses often have borders of dots or dashes round the base. The style of this enamelled decoration changed little over the years, so that late pieces can look deceptively early.

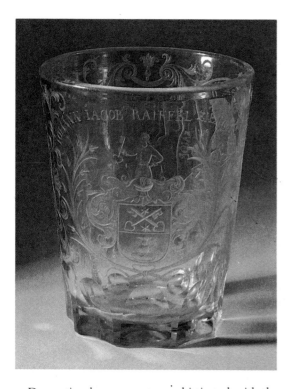

Engraved glass and Zwischengoldgläser

The first European to engrave on the lapidary's wheel since the Middle Ages was Caspar Lehmann, working in Prague at the end of the 16th century. Lehmann trained Georg Schwanhardt, who returned to his native Nuremberg in 1622. Schwanhardt sometimes supplemented his masterly wheel engraving with engraving by diamond point. He was the founder of a Nuremberg school of engraving which included Hermann Schwinger and Georg Friedrich Killinger. Nuremberg-type goblets had bowls cut with scroll-work, medallions and classical or historical scenes, and stems ornamented with a variety of knops and collars. Intaglio, in which the decoration is below the original surface, was also common.

In about 1680, experiments led to the production of a new kind of crystal glass similar to that made by Ravenscroft in England. Early pieces were made in Kassel, Potsdam and elsewhere and, like Ravenscroft's, their potash content caused them to suffer from crisselling, a network of cracks. But this crystal glass was robust enough to withstand wheel engraving, which could now be deeper, creating dramatic contrasts.

Engraving on German glass was at its best between about 1685 and 1775. Magnificent work was done in court studios by Friedrich Winter of Petersdorf, who specialized in cameo relief, his brother Martin Winter, who worked in Berlin with Gottfried Spiller, and Franz Gondelach, the genius of baroque glass engraving. Gondelach often engraved an eight-pointed rosette beneath the base of his glasses.

*Engraved glass was a Bohemian speciality; the beaker (**left**), dated 1694, is a fine example.*

Decoration became more sophisticated with the rise of the *Hausmaler*, painters who obtained undecorated glass and enamelled it, working at home. Johann Schaper of Nuremberg (1621–70) was the first well-known glass painter. He worked mainly in *Schwartzlot* (black enamel) and *en grisaille* (grey), with red and gold touches. *Commedia dell'arte* figures were among his favourite themes. His most favoured vessel was a cylindrical beaker on bun feet. Schaper's followers in Bohemia and Silesia included Daniel Preussler (1636–1733), his son Ignaz, and Johann Ludwig Faber. *Chinoiserie* decoration, often used in combination with baroque scrolls and shells, was added to the repertoire of the *Hausmaler* from early 18th century.

Left; these four beakers, dating from the late 18th to the early 19th centuries, demonstrate facet-cutting and the refined standard of enamelling that was reached at that time. The silhouette beaker, with gold leaf enclosed within the glass, is an example of Zwischengoldgläser.

The Bohemian workshops were at their height between about 1700 and 1730. Bohemian decoration progressed from small formal flowers and foliage over the entire surface of a vessel (common from 1700 to 1710) to baroque strapwork and foliage sometimes interlacing with pseudo-Chinese figures (dating from about 1720). The repertoire of strapwork, foliage and Chinese-style figures was also taken up by decorators working elsewhere, notably Anton Wilhelm Mäuerl, of Nuremberg. By the 1730s, Bohemian work had begun to look mass-produced. Almost simultaneously, Silesia became the dominant glass-making centre. Silesia produced lobed goblets with petalled bases, and many were engraved with views.

Some of the best engraving was done by Christian Gottfried Schneider (1710–73) at Warmbrunn.

Some glasses known as *Zwischengoldgläser* were made in Bohemia from about 1730. *Zwischengoldgläser* were decorated with gold leaf sandwiched inside two layers of glass, the two layers being fused together and the edge gilded. The most common shape was the straight-sided beaker, decorated with a hunting, commemorative or domestic scene.

In the late 18th century, baroque-rococo engraving gave way to facet, or brilliant, cutting.

This fine beaker, made in about 1820 and showing a view of Meissen, is finely decorated in transparent enamels, which replaced opaque enamels in the early 19th century.

Coloured glass

In the last quarter of the 17th century, Johann Kunckel, working in Potsdam, introduced his famous ruby glass, made from a formula which included gold chloride. Kunckel's ruby glass soon became fashionable; it was frequently mounted in finely chased metal and was sometimes deeply engraved by masters such as Gottfried Spiller. Blue, purple and green glass was also made in this period. *Milchglas,* an opaque white glass, was introduced to compete with Meissen porcelain.

Right: this covered goblet, heavily gilded and enamelled, is made of Milchglas, which was intended to imitate porcelain.

Ruby glass became fashionable in the late 17th century. This selection (below), mounted in silver-gilt, shows some of the forms that it took.

A wide range of colourings was developed in the 18th and 19th centuries. The fashion for imitating Wedgwood pottery and semi-precious stones led to *Hyalith* glass, which is black or red, and *Lithyalin*, an opaque or translucent multi-coloured glass produced by Friedrich Egermann from 1777 to 1864. Cased glass, consisting of two or more layers of glass of different colours, and overlay glass (cased glass with the design cut through to the inner colour), were made in large quantities from about 1815. Souvenir glassware, aimed at the tourist market, was sometimes decorated with paintings in transparent colours depicting romantic ruins or mountain scenes. The best painted work was done by Samuel Mohn (1762–1815), of Dresden, and his son Gottlob (1789–1825), who settled in Vienna.

Art Nouveau

The glass industry in Germany and Austria responded quickly to the Art Nouveau, or *Jugenstil*, movement. Johann Loetz was an important pioneer of the new style. The Loetz factory was founded in 1836 in Klostermuhle, Austria. On the death of Johann Loetz in 1848, it was renamed by his widow the *Glasfabrik Johann Loetz-Witwe*. Loetz glass is most prized for its iridescence, introduced in the 1880s. The factory also produced glassware to designs by members of the Wiener Werkstätte. The major Art Nouveau glass designer in Germany was Karl Koepping, well known for tall pieces with curvilinear stems.

Above left: two further examples of Milchglas, with contrasting forms of decoration. Armorials, chinoiseries, and biblical and mythological scenes wre other forms of decoration frequently found on Milchglas.

Above: this range of opaque red hyalith and lithyalin glass dates from about 1830. Such pieces were often decorated with gilding, as they are here.

German glassmakers were important exponents of Jugenstil, or Art Nouveau. This vase, made of iridescent gold glass, is an example of some of the finest work of Johann Loetz's factory.

IRELAND

Before 1780, Irish glass was virtually indistinguishable from English. After that date, with manufacturers responding to changing conditions, Irish glass developed a unique style that was vital and exuberant.

The only Irish city that produced a significant amount of luxury lead glass before 1780 was Dublin. After that date, England relaxed its restrictive Acts against the export of Irish glass. Many more glasshouses were consequently established in Ireland, notably in Cork, Waterford and Belfast. The best known Irish manufacturers were Richard Williams & Co., Charles Mulvaney, and Jeudwin, Lunn & Co. of Dublin, Benjamin Edwards, the Belfast Glass Works, and Smyllie & Co. of Belfast; and the Waterford Glass House (1784–1851), in Waterford, the only glass factory there but one which made the name "Waterford" synonymous with fine cut glass. Cork boasted the Cork Glass Co., the Waterloo Glass House Co. (founded, not surprisingly, in 1815), and the Terrace Glass Works. A few of these manufacturers used a mark under the base of their products, especially decanters and finger bowls. The Irish glass factories exported on a large scale; while many of their products went to America, most were destined for England.

Most Irish glass of the 1780s and 1790s has a slight dusky tint. In the neo-classical period covered urns were a common form, often cut with shallow diamond or lozenge patterns. Irish candlesticks usually have a deeply cut trefoil rim on the sleeve to hold the candle, which in turn slips into a standing socket. Drip-pans have cut vertical edging. A characteristic of Irish vases and bowls is a turned-over rim. The lower parts of decanters, bowls and jugs tend to have moulded shallow flutes (vertical facets). Some decanters produced by the Cork Glass Co. are decorated with the so-called "vesica" pattern, resembling naïvely rendered fishes placed end to end. Bowls, for rinsing the mouth as well as the fingers, were made in large numbers.

Ewers and jugs were used by the hard-drinking lower classes in Ireland; they are sometimes engraved with barley heads, hops and vine leaves. Typical decoration on glasses includes cut stars and diamonds, sometimes with the addition of a cut shamrock. Rare items of Irish glass are linen smoothers (similar to inverted mushrooms), toddy lifters (like miniature decanters with a hole in the base) and hanging lamps. Toddy lifters acted as pipettes; they were filled through the hole in the base, the liquid being held there by a finger placed over the neck of the vessel. Hookah bases were also produced, but are now often turned into decanters.

Blown-moulded table glass, produced by blowing molten glass into a mould, was made cheaply and in large quantities in the 19th century. The shapes and designs of blown-moulded glass imitated those of free-blown and hand-cut glass.

The Irish glass industry began to decline during the second quarter of the 19th century. In 1825, an excise duty, similar to that imposed in England from 1745, hampered the export of Irish glass. The Irish glass industry suffered another blow in the 1830s, when manufacturers in England started to produce pressed glass at a much lower price than Irish hand-blown glass. Ireland's most celebrated glass factory, the Waterford Glass House, closed in 1851.

Four salts and a caddy in Irish blue glass, made in about 1785–1800. Heavy cutting, seen here, often decorates Irish glass.

Far left: this magnificent cut glass chandelier, dating from the late 18th century, was among the grandest products of the Waterford Glass Company.

Left: two typical examples of Irish glass. While the covered urn is characteristic of neo-classical Irish glassware, the decanter, of the same period, has the "vesica" pattern often associated with the Cork Glass Company.

THE NETHERLANDS

Dutch and Flemish glass is noted for its decoration rather than its form. Shapes were derivative rather than original, so that for more than a century, most of the glass made by the immigrant Italian craftsmen who had settled in Antwerp as early as 1541, and in Liège by 1569, was indistinguishable from Venetian glass.

At the beginning of the 17th century, many more glasshouses were established in towns such as Middelburg, The Hague, Rotterdam and Amsterdam. The Bonhomme family from Liège, for example, built up a flourishing glass-making business, with branches in Huy and Maastricht. By then, certain serpent-stemmed and winged glasses were becoming identifiably Netherlandish.

Most well-to-do Dutch families possessed one or two *latticino* glass and silver ornaments in the shape of fantasies incorporating windmills. Possibly in reaction against this Venetian frivolity, Netherlandish glass manufacturers were soon searching for a new glass in the style of Ravenscroft's in England. By the 1670s English craftsmen were working in Haarlem and in 1680 the Bonhommes were making flint glass in the English style. Although the distinctive English ingredient, lead,

was missing, Dutch flint glass had the crisselled appearance of Ravenscroft's products.

In the 18th century, English designs, as well as wares, were widely imported into Holland. These imports largely contributed to a decline in the Dutch glass industry. By 1771, only one factory at s'Hertogenbosch continued to make good drinking glasses; all other factories had changed over to the production of window glass, mirror glass and bottles.

Engraving

Three main kinds of decoration are seen on Netherlendish glass: diamond-point engraving, practised from about 1575 to 1690; wheel engraving, from about 1690 to 1750; and stippling with a diamond point, from about 1750 to 1800.

The Netherlands were justly famous for diamond-point engraving. It became a popular pastime, and much of the best work was, in fact, done by talented amateurs.

Anna Roemers Visscher (1583–1651) combined

*Dutch glass is justly celebrated for its fine engraving. These three glasses, dating from the late 17th to the late 18th century, show three different methods, wheel engraving (**above left**), stipple engraving (**above right**) and diamond point engraving (**far right**), each of which gives subtly different results.*

calligraphy with flowers, fruit and insects. Her work, rarely signed, was never surpassed, and the green glass roemers that she decorated are particularly prized today. Her sister Maria Tesselschade van Schurman (1607–78) produced similarly enchanting traceries on fine glass.

Other notable engravers include William Jacobz van Heemskerk (1613–92), an expert calligraphic engraver (many bottles bear his signature and a date between 1648 and 1690); a mid-17th century artist signing himself "C.J.M." or "C.F.M." (possibly Christoffel Jansz Meyer of The Hague; and G. V. Nes and Willem Mooleyser (who signed himself "W.M."), both of whom were active towards the end of the 17th century.

In the 18th century, the cruder technique of wheel-engraving, applied to thicker glass, superseded diamond-point engraving. A prominent exponent of wheel-engraving was Jacob Sang, of Amsterdam, to whom some Dutch marine subjects, foliage and scrollwork and finely engraved heraldic glasses have been attributed.

Signed wheel-engraved decoration is known from 1752–62. In the second half of the 18th century, C. C. Schröder engraved portraits on flat glass panels, copying them from 17th-century prints.

The technique of stipple-engraving, carried out by means of a diamond set in a handle and gently tapped with a hammer, was probably first refined

by Frans Greenwood, of Rotterdam. Greenwood's work dates from 1722 to 1755. Contemporaries of Greenwood who used stipple-engraving were Aert Schouman, who worked in the 1750s, and G. H. Hoolart, who flourished between about 1775 and 1780.

Glasses with stipple-engraving are known as "Wolff glasses" after the engraver David Wolff. Wolff's own signed work, with dates between 1784 and 1795, appears rather laboured by comparison with the work of some of his imitators. Artists who worked in the style of Wolff include William Fortuyn, C. Adams and another who is known only by his signature, "V.H.". Important 19th-century engravers, such as Andries Melort (1779–1849), of Dordrecht and The Hague, decorated flat sheets of glass in the style of the Dutch Old Masters.

SCANDINAVIA

The oldest surviving Scandinavian glass was made in Sweden. Glass was first made in Sweden in the late 17th century and Sweden has been a great glass-making country ever since. Glass was made in Norway from 1741, and Norway supplied Denmark during the later 18th century.

Sweden

The first surviving examples of Swedish glass were made at Kungsholm Glasbruk, in Stockholm. The factory was founded in 1676 by an Italian, G. B. Scapitta; after 1678, it was administered by Swedes and continued until 1815.

The early products of Kungsholm were similar to Venetian glasswares, but the glass was thin and often of poor technical quality. Some goblets had stems formed into royal initials, and royal crowns were sometimes used as handles on goblet covers, perhaps reflecting the fact that the factory enjoyed royal patronage. In the early 18th century, Bohemian influence predominated; goblets, now fashioned out of thicker metal, were also given

shorter stems. However, some Venetian features survived, notably the fold-over foot (in which the rim was folded under) and the "squashed tomato" swelling in the stem. Wheel-engraving was introduced by Kristoffer Elstermann, a German, who arrived at the factory in 1698 and died in 1721. Coats of arms were the main type of wheel-engraved decoration.

The other 17th-century Swedish glass factory was Skånska Glasbruket, whose working period spanned the years 1691–1762. Unlike Kungsholm, Skånska did not have royal patronage and its products show less aristocratic tendencies. Skånska's glass was mainly functional at first, although production of decorative glass started in the early 18th century. The factory's later glassware imitated Kungsholm in its decoration. Glass from this factory has a certain "folk" character. Patriotic sentiments were sometimes expressed by the use of the royal monogram engraved on ordinary wares.

The third of Sweden's historic glass works was Kosta, in Smaland, founded in 1742 and still in operation.

Above left: *this glass bowl and cover, about 1750–1800, was among the earliest products of Kosta Glasbruk.*

Above: *Venetian influence on Swedish glassmaking produced such dainty wares as this ceremorial goblet. The stem is formed of royal initials, and it was made at Kungsholm Glasbruk in the late 17th century.*

Far left: *Art Nouveau provided the inspiration for this bowl, which Gunnar Wennerberg made at Kosta Glasbruk in 1900. Red and green glass were chosen for this design.*

Above: this lidded cup, made at Orrefors in 1924, is an example of the fine engraving of which Swedish craftsmen were capable..

The factory's products were mostly unpretentious, its most notable wares being perhaps small chandeliers. At the beginning of the 20th century, Kosta, along with Reijmyre, were the two most important glassworks in Sweden. They produced wares in the Art Nouveau style, employing artists such as Gunnar G. Wennerberg and Alf Wallender, whose cased glass techniques, involving two or more layers of different coloured glass, owed much to the example of Gallé. Good Art Deco glass was made at Orrefors.

Norway

The Norwegian glass industry was founded by royal decree at Nöstetangen in 1741 and the glassware produced during this early period was in the German style. In 1753, the Norwegian glass industry was overhauled, and new factories were built to cater for the needs not only of Norway itself but of Denmark as well. The Nöstetangen factory was enlarged and modernized. Excellent German craftsmen were employed and an Englishman, James Keith, from Newcastle, was taken on. A cutters' and engravers' workshop was also set up, with the German engraver and designer Heinrich Gottlieb Köhler in charge; Köhler, who had previously worked at Copenhagen, was a brilliant exponent of the Silesian style.

During Nöstetangen's best period (1760–70), two kinds of glass were made: a clear, bubbly, pinkish soda glass; and a more expensive crystal-like English lead glass. In the latter, baluster stems of Newcastle type were common for expensive drinking-glassses, Larger items were often embellished with trailed threads and moulded effects.

On the closure of the Nöstetangen factory in 1777, production of crystal glass was moved to Hurdals Verk where the prevailing style turned from rococo to neo-classical, and coloured glass was frequently used. When Hurdals Verk closed in 1809, production was transferred to a less ambitious factory, Gjovik Verk, which continued until 1847.

SPAIN

Catalonia

From an early date, the principal glass-making area in Spain was Catalonia. Catalan blown glass, Venetian in style though less dainty and diaphanous, was much prized between 1500 and 1650. Venetian decorative techniques, such as crackling and *latticino*, were also used elsewhere in Spain. Certain shapes were unique to Catalonia, and among them was the covered jar in the shape of an inverted bell; the aspersorium, or holy water bucket (a bowl-like vessel with a bail handle); and the *almorratxa* (a rose-water sprinkler with four spouts).

The Catalan glass industry declined after about 1650. Venetian styles were then replaced by the traditional Spanish *cántir* and *porrón*, both spouted drinking vessels. And by the 18th century, the *almorratxa* was being made with a narrow bottle neck and shorter spouts than in the earlier type.

Southern Spain

The glassworks of Almería, Castril and Cartagena looked to Muslim culture for inspiration.

These southern Spanish glassworks did not make crystal glass; most of their work was green, full of tiny air bubbles and Arabic in style, with short, narrow necks and bulbous bodies taken in the middle, with rims often cut off and melted smooth. There was sometimes a thick thread round necks.

Venetian influence did, however, reach as far as Seville, where some Venetian-style glass was made. By the early 18th century, as in Venice, Bohemian glass dominated the industry in southern Spain, and a few decades later the Catalonian influence was also evident in the south.

Castile

By the early 16th century, another important centre of Spanish glass-making was Cadalso, in the province of Madrid (Castile). During the 17th century, Italian and Flemish glass-workers flocked to Spain, many to Castile, and in 1608, a furnace was built at the Escorial under the direction of the glassblower Domingo Barovier. A factory was eventually opened at Castilla la Nueva in 1689 by Guglielmo Toreata, an Italo-Fleming.

Most of the Madrid based factories produced coarse versions of Venetian-style wares, which declined around 1700 with the fashion for wheel-engraved glass introduced by Philip V. However, from 1720 until about 1728, Juan de Goyeneche made wheel-engraved glass at Nuevo Baztán.

San Ildefonso

In 1728, a Catalan glassworker, Ventura Sit, set up a furnace at San Ildefonso, near the palace of La Granja. Queen Isabella built him a factory on the royal estate and Philip V encouraged him to make large plates of glass for palace mirrors. Other workmen came to San Ildefonso from Germany and Sweden and among them was Sigismund Brun, from Hanover, who by the late 18th century was making fine crystal glasses.

Characteristics of the San Ildefonso glass-works also included coloured and opaque white glass and gilt floral decoration. The typical "San Ildefonso jar", with its Arab shape and cone-like cover topped by a knop or mushroom, was decorated in enamels.

By the early 19th century, the royal glass factory of San Ildefonso was suffering badly from English and Irish competition. It closed in 1829.

Far left: an 18th-century Catalan porrón of typically Spanish form. The latticino decoration to the neck, however, is the result of Venetian influence.

Left: in this group of Spanish glassware, the 16th-century Catalan cruet bottle and 18th-century wine jug appear unrefined in comparison to the finely gilded jar, typical of those made at San Ildefonso in the 18th century.

VENICE (ITALY)

It is not known precisely when glass-making first began in Venice. Glass-makers were certainly working there by the 11th century, and by the middle of the 13th century there were enough of them to form a guild. Because of the risk of fire from their numerous furnaces in the city, the glass-makers were moved to the island of Murano.

It is likely that the Venetians; perhaps before the 15th century, discovered how to decolorize glass by using manganese, certainly it was on Murano that the resulting clear *cristallo* was made. This was a prized novelty, and by the 16th century Venice was exporting her crystal glass to the rest of Europe. The Venetian monopoly might have continued were it not for one Jacopo Verzelini, a Venetian who began making clear, Murano-style glass in London in the 1570s.

Though markedly clearer than most Renaissance glass, Venetian *cristallo* is rarely without a smoky brown tinge. Intentionally coloured glass was made in green, blue and purple, and semi-precious stones, especially onyx, agate and chalcedony were imitated. Up to the end of the 15th century, the shapes of the pieces tended to be based on the silver wares fashionable at the time.

Soda glass remains malleable as it cools, lending itself to being worked with pincers and tongs. The Venetian glass-makers of the late 16th century took advantage of this fact to produce fanciful wares such as wineglasses with convoluted winged stems or with motifs based on sea-horses. Bodies of vessels were dynamically waved or crumpled, or made to resemble flames. The most extravagant creations, reflecting baroque tendencies, date from the 17th century. Simpler wares were made for export.

Decoration on Venetian glass characteristically took the form of *latticino*, threads of opaque white glass embedded in the body of a wineglass, ewer or *tazza* (ornamental cup). In *vetro a reticello*, the opaque threads criss-crossed to form an overall diamond lattice; in *vetro a retorti*, the threads formed intricately twisted parallel "canes". Occasionally, coloured threads were used instead of white. A more rare decorative technique was

This cristallo *reliquary, with characteristic enamel decoration, is an impressive example of the prized glassware made in Venice in the 15th and 16th centuries.*

produced by "crackle-" or "ice-glass", in which a random pattern of tiny cracks was obtained by plunging the hot glass into water for a moment and then re-heating it.

Enamel decoration was also used, notably for armorials. *Lattimo*, opaque white glass, was especially suited to decoration in enamels. In the 17th and 18th centuries, *lattimo* was sometimes used as a substitute for expensive porcelain, and was painted in porcelain style, sometimes with views of Venice after Canaletto. Engraving was rare, perhaps because of the value placed on the clarity of *cristallo*.

The quality of Venetian glass declined in the 18th century. Bohemian glass, made in the mountainous region of the borders of Bohemia and Silesia, was now a formidable rival; in 1736, Giuseppe Briati obtained a patent to make glass in the Bohemian manner. The Venetian industry was, for a time, eclipsed by the rise of English and Irish cut glass.

However, the mid-19th century saw a recovery of the ancient Venetian glass industry. Antonio Salviati, for example, revived Renaissance styles, though in somewhat sentimental wares. Other craftsmen imitated or adapted 17th- and 18th-century styles. Murano thus recovered its former importance, and glass is still made there today.

Enamelling, practised in Venice before the 15th century, became fashionable again in later periods; this mid-18th-century flask (above) is an example of enamelling on clear, rather than opaque white, glass.

Far left, above: *latticino, embedded threads of opaque white glass, swirl round this typically Italian tazza, or cup.*

Far left, below: *this 18th-century plate, consisting of lattimo, or opaque white glass, decorated in enamels, could almost be mistaken for porcelain.*

Left: *the virtuosity of 16th-century Italian glass-making is re-created in this elaborate goblet made by Antonio Salviati in 1869.*

CLOCKS
& WATCHES

The development of the first mechanical clocks marked a vast
improvement in timekeeping over such simple devices as sundials
or water clocks. As decoration was lavished on them, so clocks
became magnificently decorative as well as functional pieces, or, in
the case of watches, jewel-like pieces of personal adornment. Here,
a simple account of how clocks work precedes a brief history of
clockmaking in ten countries.

HOW CLOCKS WORK

The earliest timekeepers were non-mechanical devices such as sundials and water clocks. It is not known when mechanical clocks first came into use; Dante describes a clock's motion in his *Paradiso* of 1321, and an astronomical clock was in used in Strasbourg by 1350.

A clock's mechanism is driven either by weights or by springs. The gravitational force of the weights, or coiled force of the springs, drives a system of meshing toothed wheels, which in turn move the hands of the clock. But in order for the clock to keep accurate time, the power provided by the weights or springs must be released at a controlled, even speed. This essential control is provided by a device known as the escapement.

There are two kinds of escapement: verge and anchor. The verge escapement was universally employed until 1670, and the earliest type of verge escapement consisted of a horizontal bar (foliot)

with adjustable weights on each end; the foliot was mounted on a vertical rod (the verge). Along the length of the verge were two flags (pallets) set at right angles to one another. The pallets released the escape wheel at the rate of one tooth per swing of the foliot. In a later type of verge escapement, the foliot was replaced by a balance wheel (a).

The use of a coiled spring, as opposed to weights, to drive a clock's mechanism is recorded as early as the 15th century. In order to equalize the force of the uncoiling spring, early German makers used a device called a "stackfreed". A simpler and more efficient means was a cone-shaped gear known as a fusée (c) invented in about 1460–70 and still used today. The fusée is a cone-shaped part linked by a small chain or length of gut line to the barrel containing the spring.

Until the middle of the 17th century, few clocks were accurate to within a quarter of an hour per day. The minute hand was not used until after the middle of the 17th century, when timekeeping was vastly improved. This improvement was brought about by the introduction of the pendulum by the Dutchman Christiaan Huygens in 1657. Because a pendulum swings with an even beat, it could be used to ensure that the escapement worked evenly also. Most old clocks were converted to the new method; few retain their original foliot or balance wheel. The pendulum was initially used with verge escapement, but English makers shortly afterwards devised a new escapement, the anchor, which allowed for a longer pendulum (b). The second pendulum, beating at an interval of exactly one second, was developed. The longer pendulum caused the rise to popularity of the longcase, or grandfather clock. Among the various types of pendulum specially designed to stay at a constant length regardless of temperature were the "mercury" and the "gridiron" pendulum.

Bracket clocks, as the name implies, were originally designed to rest on a bracket, which sometimes matched the frame, although they were also often placed on any convenient piece of furniture. They generally also had handles to enable them to be moved from room to room. As the

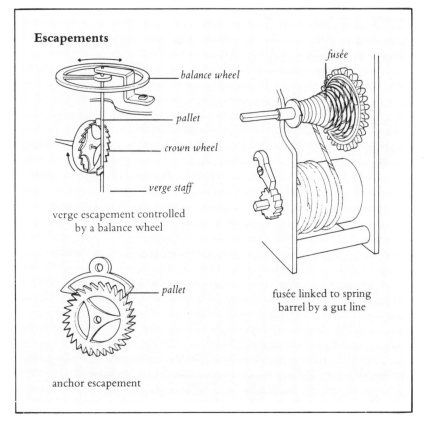

Escapements

fusée

balance wheel

pallet

crown wheel

verge staff

verge escapement controlled by a balance wheel

pallet

anchor escapement

fusée linked to spring barrel by a gut line

*Left: an ebony-veneered bracket clock made by Thomas Tompion in about 1680. Also shown are the clock's engraved backplate (**far left, above**) with Tompion's signature, and the mechanism behind the backplate (**far left, below**), featuring a verge escapement.*

Below: this ebony-veneered bracket clock, made by Joseph Knibb in about 1675, has a grande sonnerie striking mechanism, allowing it to sound the hours and quarters at each quarter.

fashion of using brackets faded, bracket clocks became known as mantel clocks since they so often occupied a central position on the mantelpiece. The portability of bracket or mantel clocks explains the survival of the verge escapement for a hundred years or so after the invention of the anchor escapement, which required more accurate levelling.

The creation of an efficient mechanism for striking the hour also exercised the ingenuity of clockmakers. Before about 1675, striking was regulated by means of a count-wheel, a disc with slots cut into the edge. Its great weakness was that the striking sequence could become increasingly out of phase with the hands. This problem was solved in 1676 by Edward Barlow's "rack and snail" construction. The rack was a T-shaped device with teeth, each one representing a blow on the bell, cut into its upper surface. The snail was a cam revolving with the hour hand, the highest point of its circumference corresponding to one o'clock, and the lowest to twelve o'clock. The *grande sonnerie*, which came in about 1660, was a type of striking in which the hours and the quarters were struck at each quarter.

AMERICA

Although clocks were to be found in the homes of the wealthier early colonists, it is likely that such timepieces were imported from Europe, and not made in America.

By the beginning of the 18th century, however, clockmaking was becoming established in America. Among early makers were Thomas Nash of New Haven, Connecticut; Abel Cottey, Benjamin Chandle and Peter Stretch, all of Philadelphia; Gawen Brown of Boston; and David Blaisdell of Amesbury, Massachusetts. Most of these men came to America from England, Ireland or Wales.

David Rittenhouse (active from about 1750 to 1790) is the best-known of a group of early makers working in Philadelphia. Rittenhouse made some of the finest American longcase clocks. Most clocks made in America in the 18th century were of the tallcase type, initially made to order, and had a brass eight-day movement. From the mid-1740s, some Connecticut craftsmen used wood instead of

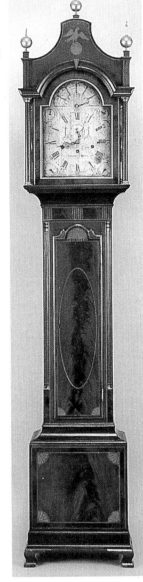

A tallcase clock by the Boston maker, Gawen Brown. The case of this mid-18th century example is decorated with an imitation of Oriental lacquer known as japanning.

DAVID RITTENHOUSE 1732–1796

Born in Paper Mill Run, Pennsylvania, where his grandfather had established America's first paper mill in 1690, David Rittenhouse displayed an early interest in mathematics. At twelve he inherited the mathematical library and tools of an uncle, and proceeded to teach himself clockmaking. He later worked on compasses, levels, thermometers, barometers and surveying instruments, and in 1763 he was commissioned to survey the first part of what was to become the Mason-Dixon Line. A keen astronomer and physicist, he also became the first director of the US Mint.

Between 1750 and 1790, David Rittenhouse of Philadelphia produced some of the best longcase clocks made in America.

Only 67 musical clocks made in America before 1820 survive today. This tallcase example with inlaid mahogany case was made around 1790 by Aaron Lane, clockmaker and silversmith of New Jersey.

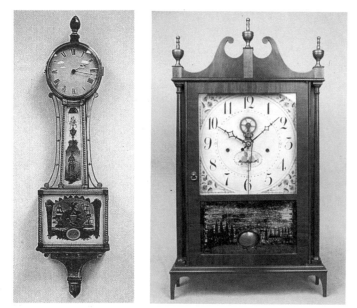

Far left: the Willards were a leading Boston clockmaking family. Simon Willard patented the popular banjo shape. This clock was made in 1815.

Left: one of Eli Terry's pillar-and-scroll shelf clocks with 30-hour wooden movement. Made in Plymouth, Connecticut, around 1820.

Right: a "sharp Gothic" clock by Birge & Fuller.

Below: a mid-19th-century acorn shelf clock with eight-day movement which was made by J. C. Brown of Bristol, Connecticut. This style is quite rare.

brass, which had become expensive. Notable Connecticut clockmakers include Timothy Cheney, Gideon Roberts and John Rich.

In Boston, Massachusetts, the Willards were a prominent clockmaking family. The brothers Benjamin, Simon, Ephraim and Aaron were noted clockmakers each of whom ran independent clockmaking businesses. In 1802, Simon Willard patented the banjo-shaped clock, a non-striking timepiece which enjoyed long popularity. Aaron Willard is notable for his shelf clocks, while his son, Aaron Jnr, is credited with the creation of the lyre-shaped clock, a rare type made in Massachusetts between about 1820 and 1840. Other 19th-century clock styles include the lighthouse shelf clock, patented by Simon Willard in 1822, and the girandole wall clock, designed by Lemuel Curtis. The girandole clock, a very rare type, was an elaborately decorated banjo clock with a circular box at the base.

Another notable clockmaker was Thomas Harland, an Englishman who settled in Norwich, Connecticut, in 1773. Harland's ability was surpassed by that of his apprentice, Daniel Burnap, who opened his own shop in East Windsor in approximately 1780. Burnap in turn was outshone by his famous pupil Eli Terry, who in the early 1790s began making wooden clock movements in the town that is now Plymouth. Terry's movements were sold uncased, and while the buyer had the option of having a case made, many of Terry's clocks were left uncased, to serve as "wag-on-the-wall" clocks. Terry's major contributions to American clockmaking were the use of standardized wooden parts, and the evolution (with his brother Samuel) of the influential pillar-and-scroll shelf clock; this had slender side pillars, a scrolled pediment and urn-shaped finials.

The cases for Terry's shelf clocks were initially made by Chauncey Jerome. By 1827, however, Jerome had formed a partnership with Elijah Darrow in Bristol, Connecticut. In the 1830s, Jerome was absorbed in the manufacture of cheap 30-hour brass movements. Being cheaper and far superior, brass movements rendered their wooden prototypes obsolete by the early 1840s. Among Jerome and Darrow's products were Empire-style clocks some of which were stencilled with bronze powders (replacing the gold leaf used earlier) and fitted with a looking-glass beneath the dial.

In the first half of the 19th century rapid strides in the development of brass and steel movements were made by Joseph Ives. In approximately 1825, Ives introduced a "wagon spring" clock, powered by a flat-leaved spring, which became the basis of numerous examples made later by Birge & Fuller, of Bristol, Connecticut. Around 1830, Ives also developed the rectangular "O.G."-style case, so-called because of its ogee, or S-shaped, mouldings. This type of case was very widely copied. Ives, like many other Connecticut makers, also produced hour-glass clocks, which as their name implies followed the general shape of an hour-glass, powered by means of a coiled spring. Other Connecticut styles include the rare "acorn" and the commoner "beehive", or "flatiron", shelf clock.

Mid-19th century neo-Gothicism spawned the "sharp Gothic" case, with pointed gable and pinnacles, and the "round Gothic" case, sometimes with a rippled effect along the round arch.

ENGLAND

England boasts the two oldest surviving mechanical clocks in the world. The oldest is in Salisbury Cathedral, for which it was made; the second oldest, made for Wells Cathedral in 1392, is now displayed in the Science Museum, London. From then until the 16th century, little is known about English clockmaking.

The earliest clocks generally available to collectors date from the reign of Elizabeth I (1558–1603). By about 1600, the familiar lantern clock had become popular. The name was a corruption of *latten*, meaning brass, but also conveniently describes the clock's lantern-shaped frame. The numerals were engraved on the dial and the hour was indicated by a single hand, and there was usually a hemispherical bell on which the hour was struck. Until the pendulum was introduced, in 1657, the escapement was normally of the verge and balance variety.

In 1631, Charles I granted permission for the London clockmakers to form their own "company", with strict enforcement of quality control. The first English pendulum clocks were made in 1658. The pendulum was fitted to hanging wall clocks, which were fixed to the wall, the pendulum swinging below. The pendulum was eventually cased, leading to the development of the longcase clock.

As well as fulfilling their primary function – that of telling the time – longcase clocks were also regarded as important pieces of furniture. The design of their cases, hoods and dials were the subject of lavish attention, and tended to follow current fashions in the design and decoration of other pieces of furniture.

The earliest longcase clocks, which date from about 1670, were generally given oak cases and stood only six and a half feet high. The case tended to be narrow and the hood of relatively simple, architectural design. In later examples, dating from about 1675–80, the oak case was sometimes veneered in ebony or walnut and the hood was given barley-twist pillars each side of the dial. Master cabinet-makers were now employed to make the finest cases.

Right: with its single hand, engraved numerals and hemispherical bell, this is a typical 17th-century lantern clock. The fretwork above the dial, often incorporating dolphins, as here, was a common decorative feature in lantern clocks.

By the end of the 17th century, longcase clocks had reached a height of seven feet seven inches and frequently had a bull's eye glass (a circular or oval window) in the centre of the case through which the pendulum could be seen.

Marquetry decoration on longcase clocks was in vogue from the late 17th century until about 1715; its early type, consisting of bold floral motifs, progressed to the finer, more abstract "seaweed" type. In the first two decades of the 18th century, longcase clocks stood to the remarkable height of eight

feet or more, and seaweed marquetry often covered the hood as well as the case. Japanned cases were popular until about 1760. Walnut, however, remained the fashionable material from about 1770. From then, mahogany superseded other case material as the most fashionable and prestigious wood.

The hoods of cases were subject to evolution; being gabled from about 1660–70, they became flat, with spiral columns flanking the dial; from about 1675, they were crested and, from about 1720, arched. From the early 18th century, the "breakarch" dial, a square dial arched at the top, came widely into vogue. The arch was used to accommodate the strike/silent lever (activating a mechanism that would stop the clock striking if desired), or a plate bearing the name and town of the maker. Somewhat later, the arch was used to take a dial indicating the phases of the moon.

Night clocks, allowing the hour to be seen in the dark, were made both in longcase and table versions from the 17th century to the middle of the

These two ornate bracket clocks, date from the first half of the 18th century. The one below was made in about 1715, and has a tortoiseshell case richly mounted in silver and is topped by a carrying handle. The one on the right, made in about 1735, is housed in an architectural frame and has two side handles. Unusually, this is a musical clock, playing one of six tunes every three hours.

19th century. They incorporated an oil lamp which shone behind a semi-circular opening, and generally had an elaborately painted dial. These illuminated clocks were abandoned in favour of a mechanism which, at the pull of the cord, sounded the time on bells to the nearest quarter-hour.

Bracket clocks, also known as mantel clocks, were portable. Many have a carrying handle for this purpose, and some originally had a bracket by which they were attached to the wall. By 1675, their brass dials and backplates were very often engraved with tulip designs in the Dutch style. Enamelled dials were introduced in about 1750. Towards the end of the 18th century, bracket clocks often had ornately pierced gilt-metal tops known as "basket tops".

The period 1650 to 1740 was the golden age of English clockmaking. The giant among craftsmen was Thomas Tompion (active 1671–1731). Tompion's achievements include his work with perpetual calendars, which allowed for the uneven extent of the calendar months and for leap years. Among other important English clockmakers are Daniel Quare (1674–1724), the Fromanteel family (whose active members spanned the years 1625–1725), Edward East (1627–97), George Graham (1674–1751), Joseph Windmills (1671–1725) and Joseph Knibb (c. 1650–1710). All worked in London.

But clockmaking also flourished in the provinces. During the 17th century, and more especially the 18th century, provincial longcase and bracket clocks were made in a variety of styles. They, too, generally followed changing tastes and

THOMAS TOMPION 1639–1713

Originally a blacksmith, Thomas Tompion's first attempt at time-keeping is said to have been a device to regulate the speed of a roasting spit. In 1664 he was apprenticed to a London clockmaker, and he was admitted to the Clockmakers Company in 1671. Within five years his reputation was such that he was appointed to make the clocks for the new Royal Observatory in Greenwich, for which accuracy was vital. Tompion was the first clockmaker for whom the accuracy and internal workings of his clocks and watches was more important than their external appearance.

fashions, although innovations usually took years, often decades, to reach the provinces from London. The fashion for longcase clocks, for example, which was almost over in London by 1720–40, continued in the provinces into the 19th century. Notable provincial clockmakers of the 18th century include William Barker (d. 1786) of Wigan, Thomas Lister (1745–1814) of Halifax, and Thomas Mudge (1715–84), a West Countryman who also worked in London.

By the Regency period (1800–30), the clockmaker's and case-maker's arts had polarized, each having become a specialized and separate activity. No longer were specific movements made for specific cases. Instead, identical cases were given movements by a range of makers. A leading early 19th-century London clocksmith, the last of the old breed, was Benjamin Lewis Vulliamy (1809–54). For his cases, Vulliamy adopted a succession of Gallic styles which ranged from the Boulle marquetry and ormolu mounts beloved of Louis XIV to the porcelain and marble of French neo-classicism.

A favourite ornamental clock of the 19th century was the skeleton clock, with its mechanism under a glass dome. From the 1830s, the Gothic revival influenced the design of clock cases.

The fascination of skeleton clocks, like this 19th-century example, lies in the total visibility of their mechanism rather than in the beauty of an ornate case.

FRANCE

Small, spring-driven clocks were being made in France by the 16th century. Silver, and even gold, were often used by French clockmakers; but such early clocks are rarely seen today, as they have been dismantled for their precious metals.

In France, the most popular timepiece in the 16th century was hexagonal in plan, with a column at each corner and a pierced dome over the bell. In the period 1590–1610, the hexagonal shape was abandoned in favour of the more familiar square form.

Early pendulum clocks were made in imitation of Dutch examples. Under Louis XIV (1643–1715), pendulum clocks known as *pendules religieuses* were decorated with elaborate tortoise-shell veneers and silver and brass inlays. André-Charles Boulle excelled at this manner of decoration. In the 1690s, an enamelled plaque bearing a numeral for each hour was added to the dial. In the

early 18th century, the pedestal clock came into vogue, and was often a superb piece of furniture. The French made relatively few longcase clocks, however; they are known in French as *régulateurs*, and most surviving examples were made in the provinces. Much more typical of French clock-making were bracelet clocks. These are characteristically waisted and were fitted with specially made consoles. Also typical were wall-hung cartel clocks and clocks incorporated into a piece of luxury furniture. Clock cases were almost always topped by an ormolu figure; favourite representations were Time with his scythe, and Diana.

In the reign of Louis XV (1723–74), clocks were ornamented with a profusion of rococo scrolls, shells and flowers. Porcelain cases were often used, with ormolu mounts. By now the mechanism of clocks had become standard; power was supplied by "going barrels", from which a cord slowly unwound, and the striking mechanism was regulated by a count wheel, a disc with slots cut into its edge. The 18th century also saw great technical innovations, which were made by Julien Le Roy (1686–1759), his son Pierre Le Roy (1717–85), Jean André Lepaute and others.

In clock cases, the excesses of the rococo were curbed by the neo-classical tastes of the age of Louis XVI (1774–93). Unglazed porcelain (known as biscuit porcelain) made an appearance, and urns and human or animal figures were among the most fashionable motifs. By now also, bracket and cartel clocks were gradually replaced by mantel clocks. A particularly elegant variety of mantel clock was that made in the form of a lyre. In the Empire period (1804–15), decoration often included Egyptian and Classical forms in low relief.

France is particularly well known for its carriage clocks which were made from about 1770 to 1910. Their antecedents were the round-dialled *pendules d'officier* used mainly by military officers while travelling. Carriage clocks proper had a rectangular gilt case, glass panels, a rectangular face and a fairly large carrying handle. They were sparsely ornamented. Miniature versions were also made. Some of the earliest carriage clocks were made by

Above: enamelled plaques on an early 18th-century clock face, typical of those introduced in the 1690s.

Right: a fine example of a pendulum clock, c. 1685, with ornate case by André Charles Boulle. The marquetry and ormolu, for which Boulle is famous, is particularly fine.

Abraham Louis Breguet (1747–1823), one of the most talented of French horologists. Lastly, the wall-hung Morbier clock was a notable provincial design, made in large numbers from the end of the 18th century in the Jura region of eastern France. Most Morbier clocks had an inverted verge escapement. The striking was double at each hour (the second time two minutes after the first), and the usual French practice of striking once on the half-hour was followed.

The Revolution did not totally disrupt clock-making in France. Breguet, for example, continued to produce very complex clocks and fine watches. Other makers turned their attention to developing French clockmaking into an industry, and carriage clocks were much exported, particularly to England.

Stylistically, the early years of the 19th century were conservative. Clocks decorated with gilt bronze figures continued to be popular, but at the same time there was also a demand for novelties such as mystery clocks and skeleton clocks. Mystery clocks took many forms; in some, a figure standing above the movement held a swinging pendulum that was not visibly connected to the movement. Skeleton clocks, in which the movement was plainly visible under a glass dome, went to the other extreme.

*The function of French clocks as timepieces was often rivalled by their extragantly decorative nature. The Louis XV cartel clocks (**above**) is heavy with rococo scrolls and figures, but the two Louis XVI mantel clocks (**above left and far left**) exude lightness and elegance. Though it is still decorative, the Louis XVI longcase clock (**above left**) with mahogany case and restrained use of ormolu, is sober by comparison.*

THE NETHERLANDS, GERMANY, AUSTRIA AND SWITZERLAND

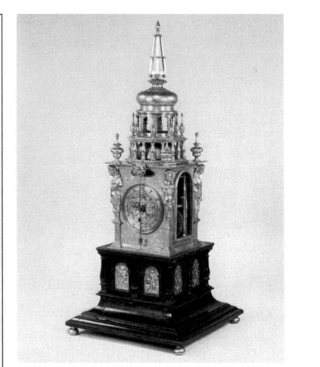

The Netherlands

A characteristic type of 17th-century Dutch clock, similar to the French *pendule religieuse*, has a movement fixed to the dial which is in turn hinged to the case. Dutch longcase clocks of the 18th century are characterized by projecting scrolls at each corner of the base and triangular panels on the dial. As well as striking on the hour, the clock struck the preceding half-hour on a higher-pitched bell.

Three distinctive types of wall-hung clocks later developed: the *Zaanse*, the *Staart* and the *Stoel*. The *Zaanse* had an elaborate box-like bracket which contained the pendulum, was fitted with pear-shaped weights on ropes and decorated with ornate brass crestings. The *Staart* had a long tail-like backboard which housed the pendulum, and the *Stoel* had a movement which rested on a wooden stool supported by the wall bracket. Many *Stoel* clocks were made in Friesland.

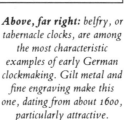

Above: a staartklok (left) and a longcase clock (right) – two examples of 18th-century Dutch clockmaking. Both have arched dials, one is painted with a landscape, the other with phases of the moon.

Above, far right: belfry, or tabernacle clocks, are among the most characteristic examples of early German clockmaking. Gilt metal and fine engraving make this one, dating from about 1600, particularly attractive.

Germany

Germany was an outstanding clockmaking region during the Renaissance. Clocks made in Augsburg were unrivalled throughout Europe. Augsburg clocks often bear the town stamp, "AG" or a pineapple. A speciality of the town was the "belfry" or "tabernacle" clock, housed in a tower-shaped case complete with turrets and spire. During the late 17th century and up to the middle of the 18th century, the ages of the baroque and the rococo, cases reached great heights of elaboration. Clocks made in Bavaria were particularly subject to these excesses.

Factories such as Meissen, Höchst, Berlin and Frankenthal made porcelain clock cases in the rococo style. David Roentgen's graceful longcase clocks often had fine marquetry on the trunk and base and generally housed movements by Kinzing.

Less sophisticated clockmaking was practised in the Black Forest. Clocks made here continued to be fitted with the verge and foliot escapement until well into the 18th century. Until about 1780, their movements were of wood, with a stone as the driving weight. The wooden dials were painted with flowers, birds, animals or figures. It was in the Black Forest that cuckoo clocks originated, probably invented in about 1730 by Franz Anton Ketterer, of Schönwald. The first cuckoo clocks were similar in style to other Black Forest clocks. It was only around 1870 that they assumed their "classic" form: a house-like case decorated with foliage, birds and other animals, and the clock-face bearing the familiar Gothic numerals.

Austria and Switzerland

During the 18th century, clockmaking expanded greatly in Austria. This was especially true in Vienna, where French and German influences were combined. The Biedermeier style, which flourished between about 1815 and 1848, was particularly fruitful in clock design.

In the 19th century, Vienna became well known for its regulators – non-striking clocks made to a special degree of accuracy. Early 19th-century examples often had a severe but elegant ebony case with stringing in lighter wood. Inferior clocks, passed off as Vienna regulators, were later made in Silesia and the Black Forest.

In Switzerland in the 18th century, P. Jaquet-Droz of Neuchâtel made magnificent French-style bracket clocks.

Far left: a 19th-century Black Forest clock. This is a plain example, made for the English market.

The bracket clock (**left**) made in about 1790, is a refined example of Swiss clockmaking. The ormolu and marquetry decoration, showing French influence, is unusually rich.

Above: an Austrian regulator, dating from the 19th century. Perhaps because of their primary function as extremely accurate timekeepers, decoration was seldom lavished on regulators.

WATCHES

The natural development of the spring-driven portable clock was the watch – the personal portable clock. Watches were first made in Europe in the 16th century. Queen Elizabeth I of England had a wrist watch and so did the Empress Josephine. But wrist watches first became generally accepted after 1850. In America, watchmaking had its beginnings late in the 18th century but did not become established until the middle of the 19th century.

Early European watches, those made in France and Germany in the middle of the 16th century, were spherical. The more familiar, circular shape was soon adopted, though watches were often made to such varied shapes as stars, ovals, octagons and crosses, and even birds and skulls. In the early 17th century, striking mechanisms, alarms or calendars were sometimes incorporated.

Although they were primarily portable clocks, watches were also items of jewellery. The materials with which their cases were fashioned included gold, silver and gilt metal; embellishment of the case took the form of embossing and damascening and, above all, enamelling. Enamelling was most expertly practised in France. Dials and backplates were often superbly engraved, and even winding keys were decorated or wrought in elegant shapes.

In Europe, important early centres of watchmaking were Nuremberg in Germany, and Blois in France. By the early 17th century Paris and Geneva dominated the watchmaking industry, but the lead later passed to England. In England, the pair-cased watch, having both an inner and an outer case, was popular until about 1830.

In the late 17th century, a mechanical invention and a fashion in dress increased the popularity of

The diminutive size of watches did not prevent them from fulfilling many functions beyond telling the time. This Swiss watch, made in 1912, records the days of the week, months and phases of the moon.

The decoration lavished on watches made them much more than personal timepieces. This Swiss example, made in about 1800, is painted in enamels and set with pearls.

Really elaborate decoration on a watch sometimes took the form of automata. In this one – a musical automaton watch made in about 1810 – a gentleman plays a cello, another a violin and a lady beats time to the music.

Not all watches were ostentatiously decorated. This one, made in London in 1812, has a case delicately decorated with flowers and scrolls picked out in varicoloured gold.

watches. The mechanical invention was the balance spring which, working in conjunction with the balance wheel, made watches more accurate. The fashion in dress was the waistcoat, which provided a convenient place to carry them. In the 18th century, Thomas Mudge devised the "detached lever escapement", which gradually superseded the verge escapement and became universal for pocket watches. The achievement of the detached lever escapement was to free the oscillations of the balance from continual interference by the escapement.

The outstanding watchmaker of all time was Abraham Louis Breguet (1747–1823), a Swiss who worked in Paris. Breguet produced an automatic winder from 1780, and was the inventor of many other complex pieces including the *montre à tact* for telling the time in the dark. Breguet also gave his name to a characteristic style of hands notable for their delicacy and simplicity.

During the 19th century, when wrist watches were becoming widely accepted, examples were mainly Swiss. By the late 19th century, Swiss watches were of unrivalled excellence.

In America, watchmaking on a significant scale appears to have begun in Shrewsbury, Massachusetts, in 1809. In that year, Luther Goddard opened a small shop. Between then and 1817, Goddard produced about 500 watches, though certain components may have been imported. In 1837, twenty years after the closure of Goddard's business, Henry and James Pitkin started to make watches in Hartford, Connecticut. The Pitkins made about 1,000 watches before competition from cheaper Swiss models forced them to cease production in about 1845.

The foundations of modern American watchmaking were laid in Boston around 1850 by Edward and Aaron Dennison, whose business became the Waltham Watch Company. This in turn became the American Waltham Watch Company in 1885. The company's earliest product was an eight-day watch made in 1850. Its later products rank among the finest achievements in watchmaking.

Another notable watchmaking concern was the New York Watch Company, founded in 1867, which was later known as the Hampden Watch Company, and, when it moved to Canton, Ohio, as the Dueber-Hampden Watch Company. In Connecticut, the firm of Benedict & Burnham made the affordable "Dollar" watch. Other makers of inexpensive watches included the Ingersoll Company, and the New Haven Watch Company.

Below far left: three views of a montre à tact, made in London in 1848, showing the face, the movement and the back of the case. The engraved numerals and revolving hand allow the time to be "read" in the dark.

Left and below: two views of a skeleton pocket watch made by Benedict and Burnham, of Connecticut, in about 1879.

Bottom: two views of a pocket watch made by the Waltham Watch Company, of Boston, in about 1901.

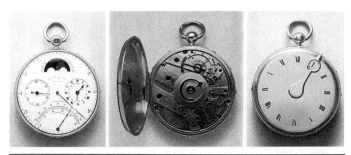

ABRAHAM LOUIS BREGUET 1747–1823

Abraham Louis Breguet's reputation as a clock and watchmaker is second only to that of Thomas Tompion. He developed a style of hands known as "moon" or "Breguet" hands that have distinctive rings near their points, which together with arabic numerals on the dial, made his watches supremely readable. Other innovations included a body with hinged front and back, and an inner perforated back which allowed winding without opening the watch fully. His watches were widely forged, so he devised a secret signature near the numeral 12.

SILVER

Silverware takes on an impressively broad variety of forms, from simple mugs and beakers to extravagant *épergnes* and centrepieces. The range and combination of decorative techniques with which silver was embellished is seemingly endless, and the sensitivity of the silversmith to changes in fashion is a source of endless fascination. The following pages describe these changing fashions and illustrate a range of forms and decorative techniques.

AMERICA

Silversmithing was the first of the European crafts to flourish in the New World. Plate (wrought silver) was more desirable than coin; in wills or after robberies, it could be identified by its shape, maker's marks or engraved arms, and it was used for pledge and even to purchase real estate.

In the 17th century, the art of the silversmith flourished particularly in the port towns of Boston and New York. In Boston in the early days, it was inevitable that English precedent should exert a strong influence. Moreover, much silver was imported from England, and some London gold-smiths came to work in America. Among them were Richard Storer, who reached Boston in 1635, and Robert Sanderson, who arrived in Massachusetts in 1638.

In New Amsterdam (now New York) the pre-dominant influence was, naturally, Dutch; the names of New York's early silversmiths – van der Burgh, Onclebagh, Kierstede, for example – reveal their origins.

Gradually, though a distinctively American style of silverware began to emerge both in Boston and New York and also in Philadelphia and Charlestown, which now had their own silversmiths. Examples of silverware produced in the later 17th

century included tankards, porringers (two-handled, covered bowls) and spoons.

New York tankards frequently had elaborate handles and mouldings to the base, and the handles of porringers were also often ornate. The earliest spoons made in Philadelphia were given trifid ends, while those made in New York generally had hoof or caryatid terminals.

In the early 18th century, American silver followed the new English fashion for comparatively plain designs so characteristic of the reign of Queen Anne in England. English silver reached America partly as gifts to colonial churches and partly brought by emigrés from England and American travellers returning from a visit to England. But then the contrastingly florid rococo style took over, dominating the design of American silver from about 1740 to the late 18th century.

After the Declaration of Independence (1776), silversmiths enthusiastically embraced neo-classicism, a style that revered Classical precedent as much as did the politicians with their Capitol and Senate. Bright-cut engraving (which owes its brilliant appearance to the graver burnishing the cut as it moves along the metal) became the vogue, and ornament in the Adam style, such as swags, rams' heads and paterae was common. The classical urn shape was also widely favoured. Philadelphia's own unmistakable idiom at this time was characterized by bold pineapple-shaped finials, small beading on most edges, and pierced galleries on the shoulders of urn-shaped pieces such as coffee-pots and covered sugar urns. The most renowned silversmith of the period was the famous patriot Paul Revere (1734–1818) of Boston.

In America in the 19th century, as in other countries, machinery was increasingly used to produce silverware. European styles and tastes, though they were still followed, played a more modest role in the design of American silver, American silversmiths continued to use neo-classical forms and neo-classical ornament though they often appear to have been experimenting with new or unexpected combinations of form and decoration.

The 19th century was generally a prosperous

*While the beaker (**above**), made in 1678, is an example of American silver reflecting Dutch influence, the later tankard (**right**), made in 1705–15, is more distinctively American, not least on account of the ornate handle and decoration to the lid and base.*

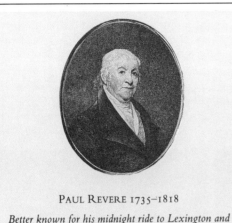

*Better known for his midnight ride to Lexington and Concord, Paul Revere was a skilful and versatile silversmith. At 16 he was apprenticed to his father, a successful Boston silversmith. In the lean years after the Seven Years War Paul became a copper engraver and a political cartoonist. One of the "indians" at the Boston Tea Party, he cast cannon and manufactured gunpowder during the American Revolution. He designed the first American coinage, the first official seal of the colonies and the State seal of Massachusetts. After the war he returned to silversmithing, until his death at 83. His silver mark (**below**) needs little explanation.*

period of the American silver industry. Output was considerable and several manufacturing firms were set up. Among them were Galt & Brothers Inc., of Washington D.C., founded in 1802, who boasted Abraham Lincoln and Jefferson Davis among their clients; the Ames Manufacturing Company, of Chicopee, Massachusetts, founded in 1829; and D. C. Bromwell, Inc., of Washington D.C., founded in 1873, who discovered how to "plate" baby shoes with precious metals.

The Art Nouveau style, with its flowing lines and use of botanical forms, was taken up in America notably by Louis Comfort Tiffany. The firm of Tiffany & Company, founded by Charles Lewis Tiffany in 1837, started to produce silver in 1868. On Charles' death in 1902, his son Louis Comfort Tiffany took on the running of the firm and it was under his direction that pieces in the Art Nouveau style were made. They included pitchers, vases, ewers and tea wares.

Art Nouveau was also embraced by other makers, as, in turn, was Art Deco. This contrasting style was developed in France around 1920, and its clean, simple outlines and minimal decoration came as the antithesis of the luxuriant idiom of Art Nouveau.

*In these three fine examples of 18th-century silver, the taste for the rococo, seen in the teapot (**top**), made by Paul Revere in 1760–65, and in the coffee pot, c. 1760, contrasts with the neo-classical features of the later urn, made in 1774.*

Left: *this bowl, made by Tiffany & Co. in about 1893, would have represented avant-garde tastes at the time.*

ENGLAND, SCOTLAND AND IRELAND

*Examples of decorative motifs on 18th-century silver and gilded silver. The waiter (**right**), made by David Willaume in 1715, has a gadrooned and foliate border and chased coat of arms. **Far right, top:** flat-chased* chinoiseries *is well displayed on this covered cup; and the tureen on stand (**below right**), made in 1789, has fluting, beading and engraved armorials.*

*The lion passant mark (**left**) used on English silver from 1542 to 1822, indicated sterling, or 92.5% purity. Britannia with lion's head erased (**right**), used from 1697 to 1864, indicated 95.8% purity.*

England

A great deal of English silver was melted down for coinage during the Civil War, and surviving silverware dating from before the Restoration (1660) is rare. But, perhaps because of their small size and consequently small silver content, a number of early drinking-cups survived that destructive demand for coinage. The earliest kind, known as mazers, were of wood, often with a silver lip and base. Mazers were superseded by standing cups – tall cups raised on a stem and with a tall cover. Salts, one of the most important types of secular silverware, became large and ornamental during the reign of Elizabeth I (1558–1603). This type virtually disappeared in the 1680s.

The Restoration of the Monarchy in 1660 brought English silversmiths new business, for, since their exile, the king and his courtiers had acquired rich tastes. But the art of the silversmith was in decline and it was not until the 1680s, after the immigration of French Huguenots, among whom were fine craftsmen, that this decline was halted. After their arrival in England in 1685, Huguenot silversmiths gradually became established, and soon English silversmiths were making fine pieces in French styles. Popular forms of ornamentation included gadrooned edging (a lobed border of convex curves), embossed acanthus leaves, spiral or vertical flutes (concave channelling) and *chinoiseries* applied by means of flat-chasing (gently hammering or punching the metal into the design).

In 1697, to prevent the melting down of coin for use in manufacture, the standard (or content of pure silver) for wrought items was raised from 92.5% to 95.8%. To distinguish it from sterling silver, used for coinage, this purer, higher-standard

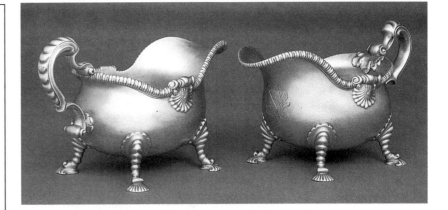

Paul Crespin's mark

Paul de Lamerie's mark

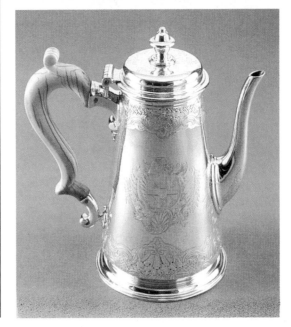

Above: applied decoration, in the form of rococo scrolls and shells, gives these two sauceboats by Paul Lamerie, 1742, a striking, eerie appearance.

Left: rococo swirls and scrolls, applied by means of flat-chasing and engraving, produce a more discreet effect on his beautifully wrought coffee pot, also by Paul de Lamerie, 1734.

silver was required to be marked with the figure of Britannia, the lion's head erased, a date letter (indicating the year of manufacture) and the first two letters of the maker's name. In 1700-01, five provincial towns – Chester, York, Exeter, Norwich and Newcastle – were appointed to assay silver of the Britannia standard, each using its own mark. Assaying involved authenticating the standard of wrought silver and awarding the five marks described above.

The use of this softer, higher-standard silver encouraged a sparsely decorated style known as "Queen Anne", sometimes incorporating cut-card work (a thin sheet of silver ornately cut and soldered onto the vessel). After 1720, when the lower, sterling standard was restored, this sparse use of decoration gave way to greater elaboration. By 1730, English silversmiths were starting to adopt rococo asymmetry. Chinese-style decoration came into vogue in about 1745.

The greatest silversmith of the 18th century was Paul de Lamerie, a Huguenot who was active in London between 1712 and 1749. Like his compatriot and fellow-Huguenot Paul Crespin, de Lamerie worked in an opulent, rococo style.

"Adam Silver", in the neo-classical style promoted by the architect Robert Adam, belongs to the period 1765–95. Oval shapes were favoured and tall pieces often took their form from the narrow-necked urn, generally without decoration after 1780. Bright-cut engraving, which owes its brilliant appearance to the graver burnishing the cut as it moves along the metal, came in during the 1780s and was much used. Among noteworthy silversmiths who worked in the neo-classical style were Matthew Boulton (1728–1809), Hester Bateman (active 1775–90), and her sons Peter and Jonathan.

From the later Georgian period, silver tends to become heavier. This fashion reached its height in

Examples of town-marks found on English silver.

London 1478–1696 and 1736–1821 (uncrowned thereafter)

Exeter 1575–1698; 1701–19th c.

Chester 1701–79; from 1780

Heavy ornamentation suited late Regency and early Victorian taste, and this silver gilt tray (**below**) would have fitted the bill. As well as prominently engraved armorials, the tray has a gadrooned border, handles modelled as oak branches ending in oak leaves and acorns, an engraved swag and paw feet.

Two contrasting examples of the work of Paul Storr. A general effect of stately elegance is reflected in this tea and coffee service (**above**), made in 1809–11. Gadrooning was not new to the Regency period, but urn shapes, paw feet and snake handles – in ivory and silver here – derived from classical sources, were novel.

Grand extravagance, however, is the effect of the magnificent candelabrum (**right**), which Storr made in 1824. Lavish design, last seen in the rococo period, was once again in demand, and Storr responded accordingly. His mark, simply "PS".

Right: a multitude of marine motifs are lavished on this early Victorian wine cooler and mirrored plateau.

the early wares of Rundell, Bridge & Rundell. Benjamin Smith and Paul Storr, whose marks appear on many of Rundell's wares, ran workshops for them before going on to found their outstanding businesses. While Smith excelled at relatively small pieces, Storr, the leading Regency silversmith, was versatile enough to produce charming beehive-shaped honeypots as well as more monumental wares.

In the Victorian era, when silverware was often preposterously showy, favourite models for designers were the Renaissance sculptor and goldsmith Benvenuto Cellini and John Flaxman, the neo-classical artist and sculptor. The Victorian period began with a rococo revival and the rise of a vigorous naturalism; vines, for example, became more lifelike and the convolvulus more convoluted. Towards the end of the 1840s, there were signs of a neo-classical revival and a tendency to base designs on Italian Renaissance metalwork.

Throughout the Victorian era, as fashions for re-creating past styles came and went, designs were generally weighty and extravagant, But if, during the 1850s and 1860s, such pomposity had become oppressive, by the 1870s it was replaced by a new and exotic decorative idiom – that of Japan. The arts of Japan became the rage not only in silver but in almost all aspects of the applied arts. In silver, "japonaiseries" were generally flat-chased or applied in relief; motifs included fans, butterflies, flowering and fruiting prunus and bamboo. The Japanese style was promoted notably by Barnard Bros. of London, and Elkingtons of Birmingham.

The 19th century was also the age of the rise of machinery and thus of the machine-made and mass-produced. Reacting against this situation, the Arts and Crafts Movement sought to protect the craftsman and encourage a return to the functional and the hand-made. The movement affected the design of silver as it did furniture, ceramics and many other manufacturing activities. Arts and Crafts silver tends to be ascetic and visibly hand-made; there is seldom an attempt, for example, to conceal rivets or smooth away hammer marks. But, as so often with new movements and changes in taste, the Arts and Crafts Movement was intellectual and avant-garde; reproductions of past styles and silverware wrought and finished by machine continued.

Art Nouveau and Art Deco also developed from relatively avant-garde attitudes. In silverware, the Art Nouveau style was probably interpreted most distinctly by Archibald Knox (1864–1933). His work for Liberty's, and particularly his pieces in Liberty's Cymric range launched in 1899, reflected his devotion to Celtic traditions. Other silver designers in the Art Nouveau style include Rex Silver, who worked in a style similar to Knox's, and C. R. Ashbee, who favoured down-to-earth hammered surfaces. Ashbee's Guild of Handicraft,

This monument to the Victorian love of showy display (below, far left) – St George and the Dragon locked in conflict atop a tankard – was made by R. & S. Garrard & Co. in 1846. The complicated strapwork is based on Elizabethan and Jacobean design and the use of silver and silver-gilt contributes to the tankard's typically Victorian richness.

This small bowl (above) – only 6 inches in diameter – was made in 1900 when Art Nouveau was at the height of its popularity. Natural forms, particularly plant and flowers are typical of this style.

The shape and motifs of this powder bowl made by H. G. Murphy in 1937 (left) are characteristic of the Art Deco period.

which began working in silver and electroplate in 1889, explored the decorative uses of precious stones and enamelling with silver.

The Art Deco idiom, with simple shapes and stark outlines, was used to good effect in silver. Ornament was rare, and tended to be confined to sparse engraved lines and simple stepped motifs. The use of this style is seen in the domestic wares of Charles Boynton, for example.

Tankards and mugs

The tankard was the most popular drinking vessel from the 16th century to the 18th. During the region of Charles II (1660–85), the most usual kind was large and plain, with a low, flat-topped cover in two steps, a thumbpiece and a splayed, moulded base. Some late 17th-century tankards are embossed around the base with acanthus leaves or spiral fluting (concave shafts). Acanthus leaves and fluting were the only types of embossing on tankards before about 1810. Other 17th-century tankards are engraved with *chinoiseries*. In the reign

of Queen Anne (1702–14), the flat cover on tankards was gradually superseded by a domed cover, and before the middle of the 18th century, a baluster-shaped tankard (of bulging, vase-shaped form) with a high moulded foot came in.

A mug is essentially a small tankard without a lid. Every vessel with a capacity of over one pint was lidded.

Porringers

The porringer was a two-handled covered cup. It had two main variants: the caudle cup and the posset pot. Early Restoration porringers often had embossed decoration on the lower half. As with tankards, acanthus or spiral-fluted embossing, and more rarely *chinoiserie* engraving, were used on late 17th-century porringers and their covers, though plain porringers were also made.

Other items associated with drinking include beer jugs, wine coasters (circular stands for a bottle or decanter, made from about 1760) and punch bowls.

*Though it is lidded and unusually plain, this well-worn mug (**above**), made in 1628, was surely a favourite with the owner whose initials "TEP" are engraved on the lid as well as on the mug itself. The silver gilt tankard (**top right**) is much grander; the stepped lid, and scrolled handle are typical of the period – 1670–90.*

Right: this aristocratic beer jug was made by the Huguenot silversmith David Willaume in 1734. Its baluster shape, stepped foot and comfortably scrolling handle are very characteristic of this period.

*Porringers were made in all styles and sizes. These two show two different forms of decoration: the example (**below right**), dating from about 1650–60, has bold engraving, while the other one (**below left**), made in 1685, is flat-chased with chinoiserie scenes.*

Coffee and chocolate pots

Coffee and chocolate pots are identical but for one detail: chocolate pots have a hinged lid or removable finial, revealing a hole for stirring. Early coffee pots had conical lids, straight spouts and rounded handles. Until about 1720, the handle was either opposite the spout or at right angles to it. By 1700, the spout had become curved and the lid rounded. Also at this time, the joints at the handle and spout were sometimes treated with cut-card decoration. Handles at right angles to the spout went out of fashion in about 1715. Apart from cut-card decoration, ornamentation on coffee and chocolate pots was usually restricted to engraved armorials.

At the turn of the century, the cylindrical body gave way to one of polygonal form, and around 1725, lids became flatter. Pear-shaped coffee and chocolate pots were introduced in about 1730, sometimes with flat-chased or embossed decoration.

In keeping with neo-classical tastes, the typical coffee pot of the 1780s and 1790s was urn-shaped, sometimes with bright-cut engraving. In the early 19th century, examples were squatly pear-shaped, often on feet and frequently standing on a spirit-lamp.

Teapots and associated items

Early teapots, dating from the second half of the 17th century, are generally small, since tea was an expensive novelty. Up to about 1780, teapots are rarer than coffee pots. The egg-shaped body of the later 17th-century teapots gave way to the Queen Anne pear shape, then, after 1710, a taller, octagonal shape became more fashionable with handles of wood.

Around 1720, a new style became popular. This was the bullet-shaped teapot – round with a flattened top and a straight spout. This was followed by the inverted pear shape.

In the neo-classical period, forms metamorphosed from cylindrical to flat-topped then to a dome-topped oval. From about 1800, a variety of rectangular forms became common. Almost all teapots from the neo-classical period onwards had a straight spout rising from near the base.

Tea or coffee urns, introduced in about 1760, generally had neo-classical rather than rococo decoration. Cream jugs were made in a variety of styles; among them were the realistic cow creamers (vessels for milk or cream in the shape of a cow) made between 1757 and 1768 by John Schuppe. Mid-18th century tea caddies were commonly embossed with *chinoiserie* designs.

Left: clean lines and sparse decoration enhance this mid-18th-century coffee pot with its classic tapering cylindrical shape. Until the rococo period, the owner's engraved armorials were often the only form of decoration.

Below left: by the later 18th century, decoration became more ambitious. The chased and moulded decoration on this teapot, shaped like an inverted pear and made in 1767, reflects the growing taste for the rococo.

Above: a tea caddy was an almost essential adjunct to genteel tea-drinking. The engraving on this one, of about 1760, is particularly delicate.

Left: this octagonal pear-shaped teapot dates from about 1715. Matching oil lamp stands were often provided as an integral part of the set in the early 18th century.

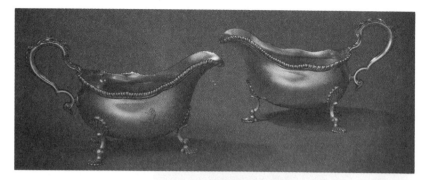

*Silver sauceboats were particularly popular in the 18th century. Though often more elegant, the earlier double-lipped, double-handled type (**right**) was probably less practical than the later variety (**above**) with single lip and opposing handles.*

Below: *this 18th-century cruet consists of three casters and four bottles held by ring frames on a shaped stand.*

Sauceboats

The earliest sauceboats, dating from the first quarter of the 18th century, are rare and have low oval bodies with two opposing lips and two handles. In the second quarter of the 18th century, this form was replaced by a boat on three legs with a handle opposite the lip. Most examples date from before 1780.

Salts, casters and peppers

From the middle of the 17th century, salts (salt dishes) were generally small circular or oblong vessels, known as trencher salts. After about 1735, salts became three-legged. From about 1760, pierced, oval ones were made, fitted with a blue glass vessel known as a liner. From about 1785, boat-shaped salts came into vogue, to be replaced by oblong tubs at the end of the century.

Casters, used for sprinkling condiments, were made in sets of three. The largest was for the sugar. Around 1705, the cylindrical "lighthouse" caster gave way to a pear-shaped form on a moulded foot. Around 1715, the upper part of casters became distinctly concave.

Flatware

Spoons are among the smaller items of English silverware that have survived from pre-Restoration times. Finials (the decorative motifs at the end of the handles) are found in great variety,

*With its stepped foot, circular bowl and applied decoration, the trencher salt (**above**) is typical of those made around 1725.*

*The fine piercing on this caster (**left**), made in 1711, was both practical and decorative. In sets of three, casters were used for sugar, pepper and dry mustard.*

but seal-top spoons, with a flat seal on a baluster (vase shape), are the commonest. Apostle spoons also survive in surprising quantities. Trifid spoons, with two notches in the end, have an elongated "rat tail" down the back of the bowl, sometimes surrounded by a lacy pattern continued on the front of the spoon.

Spoons of the Hanoverian pattern, with a ridge along the front of the stem and an upward-turning end, predominated from about 1720 to 1760. The Old English pattern, by contrast, popular after about 1760, has the ridge along the back and the end turned the other way. Another trend in the 1760s was the Onslow pattern, with a scrolled end. Early 19th-century patterns include the fiddle-and-thread and the hour-glass, named after the shapes of the handles. Handles of knives and forks generally followed the stylistic development of spoon handles.

Candlesticks

Until about 1700, silver candlesticks were made from sheet metal and consisted of a clustered or fluted column on a square stepped or polygonal stepped base. Cast candlesticks, introduced by the Huguenot silversmiths in about 1690, became standard in about 1760. Their height also gradually increased. The Queen Anne style of candlestick, common from about 1700 to 1715, had a baluster (bulbous vase-shaped) stem and a wide base. This

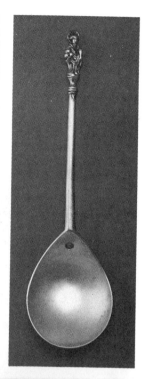

This cast candlestick, made by David Willaume in about 1690, forms one of a pair and would have been used at table.

Examples of spoons, forks and knives from the 15th to the 19th century.
Top left: *three seal-top and two trifid spoons dating from the 16th and 17th centuries.*
Top right: *an apostle spoon depicting St Philip bearing three loaves, made in 1490.*
Left: *a mid- to late 17th-century trifid spoon with rat-tail down the back*

of the bowl. ***Above:*** *the fiddle and thread pattern was just one of many patterns devised in the 18th and 19th centuries for cutlery.*

type formed the basis of many later variations. The mid-18th century saw the appearance of candle-sticks with shafts formed as caryatids and kneeling blackamoors. Shafts formed as Corinthian columns and made from sheet silver came in with the classical revival of the late 18th century. In the Adam period (1728–92), a typical design for candlesticks was a concave column with festoons on the base and rams' heads on the shoulder, which was four-sided.

Other silverware

Luxurious toilet services, consisting of up to 30 pieces and including a mirror, a ewer, a basin, candlesticks and ointment boxes, were made in the second half of the 17th century.

In the 18th century, table silver included the épergne, a centrepiece with detachable stands or hanging baskets for fruit and sweetmeats. Ink-stands, also known as standishes, were particularly common in the late 18th century and early 19th.

Above: a magnificent silver-gilt toilet service of 16 pieces, made by David Willaume in 1734 for a noble and wealthy family.

Above: rococo exuberance leaves hardly an angular line in this pair of caryatid-stem candle-sticks by Paul de Lamerie. And it was the reaction against rococo extravagance that resulted in the neo-classical restraint visible in the other pair of candlesticks (above right) with their simple gadrooning.

Right: the rococo was not always overpowering. This pierced cake basket is a relatively demure example of the style.

Wine labels, originally known as bottle tickets, were made in silver from about 1734. They were small silver tags engraved with the name of a wine or spirit and hung on chains round the necks of bottles or decanters. The earliest were of shield shape; later examples were crescent-shaped and after about 1823 vine leaf shapes were made.

Baskets for bread, cake, fruit or sweetmeats, often very delicately wrought, became common in the late 1720s.

Sheffield plate

Sheffield plate is copper plated with silver by a method which fuses the metals inseparably. Sheffield plate is said to have been invented in about 1743 by Thomas Bolsover, a Sheffield cutler. Bolsover himself used Sheffield plate mainly to make buttons; it was Joseph Hancock, another cutler, who applied the new technique to the manufacture of candlesticks, coffee pots and other domestic wares.

Some of the earliest manufacturers of Sheffield plated wares were Henry Tudor, Thomas Leader, Thomas Law, John Winter & Co., Richard Morton, Matthew Felton & Co., John Littlewood and John Hoyland & Co. At Soho, in Birmingham, Matthew Boulton was making fused plate by 1762 and three years later founded the Matthew Boulton Silver & Plate Co. Styles of plated wares drew heavily on silver forms, and often copied the grandest and most elegant silver designs, but as the price of Sheffield plate was only a third of that of silver, competition between manufacturers of plate and silversmiths was intense.

"Double plating", plating on both sides of the copper rather than on one, came in around 1763. Double plating was used particularly for drinking vessels and for dishes that were intended to hold food. Methods of decoration in the second half of the 18th century included flat chasing, "swaging" (moulding the edges with a swage, or pair of pincers) and piercing. By about 1780, silver bands or shields were often applied to plated ware to provide a suitable surface for engraving. Silver wire was sometimes added to sheared edges from the late 18th century.

Among the smaller items made in Sheffield plate were wine coasters, salt and mustard pots, inkstands and candle-snuffers with trays. Among the larger articles were épergnes, soup tureens, entrée dishes, salvers, ice pails and wine coolers. Teapots, coffee pots, hot-water jugs and cake baskets were also made. Plated wire toast racks appeared around

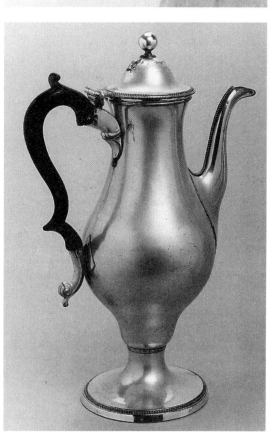

Above: a fine Sheffield plate tureen on stand by Thomas Law, whose signature, with the date of manufacture, appears on one of the dolphin-shaped feet (left). This tureen is an example of grand elegance and was probably copied from a silver original.

This pear shaped Sheffield plate coffee pot, on a raised foot, was made in about 1790. This plain, sparsely decorated piece reflects late 18th-century taste.

1780–85. Candlesticks, some of which were telescopic, and tankards were in great demand. Some church vessels were also made.

When Sheffield plate first began to be used, makers used marks for their wares that dishonestly suggested that they were solid silver. In 1773, at the request of the silversmiths of Sheffield and Birmingham, an assay office was established in those cities to control this abuse. In the same year, an Act of Parliament forbade letters to be punched on plated articles (which unfairly prevented platers from marking their wares). A further Act was passed in 1784 allowing platers to sign their products as long as silver assay marks were not used.

Electro-plating

By 1830, the introduction of "German silver", an alloy of copper, zinc and nickel, was already causing the decline of the Sheffield plate industry. But it was the arrival of electro-plating that caused its ruin. The technique of electro-plating, by which a layer of pure silver was applied to a base metal by electrolysis, enabled wares to be produced at a far lower labour cost than was required in the production of Sheffield plate. Elkingtons of Birmingham were particularly successful in commercializing the new technique.

Some of the most attractive Sheffield plate is also the plainest; this beautifully simple candlestick – one of a pair – was made in about 1790.

Scotland

While the characteristics of Scottish silver are not easily definable, it may be said that Scottish silver is more austere than English.

In Scotland, as in Europe, the beaker became a popular drinking vessel in the 17th century. Its shape was introduced by Protestant refugees and by traders from the Netherlands. Tankards, rare before 1700 and always remaining fairly uncommon, were generally large and extremely well made.

Many characteristically Scottish vessels, made in silver, date from the second half of the 17th century. Characteristic of the last decade of the 17th century, for example, was the "thistle cup", a small lobed mug of inverted bell shape with an S-shaped handle. Decoration on thistle cups, which was simple, consisted of thin lobes rising from the base. Quaiches, first made, or mounted, in silver in the second half of the 18th century, were very much a Scottish speciality. "Quaich" is adopted from the Gaelic word for a bowl or cup. The quaich was originally carved out of a solid block of wood, like the English mazer, or made of small wooden staves held together with hoops. It had

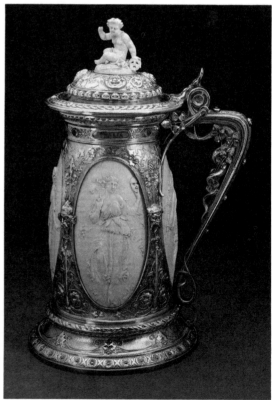

Above: *A Sheffield plate epergne and tray, one of the larger and more elaborate pieces successfully rivalling pure silver.*

Right: *this delicately ornate tankard, with carved ivory plaques and finial, is an example of Elkingtons' electro-plated wares.*

two or more handles. Silver quaiches, with engraved representations of staves, were made for the aristocracy between about 1660 and 1725. Silver-mounted wooden quaiches were always more common, however.

The finest Scottish silver dates from the 1730s and 1740s. Teapots were among the fine domestic wares made at that time. The typical Scottish bullet teapot is totally spherical, instead of being slightly flattened in the English manner. Teapots made after about 1730 often have flat-chased or embossed decoration.

Scottish mulls – large or small horns – were often mounted in silver for use as snuffboxes, especially in the early 19th century. In the High-lands, mulls were commonly made from a curled sheep's horn with silver mounts and hinge.

In Edinburgh, a hallmarking system was in operation from the middle of the 15th century. The date letter was added after 1681 in Edinburgh and, more erratically, in Glasgow. From 1784, the sovereign's head duty mark was used, though this was discontinued in 1890. Glasgow did not have an assay office until 1819.

Ireland

While some aspects of Irish silverware are quintes-sentially Irish, others are almost indistinguishable from their English counterparts. Irish tankards made after about 1660, for example, can only be distinguished from English tankards by their marks, but the "farmyard design" used on many objects, particularly sugar bowls and dish rings, between 1760 and 1780, is wholly Irish in character.

Early Irish coffee and chocolate pots were identical to English ones. However, from the mid-1730s, some national features appear such as the transverse band on the spout of the vessel, with slanted grooves above it. No exact English parallel exists for a particular type of wide-lipped, helmet-shaped cream jug. Cream jugs of this type, with a central foot, date mainly from the mid-1730s; a three-legged model was introduced later with the third leg under the lip (rather than under the handle, as in England). In about 1740, the feet of these helmet-shaped jugs were fashioned as lion masks or human masks. Human masks were especially favoured by the silversmiths of Cork and Limerick.

The dish ring, made between about 1740 and

Left: this Scottish mull, or snuff box, was made in 1832, and consists of a ram's horn mounted with silver.

Below: a shepherd and his sheep, surrounded by rococo scrolls, provide the theme for the fine decoration on this Irish dish ring, made in about 1780.

Dublin, 17th–19th century   *Cork (Eire), both 17th–18th century*   *Edinburgh, 16th–17th century (left) and from 1760 (right).*

1820, is an Irish speciality. Its function was to protect the surface of mahogany tables from the heat of bowls. Early dish rings were made of sheet silver, pierced and decorated. Dating from about 1740, they narrowly precede the craze for the rococo. In the later 1740s, the diameter of dish rings became larger at the bottom than at the top, and this style persisted until the 1770s. The "farm-yard design" was extensively used on dish rings in the 1760s. In the 1770s, chasing and *repoussé* decoration gave way to geometric piercing and bright-cut engraving.

FRANCE

It is something of a tragedy that very little French silver made before 1790 survives today. Its scarcity was brought about largely by political events. In the France of Louis XIV, nobles were required to send their silver to be melted down to subsidize wars. And in the French Revolution, church and domestic silver was seized and turned into bullion for the benefit of the Republic. Only small, lightweight pieces, such as beakers and wine tasters, escaped the effect of these events to survive in comparatively large numbers.

The Gothic style dominated French silver until the middle of the 16th century, when Renaissance ideas were brought to Paris by the Italian goldsmith and sculptor Benvenuto Cellini. Banishing the formality of the Gothic style, Renaissance influence on silver was seen in elaborate designs often incorporating strapwork and figures.

During the 17th century, the Renaissance tradition was in turn replaced by a showy baroque style in which lambrequins (ornate border patterns), vicious-beaked bird masks and elaborate chased decoration predominated. Towards the end of the 17th century, silverware became more

restrained, and with the death of Louis XIV in 1715 there began a period of simplicity. Piercing was now the fashionable method of decoration. This brief period of restraint gradually metamorphosed, by way of the Régence style, into forty years of florid rococo.

The silversmith Juste-Aurèle Meissonier (1695–1750), royal silversmith to Louis XV, is generally credited with launching the rococo style in France. Another genius among rococo silversmiths was François Thomas Germain. Germain carried out many royal commissions, among them to make a gold rattle for every royal birth from 1726. As the name of Louis XIV is synonymous with the baroque, so Madame de Pompadour's is with the rococo, but a pair of sauceboats and two mustard barrels are the only pieces of silver known to have belonged to her which have survived.

It was during the 18th century that some of the most typically French silverware was made. Many écuelles, two handled bowls with lids, similar to the English porringer, but shallower, were made between 1714 and 1770. Écuelles were often decorated with cut card work (consisting of a thin sheet

Below: an écuelle made by Thomas Germain in 1735–38, and a stand made by Antoine Plot in about 1766. Complex finials, in this case taking the shape of an artichoke, were often attached to écuelles at this period.

Below right: This candlestick, with its relatively restrained decoration, is an example of plainer silverware made during the 18th century.

of silver ornately cut and soldered onto the vessel) and given complex finials. After about 1730, *écuelles* were often also supplied with stands. Wine tasters were characteristic of the late 18th century and early 19th. They were small bowls normally fitted with one S-shaped handle, a thumbpiece or a pierced lug with a ring beneath. France was the first country to introduce double-lidded oval or rectangular spice boxes on four feet, which appeared at the end of the 17th century. French coffee or chocolate pots characteristically have a handle at right angles to the spout. Changes in taste were seen particularly well in candlesticks, which progressed from the late 17th-century restraint to rococo flamboyance, becoming asymmetrical by 1740. Some however, remained quite plain.

To return to stylistic developments in French silver, the rococo, already being overtaken by neo-classicism after the middle of the 18th century, was firmly banished from favour by the French revolution. Pedantic imitation of Roman and Greek styles was then encouraged. The most successful silversmiths of the neo-classical First Empire of Napoleon were Martin-Guillaume Biennais (1764–1843) and Jean-Baptiste-Claude Odiot (1763–1850). The late 18th century also saw reorganization in the silversmith's craft; in 1797, marks, which up until then had been regional, became common throughout France, consisting of a lozenge enclosing the maker's mark and a tax mark indicating first- or second-class silver. Annual marks, by which the year of manufacture was indicated, were introduced in 1818.

After the Empire (1804–15), French silver closely resembled English for about 30 years. By the end of the 19th century, the Art Nouveau style, which originated in France, was making an impression on silver design. The style at its purest is seen in the "whiplash-style" pieces produced by the firm of Cardeilhac.

Jean Puiforcat (1897–1945) was one of the geniuses of Art Deco. Puiforcat, influenced by painters rather than by silversmiths, was taken by Cubism, which he attempted to use in silver. Some influence may also have come from Aztec art, from which Puiforcat may have taken the idea of combining silver and rock-crystal.

Another important French silver producer was the firm L'Orfèvrerie Christofle, founded in 1839. Christofle made some delightfully whimsical novelties as well as the grand silver for the liner the *Normandie*. Tétard Frères, who, like Puiforcat, adopted Cubist ideas, produced tea wares which were perfect oblongs.

Top: *the splendour and dignity of the French Empire style is well demonstrated in this tureen, made by Martin-Guillaume Biennais in the early 19th century.*

*The freedom of Art Nouveau, producing a striking effect in the lamp stand (**left**) made by Charles Emile Jonchery in 1897, contrasts with the straighter and more severe lines of the Art Deco soup tureen (**above**), made by Jean Puiforcat.*

GERMANY

By the 16th century, Augsburg and Nuremberg were the two great centres of the silversmith's art. A large amount of silver-plated wares in the Gothic style was produced, and much of this output was exported. The history of 16th-century German silver is dominated by the Jamnitzer family. Wenzel Jamnitzer (1508–85), who has been called the Cellini of Germany, worked in Nuremberg from 1534. Among Jamnitzer's best pieces are some superb centrepieces and cups. His work is covered with relief ornament such as realistic lizards and insects. Wenzel Jamnitzer's grandson Christoph was also a fine craftsman.

Beakers were popular in Germany from the 16th century to the 18th. Those of the 16th century are often covered with plain bosses (hemispherical protrusions). Some 17th-century beakers were made in imitation of German wineglasses. An earlier type of beaker, on plain ball feet, continued to be made in the 17th century. More typical of the time, however, were heavily embossed beakers standing on moulded bases. Double beakers, forming a miniature barrel, were also made at that time.

Tankards were fashionable pieces of drinking equipment from the 16th century. Trends in their development run parallel with those in England; the small, tapering bodies characteristic of the 16th century developed into fuller forms of larger capacity in the 17th century, when the surface was also often decorated with *repoussé* designs based on scenes from the Bible or from classical mythology. From the middle of the 17th century, Bacchanalian subjects and coins set into tankards were popular. Throughout the period of their popularity, tankards were often also parcel-gilt (partly gilded).

The double cup (*Jungfrauenbecher*), a stemmed cup supporting an identical cup, was a typically German vessel. The top cup is frequently smaller than the lower, and was intended for use by the

This ewer and basin, made in Nuremberg in about 1725, are examples of the less typically German tablewares that tended to follow European styles.

ladies. Double cups are often covered with large bosses. Later ones have larger and rounder bosses with foliage and other ornament running between them. Sometimes the bosses too are decorated in relief.

A distinctively German vessel, made by no other European silversmiths, was the standing cup and cover. Being tall-stemmed and of great height, standing cups were impracticable to use and were intended chiefly for display. The most characteristic German vessel was the pineapple cup, shaped like an inverted pineapple on a stem and covered in lobes and bosses. A lot of ingenuity went into the designs of the stems, some being fashioned as tree trunks, often with attendant woodmen, others shaped as figures. Pineapple cups appeared in the latter half of the 16th century but reached their greatest popularity between about 1600 and 1650.

The German Renaissance also produced what might be called fantasy cups. Some consisted of real coconuts or nautilus shells – exotic objects at the time – mounted in silver; others took the form of silver ostriches with real ostrich eggs on their backs, figures of Atlas holding globes and charging figures on horseback.

Wager cups – double cups often with one bowl in the form of a long-skirted woman, the other as a small tumbler on pivots which she holds above her head – were made in large numbers from the late 15th century until the 1850s, especially in Augsburg. The cups were used for wagers and toasts; the aim was to drink from the bigger cup without spilling the draught in the other cup.

Sweetmeat dishes were a very popular form of silverware in the 17th century. Other notable pieces of German silverware were *écuelles* and *trembleuses*. *Ecuelles* were shallow bowls with two small handles. The small button feet on early examples gave way to claw supports in the mid-18th century. *Trembleuses* were frames, or small trays, for holding a teacup or glass; they could be extravagantly and exotically wrought, and were among the showpieces of rococo exuberance.

A date letter system, in which each year was indicated by a letter of the alphabet, was introduced into German hallmarks in 1735, but was abandoned after the middle of the 19th century.

Opposite page, left: this 17th-century Augsburg tankard, parcel gilt and decorated with repoussé motifs, is a typically ornate German drinking vessel.

Opposite page, right: too impractical to use, this heavily decorated silver gilt standing cup and cover, made in Nuremberg in about 1600, was probably intended only for display.

ITALY

By comparison with that of other European countries, Italian silver appears showy and fantastical. Nevertheless, much Italian silver is outstanding, notably that of the Renaissance. Benvenuto Cellini (1500–69), the goldsmith and sculptor, was probably the greatest craftsman in precious metals.

Italian Renaissance gold and silver work followed an essentially sculptural tradition, and sculptural qualities persist in the beautifully excuted reliefs and boldly modelled domestic wares of later centuries.

The five leading centres of silver production were Rome, Turin, Venice, Genoa and Naples.

An overpowering sense of classical grandeur is created by this richly cast and chased ewer and basin, made in Milan in 1847.

The products of each centre showed stylistic variations, and some centres had their specialities. Roman silversmiths, for example, naturally specialized in ecclesiastical silver. More often than the other centres, they also produced reliefs and statuettes depicting religious and mythological subjects. Roman silversmiths were quicker to adopt the neo-classical style, which had become established by 1770, ten years sooner than elsewhere among Italy's silver-producing centres.

Genoa was famous for its silver filigree, the decorative use of silver in thin strands, and was also the only place in Italy where *trembleuses*, stands for cups or glasses, were made. Silverware made in Turin was especially subject to French influence; *écuelles* (two handled shallow bowls with covers) made in Turin are very similar to French examples. Venetian silversmiths went in for highly embossed ornament and made superb book-bindings and picture frames, but they also produced simple tableware that seems to show English influence.

Silver from Rome, Turin, Venice, Genoa and Naples was almost always hallmarked in the 18th century. Other noteworthy towns in which the art of the silversmith flourished were Bologna, Florence, Mantua, Messina and Palermo.

THE NETHERLANDS

This windmill glass with silver mount, made in about 1570, was an ingenious and particularly Dutch adjunct to conviviality.

The characteristic early drinking vessel of the Netherlands was the horn, either mounted in silver or wrought entirely in the precious metal. Such costly cups were presented to Dutch guilds by important members for use at banquets. After the age of the drinking horn, the beaker became the commonest Dutch vessel, some being engraved with bands of arabesques and flowers, others decorated with sacred subjects.

The 17th century is the great period of Dutch silver. Some magnificent embossed work was done, with perspective cunningly indicated by variations in the depth of the relief. The Van Vianen family were the outstanding silversmiths of the late 16th and early 17th century. Adam Van Vianen (c. 1555–1627) introduced an extreme mannerist style of ornament known as *Kwabornament*. This was an asymmetrical style, and, although it was at times pretentious, *Kwabornament*, a true forerunner of the rococo, spread throughout the Netherlands, but by the mid-17th century it was dying out. Floral decoration then took the lead, reaching its height in about 1745.

Dutch standing cups of the 17th century follow German 16th-century examples. Sometimes, however, the decoration is distinctively Dutch, for example, figures of saints chased onto silver after designs by Hendrik Goltzius. Cups were popular gifts to Dutch naval heroes. Tankards, by contrast, are rare.

Peculiarly Dutch are silver-gilt stands for hold-

Marks on Dutch silver

Amsterdam, 18th century

Leiden, 17th century

ing wineglasses. These holders were tall and elegant and were made in sets of a dozen. Coconuts and nautilus shells were often turned into elegant drinking vessels or attractive ornaments by the addition of silver mounts.

Three cups in particular represent Dutch conviviality; they are the bridal cup, the windmill cup and "Hans in the cellar". Bridal cups, a Dutch speciality, were double cups, consisting of a fixed bowl and a bowl on pivots, and were made on the principle of German wager cups. The large, fixed bowl, in the form of a woman's skirt, was filled with wine, and the drinker had to drain it, then reverse the cup and empty the smaller, pivoted bowl without spilling the draught. The windmill cup, consisting of a miniature windmill on an inverted cup, was even more ingenious and must have caused much inebriation and hilarity: by blowing through a tube, the sails were set in motion, and the cup had to be emptied before they stopped.

The cup known as *Hansje in den kelder* ("Hans in the cellar") was brought out to celebrate news of a child on the way. In the centre, under a domed lid, was the figure of a baby which popped up when the vessel was filled with wine. *Hansje in den kelder* was popular from the 16th century to the 19th.

Another Dutch drinking vessel, made in the 17th and 18th centuries, was the brandy bowl, which was filled with brandy and raisins and used for family gatherings. Brandy bowls were initially seven- or eight-sided, becoming oval in the 1670s and retaining this shape for the remainder of their period of manufacture. Brandy bowls were often

fitted with handles and sometimes bore engraved decoration which might refer to family life.

Tableware such as salts, casters and candlesticks are rare, though they can be seen quite frequently in paintings by the Dutch Old Masters. Dutch candlesticks of the 17th century tend to have bulbous, hemispherical bases, and their shafts are often wrythen, or twisted like barley sugar.

In the 18th century, ordinary domestic silver items such as teapots and kettles were influenced by French styles, and there was a lot of gilding. Other practical pieces such as tobacco boxes, tea urns (from 1760) and trays were in great demand at this time.

Above: three elegant pieces of Dutch tableware. A taste of rococo is seen in the engraving on the beaker, made in 1669, and in the chasing on the casters, made in 1765.

Left: the plain outlines of this teapot, made in 1792, were inspired by a taste for neo-classical order which arose towards the end of the 18th century.

RUSSIA

In silverware, three distinctive vessels – the *bratina*, the *kovsh* and the *charka* – and one decorative technique – *niello* – are essentially Russian. The *bratina* was a loving cup with cover but no handles. After the death of a royal prince or princess, a favourite *bratina* was placed on his or her tomb in a church and was sometimes consecrated afterwards and used as an incense-burner.

The *kovsh* was a boat-shaped vessel with a bent handle extending from it like the prow of a Viking ship. Its original purpose was for ladling and drinking, but it later acquired a commemorative or symbolic function, being presented as an acknowledgement of service to the State or as a reward for military, diplomatic or commercial achievement. The *charka* was a small cup, usually with one handle, for strong liquors and brandy. Some are entirely of precious metal, others ornamented with rock crystal and semi-precious stones. Coloured enamels were sometimes used in the 17th century.

Niello, a black inlaid enamel, was used to decorate and letter Russian gold and silver wares in the 16th and 17th centuries. It was also used especially at Tula, St Petersburg and Novgorod in the 18th century. In the 19th century, *niello* was most frequently used on silver snuffboxes.

Filigree was another Russian speciality, used from the 17th century not only on its own but also with polychrome enamels, white, blue and yellow being the most usual colours. Another 17th-century decorative technique on Russian silver was chasing with delicate plant motifs which became

*While Western European influence is seen in the lidded tankard, c. 1680, (**right**), the beaker (**far right, above**) and charka (**far right, below**) are typically Russian vessels. Both date from the 18th century and are parcel gilt with niello decoration.*

more complex as the century progressed.

In the early 18th century, drinking cups of Western European style and large lidded tankards started to be made in Russia. This was also the period of the ascendancy of St Petersburg silver, largely brought about by foreign silversmiths brought there by Peter the Great, who also introduced compulsory hallmarking in 1700. By the end of the 18th century, Western styles were being rejected in favour of a return to earlier, native Russian styles and models, and the particularly Russian use of filigree, *niello* and enamelling was also re-adopted.

Perhaps the best-known Russian craftsman is Peter Carl Fabergé (1846–1920), a descendant of the Huguenot Fabergés who fled from France in 1685. In 1870, Peter Carl inherited the running of his father's shop in St Petersburg. Receiving the Royal Warrant in 1884, the firm then moved to Moscow. The house of Fabergé is renowned principally for its jewellery and richly-jewelled decorative objects, but the firm also produced fine silver wares among which were examples of the *kovsch* and a range of boxes, candlesticks and tablewares, finely ornamented desk clocks, cigarette cases and match cases, many finely enamelled.

Below: on account of its lavish ornamentation, this silver gilt and cloisonné enamel kovsh, *made in Moscow 1899–1908, could only have had a symbolic function.*

Right: this lidded tankard, made in St Petersburg 1899–1908, is an example of extravagant neo-rococo style, which had first been fashionable in Russian in the 18th century.

Above: interlacing Art Nouveau motifs decorate this silver and enamel desk folder, made by Fabergé at the beginning of this century.

SCANDINAVIA

Denmark

As in the Netherlands, the most popular early drinking vessel in Scandinavia was the horn, which was often mounted in gilt copper and sometimes silver. Also as in the Netherlands, horns were replaced by beakers. In both Denmark and Norway, which were united until 1814, beakers were commonly decorated with an open band of flowers and foliage encircling their circumference.

In the 17th century, shallow two-handled silver bowls, for serving hot brandy and liquor, were made in Denmark, as well as in Norway, Sweden and Holland. They were often engraved all over with formalized arabesques in the baroque style.

Engraving, lightly executed, was also seen on 16th- and early 17th-century Scandinavian tankards. The tall cylindrical bodies of these tankards later became shorter and wider and came to be fitted with three, or in rare cases, four feet. The distinctive Scandinavian peg tankard, made from about 1650, had eight pegs evenly spaced down the inside behind the handle as a guarantee of equal shares or for use in wagers in which the aim was to drink exactly one "peg measure".

In the second half of the 17th century, English cups of Charles II style were copied, down to the granular finish sometimes favoured. In the early 18th century, French rococo influence affected Danish silver styles, although English influence persisted alongside it. Scandinavian pieces of the rococo period often have twisted ribbing.

Sweden

Under Gustavus Adolphus, the hero of the Thirty Years War, Sweden was a great power in the 17th century. But his exploits were less celebrated in Swedish silver than in German.

Swedish domestic silver of the 17th century is often German in style. The main difference between the late 17th- and early 18th-century Swedish tankards and those of Denmark and Norway is that, in Swedish examples, the bodies are shorter and tend to taper downwards while the covers are lower and broader and project outwards over the lip. The ball feet and thumbpieces of Swedish tankards are also larger and much decorated – again in German style. Beakers were also popular in Sweden and are characterized by wide mouths tapering to narrow bases. In the second half of the 17th century, vessels were often made in filigree – fine strands of silver used decoratively, in this case on a solid base. Notable filigree workers included H. V. Torell of Gothenburg, and Rudolph Wittkopf and John Stahle of Stockholm.

Far left: a Norwegian "wager" cup of 1794. This is in fact two drinking vessels; the cup can be up-ended so that the woman's skirt becomes a goblet.

*In the late 17th century filigree decoration was fashionable in Sweden. This cup (**left**) is the work of one of the finest exponents of the craft, Rudolf Wittkopf of Stockholm.*

Norway

Norwegian tankards are similar to Danish ones, but they are usually bolder. Late 17th-century examples often have a flat-topped cover, larger in diameter than the tankard itself and sometimes set with a coin or medal. Among the makers of such tankards was Romanus Fridrichsen Möller, of Christiania, an important centre of silversmithing, particularly during the early and late decades of the 18th century. Another Christiania tankard-maker was Berendt Platt. Albert Groth (active 1706–17), of the same city, favoured acanthus-leaf decoration on his tankards. Groth also imitated English wares.

Complete sets of marks, consisting of the town mark, maker's and warden's mark, and the marks for the year and month of production, are occasionally found on Norwegian silver dating from the early 18th century onwards.

GLOSSARY

Acanthus decorative leaf motif

Air-twist stem Stem of drinking glass with hollow spiral core.

Albarello Drug pot made of tin-glazed earthenware.

Arita A centre of Japanese porcelain production.

Armoire Large cupboard or wardrobe, originating in late 16th-century France.

Armorial Coat of arms applied to silverware, ceramics, etc.

Arts and Crafts Movement An attempt to revive interest in craftsmanship in the late 19th century.

Aumbry An early form of food cupboard, sometimes with doors for ventilation.

Baluster Bulging vase-shaped form, commonly used for stem of drinking glasses, etc.

Ball and claw foot Foot consisting of paw grasping ball, commonly used on cabriole leg.

Baroque Grandly exuberant decorative style, originating in 17th-century Italy.

Basalt Unglazed black stoneware developed by Josiah Wedgwood.

Bianco sopra bianco Decoration on earthenware, in white on a pale grey or lavender ground.

Biedermeier Solid homely style, seen particularly in furniture, popular in Germany and Austria c. 1820–40.

Biscuit Unglazed porcelain (or pottery).

Blanc de chine White porcelain of a type first made at Dehua, China.

Block front The front of a piece of furniture, consisting of an inward curve flanked by two outward curves, and typically American.

Blown-moulded glass Glass decorated and shaped by blowing into a mould.

Blue and white Style of underglaze ceramics decoration, originating in China.

Blue-dash charger Delftware dish with border of blue brush strokes, and usually with bold polychrome central decoration.

Bocage Modelled leaves and flowers used as background to pottery or porcelain figures.

Bombé Exaggeratedly curved, usually applied to case furniture.

Bone china Hard-paste porcelain containing bone ash.

Boulle work Marquetry of tortoiseshell and, usually, brass perfected by André-Charles Boulle.

Bracket clock Portable clock fitted with carrying handle and, originally, made to stand on bracket fixed to wall.

Break-arch dial Clock dial with arch-shaped top.

Bright-cut engraving Decoration on silver in which graver burnishes as it cuts.

Bureau-bookcase Fall-front desk surmounted by an enclosed upper stage.

Bureau plat Flat-topped writing table.

Burr walnut Intricately figured walnut veneer.

Cabriole leg Furniture leg shaped like an elongated S.

Carriage clock Travelling clock in a rectangular case with a handle.

Cartel clock Flamboyant wall clock.

Caryatid A female figure used as a column, especially in furniture.

Cased glass See Overlay glass.

Celadon Chinese porcelain ware with greenish or bluish felspathic glaze.

Chasing Hammered decoration on metal.

Cheval glass Full-length mirror suspended between two uprights.

Chiffonier In France, a tall chest of drawers or a kind of small commode on legs; in England, a low cupboard with shelves for books, etc.

Chinoiserie Decoration on European furniture, silver and ceramics, etc., based on Chinese motifs.

Cloisonné Type of enamelling, with metal "cells" forming the design.

Commedia dell 'arte Popular comedy performed in 16th-18th-century Italian theatres, whose stock characters were often portrayed in porcelain figures.

Commode French chest of drawers.

Console table Side table permanently fixed against a wall.

Court cupboard Cupboard with lower stage open.

Creamware Fine-grained creamy-white earthenware perfected by Josiah Wedgwood.

Credenza Italian sideboard.

Crest Carved ornamentation usually on top of clock, mirror-frame, etc.

Crisseling Cloudy defect in early glass.

Cristallo Early Venetian colourless glass.

Crystal Fine, colourless glass.

Cut-card work Flat, applied decoration on silverware.

Damascening Inlaying of iron or steel with gold or silver.

Delftware Tin-glazed earthenware made in England and the Netherlands.

Deutsche Blumen Naturalistic floral decoration on ceramics, used at Meissen and other German factories.

Diamond-point engraving Decoration on glass produced by scratching the surface with a diamond.

Directoire Neo-classical furniture style current in France c. 1790–1804.

Drop front, or fall front Hinged flap on desk.

Earthenware Baked clay.

Ebéniste French cabinet-maker

Ebonized Stained black in imitation of ebony.

Empire Neo-classical style current in early 19th-century France, characterized by Egyptian motifs, drapes and glorification of Napoleon.

Enamel Glass coloured with metallic oxides used to decorate metals, ceramics and glassware.

Epergne Table centrepiece with various small containers, usually of silver or glass.

Escritoire French writing cabinet.

Façon de Venise Glassware imitating delicate Venetian styles.

Faïence Tin-glazed earthenware, especially that made in France.

Fall front See "Drop front".

Famille rose Style of decoration on Chinese porcelain, in which rose-pink predominates.

Famille verte Style of decoration on Chinese porcelain, in which a brilliant green predominates.

Federal style American furniture style showing Hepplewhite, Sheraton, Directoire and Empire influence, current c. 1785–1840.

Feldspar A mineral containing silicates, used to make hard-paste porcelain.

Feldspathic glaze Glaze containing feldspar.

Figure Natural pattern in wood.

Filigree Decoration made from thin interwoven metal or glass threads.

Finial Terminating ornamental knop, on teapot lid for example.

Flambé glaze Rich red glaze with splashes of blue.

Flat-chasing Relief decoration on metal obtained with punch and hammer.

Fluting Decoration in the form of shallow, concave, parallel grooves.

Gadrooning Decoration in the form of lobes, usually used as a border pattern.

Gate-leg table Circular or oval table with hinged leaves on gate-like supports.

Gesso A wood substitute consisting of plaster, used for elaborate gilt decoration.

Girandole Small wall mirror with candle-holders; or American circular convex mirror surmounted by eagle; or a type of banjo clock.

Glaze Glassy coating applied to ceramics.

Hard-paste porcelain True porcelain, made of feldspar and kaolin ("china-clay") in the Chinese manner.

Indianische Blumen Orientalized floral decoration on ceramics, used notably at Meissen.

Inlay Decoration consisting of pieces of wood, etc., set into recesses.

Intaglio Design carved out from surface of object.

Jacobean Style of furniture current in England and America, usually understood to span the reigns of James I (1603–35) and Charles I (1625–49).

Japanning Western imitation of Japanese lacquerwork.

Jasper Fine-grained stoneware, usually stained blue, sage green, lilac or yellow, perfected by Josiah Wedgwood.

Kakiemon Asymmetrical style of decoration in bright colours on Japanese porcelain.

Kaolin White china clay used with feldspar to produce hard-paste porcelain.

Knop Decorative swelling on stem of drinking glass, etc.

Lacquer Decorative varnish of Oriental origin.

Lacy glass American pressed glass with design in relief.

Lambrequin Baroque border pattern

Lantern clock Early English brass clock.

Lattimo Opaque white glass.

Latticino White interlacing patterns embedded in clear glass.

Lead glass Glass consisting of lead oxide, flint and potash.

Lead glaze Ceramic glaze consisting of silica and lead oxide.

Longcase clock Correct term for grandfather clock.

Maiolica Tin-glazed earthenware made in Italy and Spain.

Majolica Victorian earthenware with thick, coloured glaze.

Mannerism Sophisticated, fanciful treatment of Renaissance styles developed in 16th century Italy.

Marquetry Decorative veneers applied to furniture, clocks, etc.

Millefiori Rods of glass bearing tiny floral designs, embedded in clear glass, eg for paperweights.

Mudéjar Decorative style used by Moslems in Spain.

Neo-classicism Style current in later 18th century, inspired by classical antiquity.

Niello Black alloy inlaid decoratively on silver.

O.G. American 19th-century style of clock case.

Opaline glass Translucent milky glass, popular in 19th-century France.

Ormolu Gilt bronze.

Opaque-twist stem Stem on a drinking glass with white spiralling core.

Overlay glass Superimposed layers of different-coloured glass, with "windows" cut through to show the lower layers.

Palladianism Architectural style of strict classical proportions, defined in 16th century by Andrea Palladio.

Parcel-gilt Partially gilded.

Parian ware White, unglazed porcelain resembling marble.

Parquetry Geometrical marquetry.

Pâte-sur-pâte Relief decoration on porelain achieved by building up layers of white slip.

Patina Mellowed surface on furniture.

Pediment Gabled top on bookcases, clocks, mirrors, etc.

Pembroke table Small table with short drop leaves.

Petuntse Feldspathic rock, used in Chinese porcelain.

Pier glass Tall mirror designed to hang between two tall windows.

Pietra dura Semi-precious stone inlaid on table-tops, etc.

Porringer Small, two-handled bowl, usually of silver.

Posset pot Vessel for posset (spiced hot milk curdled with wine or ale).

Press cupboard Cupboard with upper and lower stages, both closed by doors.

Press-moulding Technique of shaping ceramic vessels by pressing moist clay into moulds.

Pressed glass Glass shaped while molten by a mould and plunger.

Prunt Decorative blob applied to stem of glass goblet.

Putti Naked baby-like figures of boys used as decorative motifs.

Redware Simple type of English and American domestic pottery.

Régence In France, the first phase of rococo style.

Regency English late neo-classical style current in early 19th century.

Renaissance Rebirth of Ancient Roman ideals, and of art and literature, after end of Middle Ages.

Repoussé Designs raised on metal by beating from the underside.

Reserve In ceramics, a surface left plain to receive decoration.

Rococo Lively, delicate 18th-century style, often asymmetrical with s-shaped curves.

Romayne work Carved roundels on furniture depicting profile heads.

Salt Salt cellar

Salt glaze Hard, glassy glaze obtained by throwing salt into kiln at hottest moment of firing.

Schwarzlot Black enamel decoration on glass or ceramics.

Sconce Wall-light with candleholders.

Seaweed marquetry Veneers in foliate patterns resembling seaweed.

Sécretaire Various types of writing desk.

Secretary American term for bureau-bookcase.

Serpentine Swirlingly convex.

Sgraffito Decoration on pottery obtained by cutting through slip to expose body underneath.

Silesian stem Shouldered stem on drinking glass.

Skeleton clock Clock with exposed mechanism under a glass dome.

Slip-casting Technique of making ceramic figures by first pouring slip (clay and water) into moulds.

Slipware Earthenware decorated with slip.

Soaprock porcelain Porcelain made from soaprock and clay.

Soda glass Glass consisting of seaweed and silica.

Soft-paste porcelain Imitation porcelain made from various clays and ground glass.

Splat Vertical central section of chair-back.

Sterling Standard of purity in British silver.

Stipple engraving Method of decorating glass by tapping surface with a diamond to produce tiny dots.

Stoneware Hard, non-porous pottery.

Stretcher Horizontal member joining chair or table-legs.

Style rayonnant A radiating pattern of symmetrical motifs, used particularly on faïence.

Sulphide Glassware embedded with plaque of white porcelain.

Tin glaze Lead glaze made opaque by addition of tin.

Transfer printing Printing from engraved plates onto ceramics by means of paper transfers.

Trembleuse Saucer with raised ring to steady cups.

Turning Shaping of furniture legs, etc., on a pole lathe.

Twist turning Spiral turning on "barley-sugar" furniture legs.

Underglaze Colours applied to ceramics under the glaze.

Veneer Thin layer of wood of the type glued to furniture carcases, usually for decorative purposes.

Vernis Martin 18th-century French japanning on wood.

Verre eglomisé Glass decorated on the reverse in colour and gold and silver foils.

Wainscot chair Panelled or planked chair common in 16th and 17th centuries.

Wheel-engraving Method of decorating glass by holding it to an abrasive rotating wheel.

Windsor chair Chair with spindled back.

Zwischengoldglas Glass decorated with gold cased inside another layer of glass.

Italic numerals refer to captions

ACKNOWLEDGEMENTS

T = top, B = bottom, C = centre, R = right, L = left.

AISA, Barcelona: 51TL, 52TL/BL; Richard Bryant/ARCAID: 146; Armitage, London: 162/3, 166TR/BR, 168BL, 170TC/L/TR/BR, 171T/CL/CR/B, 172BR, 173L, 174TL/TR/BL, 179T; E. Armstrong: 67TCR, 85B, 109C/R, 153R; Bonhams, London, 8BCL, 9L, 11, 23TR, 28T, 29BR, 30TL, 31R, 33B, 46BL & inset, 56BL, 70TL, 71T, 93T, 94T, 116, 121BR, 127B, 132/133T, 133, 154R, 158C, 172BL/CB; The Bennington Museum Bennington, Vermont: 64B; The Bridgeman Art Library: 35CR, 43B, 45L, 66R, 70C, 75, 77TL, 80BL, 82T/TC, 83L, 98TL, 104TL, 108L, 115R, 143, 144, 152, 159BL, 161BL, 177T, 183BL;/Hanley Museum and Art Gallery: 60; /National Museum of Wales, Cardiff: 84C; /Bristol Museum and Art Gallery: 124BR; /Cecil David Ltd.: 138B; /Bethnal Green Museum: 145C; /Kingston Antiques: 155BR; /S.J.Phillip: 180TR; from Thomas Chippendale's "The Gentleman and Cabinet Maker's Director: 26BL/CT/CB; Christie, Manson and Woods, Geneva: 9CBR, 104B, 105L/TR/BR, 106TL/R/B, 158R, 160CL/CR, 161CBL, 166L, 180TL, 184L, 185T/BL; Christie, Manson and Woods, London: 7, 42BL/BR, 56T, 57TR/BL, 67B, 70R, 71CR, 71B, 76TR/BR, 77TL, 79BR, 81TL/BL/BR, 87T, 88T/B, 89BL/BR, 90TL/TR/C/BR, 91, 92TR, 93C/BR/L, 96BR, 102T, 103T, 107T, 108R, 109L, 114L, 134BR, 145TR, 154L, 167T, 16BR, 170L, 171CL, 174BR, 183T; Christie, Manson and Woods, New York: 12TR, 13T, 37, 42TL, 45BR, 56R, 58TL, 59R, 67CBR, 80L, 84B, 96TL, 97TR/C/CR, 99BL/CR/BR, 100T, 101BL, 103C, 115L, 121T/CR, 130CR/BR, 131BL/BC/BR, 132L, 153L, 156L/R, 157TC/TR, 160L/R, 165B, 167CR, 168TL/TR, 170BC, 178BR; Cincinnati Art Museum, Mr. and Mrs. John J. Emery

Memorial and miscellaneous funds: 63R; The Corning Museum of Glass, Corning, New York; 118, 119L/R, 120TR/B, 121BL/CR; Daughters of the American Revolution Museum, Washington, D.C./Photo: Helga Photo Studio. (Acc. 58. 39): 65T; The Design Council: 35BL; Jacqueline Guillot/Edimedia: 128/9B; Musée des Cristallines de St. Louis/Edimedia: 130BL; East Liverpool Museum of Ceramics, Ohio: 64TR, 65B; E.T.Archive: 18T/TC, 74B, 123T, 179CR; Lauros-Giraudon: 117C, 128T; Goldsmiths Company: 169BC; Paul Rocheleau/Hancock Shaker Village, Pittsfield: 16CL; Claus & Liselotte Hansmann Kulturgeschichtliches Bildarchiv A-Z: 137BR, 179BC; from George Hepplewhite's "The Cabinet Maker and Upholsterer's Guide": 30CTL, 58BL; Angelo Hornak Photograph Library: 36L, 51BR, 100BR, 122L, 142BL, 145TL/BR, 159TR; Jonathon Horne: 67TCL from Thomas Hope's "Household Furniture and Interior Decoration": 32B Liberty: 35BR; Mallett & Son Ltd., London: 18B; The Mansell Collection: 35TL, 155TR, 165TL; Musée des Arts Decoratifs, Paris: 103B, 129TR, 130TL; Museum of the City of New York: 164T; Museum of Fine Arts, Boston: 165TR; Collection of the Museum of the National Association of Watch and Clock Collectors, Inc.: 151TC/CR, 161TC/TR/CBR/BR; The National Portrait Gallery, London; 25TL, 33T; The National Portrait Gallery, Smithsonian Institution, Washington, D.C.: 150CL; The National Swedish Art Museums: 50B, 141, 142TL, 186R, 187R; The National Trust Photographic Library: 58R, 110, 111B; Photo J.Whitaker: 10, 26/7B, 27BR; Photo J.Bethell: 28C, 29T. 32CL, 67TCR; New Jersey State Museum, Trenton, N.J.: 65C; The Historical Society of Pennsylvannia: 150CR; The Philadelphia Museum of Art: 165C/CR; Phillips, London: 71TR, 74TL; Pilkington Glass Museum: 8CR, 125R,

126BC, 136T, 140R; Princeton University Art Museum, the gift of Roland Rohlfs: 17TR; Royal Copenhagen: 113; Royal Doulton Ltd.: 72, 73TL/BL, 74TC, 76TR, 78TL/TR/B, 79BL/T, 85TL/TR/C; Hugo Ruef, Munich: 135T; Courtesy of the Seamen's Bank for Savings FSB: 151TL; from Thomas Sheraton's "Design for Household Furniture": 31TL; S.J.Shrubsole Ltd. London: 172T/C, 173TL/R/C/BR, 175T/C/B, 176T/BL; Somervale Antiques, Bath, 125L, 126TL/R, 127T; Sotheby's Geneva: 178BL, 180B, 184TR/BR, 185BR; Sotheby, King & Chasemore – The Pulborough Saleroom: 177B; Sotheby, Parke Bernet, London: 8TCL/R, 9CL/TCR, 18TR/C, 19R, 20L, 21L/R, 31C, 49L, 61, 66 TCL, 73BR, 81B/C, 87BL/CR, 88BL, 89T, 90BL, 92L/R, 102C, 120TL, 123B, 124CL/B, 126BC, 131TL/TC/TR, 134TL/BL, 135B, 136BL/BR, 137TR, 147, 149T/B, 153CL 169L, 176BR, 181; Sotheby, Parke Bernet, Monaco: 2, 94BL/BR, 95L/R, 96BL, 97TL, 114R, 157BR; Sotheby's Munich: 99TR; Sotheby, Parke Bernet, New York: 13BL, 16BL/BR, 32TR, 47BR, 150R; Sotheby's Winchester: 57TL; Sotheby's Zurich: 153CR, 157L, 159BR, 161TL; Spink and Sons Ltd.: 169R; Time Museum, Rockford Illinois: 1, 151TR; Earle D.Vandekar or Knightsbridge Ltd.: 70BL, 97B, 101T, 102B, 107B, 109C/R, 111T, 112, 137TL; Victoria and Albert Museum: 76BL, 83R, 84T, 139TL, 140TC/TL; Courtesy Victoria and Albert Museum/Photo Eileen Tweedy: 167CL; Courtesy Victoria and Albert Museum/MB: 182BC, 187L; Trustees of the Wedgwood Museum, Barlaston, Staffordshire: 68, 69, 73TR; The Henry Francis du Pont Winterthur Museum, Winterthur, Delaware: 12BR, 54T/B, 55TR/BL, 62T/L/R, 63L/R, 64TL, 150L; from the Richard and Gloria Manney Foundation: 17TC; Yale University Art Gallery/ The Mabel Brady Garvan Collection: 164C.